Presented To
A. J. Ritchie
December 1981
by
Dumfries and Galloway
Head Teacher's Association.

A FOURTH INNINGS WITH CARDUS

A FOURTH
INNINGS WITH
CARDUS

Neville Cardus

SOUVENIR PRESS

ISBN 0 285 62483 0

Printed in Great Britain by
Ebenezer Baylis and Son Ltd
The Trinity Press, Worcester, and London

To
Ken Murphy
in gratitude for all his help

ACKNOWLEDGMENTS

The publishers are grateful to the editors of *The Guardian, The Spectator* and *The Sunday Times* and to William Collins for their co-operation in the assembly of articles in *A Fourth Innings with Cardus*. The publishers are particularly grateful to Margaret Hughes for her generous assistance in planning and compiling the book.

CONTENTS

Acknowledgments	7
Stumps Pitched *(Spectator)*	11
Characters for Our Delight *(Spectator)*	14
J. T. Tyldesley *(Guardian)*	17
A Request for Cricket *(Sunday Times)*	22
The Sorcerer's Apprentice *(Sunday Times)*	24
Jessop the Croucher *(Guardian)*	26
Ghosts from the Past *(Sunday Times)*	28
George Hirst *(Guardian)*	31
The End of Summer *(Spectator)*	33
Duleepsinhji *(Guardian)*	35
A Century for the Connoisseur *(Sunday Times)*	38
Leyland, a Lovable Fighter *(Guardian)*	40
Enter the Boy Trueman *(Sunday Times)*	43
Cricket Laws and Facts *(Spectator)*	45
Some Thoughts—England *v.* Australia 1948 *(Sunday Times)*	49
Woolley: an Appreciation *(Guardian)*	77
An Innings from Yardley *(Sunday Times)*	81
Bill Worsley Straight from the Pits *(Guardian)*	82
An Innings from Hutton *(Sunday Times)*	85
McCabe, Batsman of Poise and Chivalry *(Guardian)*	88
An Innings from Bailey *(Sunday Times)*	90
Greatest of All Cricketers *(Guardian)*	94
Martin Donnelly A Pedigree Batsman *(Sunday Times)*	97
D. R. Jardine *(Guardian)*	101
Frank Worrell *(Guardian)*	103
Great Indians *(Spectator)*	105
Cricket's Coronation Year *(Spectator)*	109
The Caribbean Flavour *(Spectator)*	112
Green Caps and Demons *(Spectator)*	117

CONTENTS

The Test that Never Was *(Spectator)* 121
Surrey Heroes *(Spectator)* 123
Good Lancashire Men *(Guardian)* 126
Conversation with Rhodes 1950 *(Cricket All the Year)* 129
Some Thoughts—England *v.* Australia 1956 *(Guardian)* 137
Old Trafford's Century *(Guardian)* 164
England *v.* Australia 1926 *(Guardian)* 170

STUMPS PITCHED

PREPARATIONS for the cricket season are going busily forward up and down the land. Groundsmen are again at their fell work. Bats are being oiled, and turnstiles, too. Score-boards are waiting to record history. At the Oval and Nottingham, I believe, they are erecting score-boards built after the Australian model, those that tell you all, if not more, than all: the bowler's analysis over after over; and there's an electrical light that flickers here and there, appearing at the side of a fieldsman's name every time he moves an inch or raises an eyebrow. These score-boards are rather loquacious; I prefer the old-fashioned English ones, which need some co-operation from and collaboration with a card and a pencil. It is pleasant to write down for oneself and to find out for one's self what has happened.

In a week or two the evening papers will be printing the cricket scores, and as we come from Lord's at close of play we'll be able to read the tea-time scores in the 'extra late night final'. I hope they will give us all the details, and not fob us off with 'Surrey out, 257'. Let us have the tables and columns of old again, so that we can repeat, like rubric in ritual, noble numbers. When I was a boy it was poetry and nothing less to read or murmur: 'c Maclaren, b Brearley', 'c Tunnicliffe, b Rhodes'. There was magic in the necessarily abbreviated 'c R'nj'ts'nji, b L.'ckw'd'. Let us soon be given a chance to intone, 'c Compton, b Sims', or even 'c C'pt'n, b S'ms'.

When cricket returns to us each year we welcome it with a warm and almost mystical devotion not given to other games; for it is part of the springtime and the renewal of things. Old men in the clubs emerge and go to Lord's in taxis—though I know one stalwart who walks three miles there and three miles home every day—and the fresh air enlivens them. Before long they are telling us, forcibly as ever, that the game is going to the dogs. They wield their rolled umbrellas to show us what a bat was made for.

North, south, east, west, the familiar names will be affectionately pronounced as local giants manifest themselves after winter obscurity. In Yorkshire it will be Hutton this year more than ever; and if Denis

11

Compton should kick the winning goal in the Cup final his greeting on his first appearance at Lord's, a few days hence, may easily beggar description. But in all the counties, weak or strong, the crowds and regional patriotism create their own heroes. No Somersetshire lad, whatever his age, looks upon Hutton or Compton with quite the same light in his eyes as shines when he gazes on Gimblett, who no doubt will die in the belief that a maiden-over bowled at him is an insult to family and county pride.

The spirit of 'Sammy' Woods still has influence down at Taunton and Bath, not forgetting 'Prophet' Daniell and the wonderful wild things he said and did while he wore that disreputable hat—a 'Trilby', if I am not mistaken. It is possible—all things are possible in Somersetshire—that even the example of Ernest Robson remains an inspiration in a generally dowdy world. It was Robson, a professional of rare vintage, who once came in last when eight runs were needed for a Somersetshire victory. He was at last a veteran; his moustache was grey, though after a droop downwards it curled genially, if not belligerently, up, as ever. When Robson arrived at the wicket in this crisis, the batsman at the other end was Mr R. C. Robertson-Glasgow, who had by this time come to the conclusion, by inference, that it was for him to win the match, if the match were now to be won at all.

Alas, after Mr Robertson-Glasgow had scored two of the eight runs, some misunderstanding between the wickets delivered Robson to the enemy, a desperate fast bowler. Ernest 'took guard' and surveyed the field, stroking his moustache. He patted his blockhole, surveyed the field yet again, and yet again he stroked his moustache. He drove the first ball hurled at him clean over the pavilion, and as the ball soared into the westering sun he watched the course of it, all the time stroking his moustache. Then he looked down the wicket and said: 'I believe, Mr Robertson-Glasgow, that that is the winning hit.'

It is the way cricket is played matters most; and nowadays we make too much of the technical apparatus of it all. If a cricketer's mind and every nerve are awake and all his wits, there can be no dullness, whether the scorers are active or not. Makepeace of Lancashire used to stonewall quite passionately. Cricket, more than any other of our manly field sports, depends on individual zest, will, temper—yes, temper! Remember Macaulay, of Yorkshire, eyes popping out of his head if an umpire rejected an appeal or demand for leg-before-wicket, or if he were hit to the boundary from the leg-stump? He was a man outraged—but give him the ball, wait for another over; he would be revenged, so help him; he would do such things—what they were yet he knew not—but they should be the terror of the earth. I am much too much of a North-countryman to take the view that 'winning doesn't matter' in cricket, and I have no use for the saying: 'May the best side win.' The best side is always *our* side. But I am satisfied and convinced that the game is at any time as great as the players themselves make it by character first of all.

The *material* contribution comes next. When G. L. Jessop, at Kennington Oval in 1902, went in to bat, England in their second innings had lost five wickets for less than fifty, and spectators were leaving the ground sick at the 'certainty' of another humiliation before the cock-a-hoop and dreadfully efficient Australians. It is well known to students of the more epic pages of cricket's history that Jessop that day scored 104 in an hour and a quarter. It is not generally known, though, even yet, that this remarkable innings didn't just occur by the 'accident' or chance of the game; it was the result and consequence of the will of a man who was at the moment in a condition of much liveliness of mind. It is said that he went to the wicket with his chin more aggressively thrust out even than was usual with him. He was probably livid with rage.

Jessop, of course, was a law—or rather a power—unto himself. Besides, none of us wants rhetoric all the time on a cricket field. But vitality must certainly be there all the time, with no routined standardized contribution at all, either of service or of skill. Every player should keep faith with his natural impulses; let the stone-wallers stonewall, the hitters hit, the fast bowlers bowl their fastest—but not compromise to a formula! What's bred in the bone will come out in the shortest innings; and breeding will count for most in the end—if it is another Woolley we are waiting for, another Sutcliffe, another Spooner, another George Lohmann, another Maurice Tate, another 'Patsy'.

I wonder if any of these learned to bat on a concrete wicket. . . . I am of what I might call the 'green-grass' school; I don't object even to a few rough places in the earth—if it is genius I am searching after—(though, of course, this is not to say that a poor boy playing in a park should need to look to his shin-bones or his skull for want of a good roller on the premises). If it is argued that Bradman practised when young on a concrete wicket, I am inclined to ask—with the accent of Mr. Robey—and what OF it? Bradman was a genius and a prodigy; but as he made his double and triple centuries, didn't they suggest something 'contracted' about them, built to plan, and

13

substantially concrete, not to say massive? I preferred George Gunn, who, whether performing strokes that astonished eyesight, or whether (at his pleasure) not scoring at all for hours, never for a moment held back the essence of himself from the game. Once he began a Nottinghamshire innings at Trent Bridge on a day of burning heat. The wicket was perfect, the opposition weak. After he had flicked three or four fours here and there, George suddenly sent a simple return catch to the bowler, and was out. When he reached the shade of the pavilion, his captain, not unreasonably curious, asked him why he had got out to such a silly stroke. 'Too hot, sir,' said George.

These things—of the spirit and the humorous—can't be referred to, or estimated, on the score-board, not even on the comprehensive and communicative score-boards of Australia. But they are matters of individual essence, and just now we shall do well to look after them.

CHARACTERS FOR OUR DELIGHT

MOST cricket reporters nowadays depend for statistical details on Mr Bill Frindall, the kindly, reliable Press Box computer. When I first reported cricket matches in 1919, the Press had to work out their own statistics. The reporters made a ball-by-ball analysis, by pen or pencil, noting every run scored, in which direction the stroke went, and from which batsman or bowler. At the age of twenty-six I faithfully followed this clerical fashion, until I began to get absorbed in the players as men, as 'characters'. Christopher Martin-Jenkins, summing-up the MCC team in the West Indies 1974, refers to it as a 'team short of "characters" if not of character'. 'Characters', no doubt, are missing from contemporary English county cricket. The present England XI is constantly praised by the 'media' for its efficiency: 'they do a good job of work.' Maybe. But the plumber who comes to my flat to put my bath tap right also does a 'good job of work'. None the less, I don't want to pay to watch him doing it.

In his closing assessment of the MCC's performances in the Test matches against the West Indies, Martin-Jenkins is rather baffled that a company of players generally mediocre should, at the pinch, salvage a rubber nearly sunk with all hands, against a team extremely gifted individually: 'But their brave and honourable finish to the tour, and their win on merit in the final Test, did not alter the belief that to have earned a half-share in a series dominated by the West Indies was something like daylight robbery.'

I sympathize with him in his searchings for characters in our first-class cricket at the moment. Frankly, I think they are there, present embryonically. Emmott Robinson, Rhodes and Herbert Sutcliffe, were not actually the rounded 'characters' looming large in my accounts of Lancashire *v.* Yorkshire matches. They provided me with merely the raw material, so to say; my histrionic pen provided the rest. I have often told, in print, of a wet morning at Leeds, a Yorkshire *v.* Lancashire match. Then the sun came forth hot and sumptuous. At half-past two Rhodes and Robinson went out to inspect the wicket, I with them. Rhodes pressed a finger into the soft turf, saying, 'Emmott, it'll be "sticky" at four o'clock.' Emmott simply replied, 'Aye, Wilfrid,' which was not good enough for me, not good enough for Robinson. So I, in my report, made him reply to Rhodes's 'It'll be "sticky" at four o'clock,' 'No, Wilfrid, half-past.' I put words into his mouth that God intended him to utter.

Take the incident of the run out in the West Indies when Greig caused a great hullaballoo. Officials of the West Indian Board, and Mr Donald Carr, representing the MCC, held solemn conclave, at last issuing a statement as momentous as any from the United Nations . . . 'Whilst appreciating that this is not strictly within the laws of cricket, England's manager, Donald Carr, and Mike Denness, captain, have in the interests of cricket as a whole, and the future of this tour in particular, requested that the appeal against the batsman be withdrawn . . .'

I cannot help feeling that such a mix-up in the cricket field would once on a time (and not too long ago), have been settled on the spot with some sense of humour and proportion. During the 'thirties the turf and pitches at Old Trafford, Manchester, were so perfectly moulded for batsmen, that a Lancashire and Yorkshire match was seldom brought to a decisive conclusion in three days. Each team played mainly with intent not to lose. 'We've won toss, lads,' Harry Makepeace would say to his professional colleagues in the dressing-room—and he was the power behind the throne occupied by the amateur captain—'We've won toss, lads. Now, no fours before lunch.'

I one day protested to Maurice Leyland, great Yorkshire batsman and representative Yorkshireman, that this sort of cricket was 'killing the game'. 'It's all reight,' he assured me, 'but what we need in Yorkshire–Lancashire matches is *no umpires*—and fair cheatin' all round.' Lancashire and Yorkshire batsmen, on being struck on the pads by the bowler, immediately withdrew legs away from the stumps, so that the umpire would be hard put to it to deliver a leg-before-wicket decision. No truly-born and bred cricketer of Lancashire and Yorkshire would have dreamed of 'walking', of leaving his crease way back to the pavilion in advance of an umpire's decision. Yet, wonderful to relate, it was in a Lancashire and Yorkshire match, at Old Trafford, that burly Dick Tyldesley so far forgot the rigour of the game that after making a sharp catch at short-leg announced to the umpire, who was about to raise his hand for dismissal, that the ball just touched the ground before the apparent catch had been accomplished. I congratulated Tyldesley, at the end of the day's play, on his sportsmanship. 'Thanks very much,' he replied, in broad Lancashire accent, 'Westhaughton Sunday School, tha knows.' (Did he really say it, or did I . . . ?). .

Martin-Jenkins is able to appreciate the difference between competence and individual style. Despite a young man's natural patriotism, he was not really happy that the West Indies did not win this rubber. 'At the crunch,' he writes, 'England's icy professionalism had overcome the more fitful talents of the West Indies.' Obviously he shared the mystification of the small West Indies boy, who, after England's rather kleptomanic victory in the Fifth Test, asked him, 'Mister, how *could* West Indies lose that game?' And Martin-Jenkins admits, 'I did not know how to answer him.'

Sometimes there should be two ways by which honours in a cricket match are awarded—by competitive and aesthetic valuation. Of all games cricket at the top level is the most appealing to the aesthetic sense (this is why it has inspired a literature such as no other outdoor sport has inspired). Bloggs of Blankshire has scored more runs in a Test match series than were ever scored in a series by Victor Trumper, Denis Compton or Tom Graveney. And Stockhausen has written more notes in a single composition than Mozart. So what?

I am often told that I live my cricket in the past, enchantment of distance glorifying disproportionately cricketers in action decades ago. But let me see, today, Barry Richards at the wicket, or Kanhai, or Sobers, or Clive Lloyd or Kallicharran, to pick on a few un-English names, and I know I am watching cricketers as gifted in skills, as fascinating and personal as any exhibited by my heroes in the past.

Emmott Robinson once said to me, 'Tha writes some funny stuff about us, flowery-like; but only this mornin' my missus said to me "but there's summat in what he says—and me and mi mother 'as been tellin' thi same thing these many years . . ." '

J. T. TYLDESLEY

IN July, 1895, a young cricketer, playing for Lancashire against a strong Gloucestershire XI, batted with an assurance that moved W. G. Grace, in his position at point, to paternal interest and approval. 'Eh, eh,' commented his high voice, 'he's a good lad, and when he learns to play with a straight bat he'll do.' The young cricketer, though he never learned to play with the straight bat (it wasn't in his line), became one of the greatest professional batsmen we have ever had. 'What's his name?' asked Old Trafford on that July day. 'Ty'des-ley, Tyl-desley, Ty'd-dle-sley?' The progress of this cricketer to a popularity with the Old Trafford crowd far beyond that ever known by any other Lancashire player was marked by the changes in the name the crowd knew him by, each change denoting a more and more intimate notion of him. First it was 'Ty'd'sley', then 'J.T.T.', and finally 'John Tommy'. He became one of the county's common possessions—institutional. 'Mornin', Johnny,' somebody would say to him as he stood at his place on the boundary, and when he let it be understood by a glance over the shoulder that Familiarity had not gone out to the winds over his head, then Familiarity preened itself and said to the multitude around: 'Nice feller.'

A lot of people, it seemed, knew him very well—met him on the train from Monton every morning and even went to the same barber's. He really was everybody's business. Mature men, working at grey cloths in George Street on hot afternoons, used to ask, on hearing Lancashire's score was 157 for 5: 'How's Johnny gone on?' A great man does not come to this kind of easy familiarity with average folk unless there is nature as well as art in his achievement. Nobody on the sixpenny side ever shouted right from his heart, 'Hello, Charlie!' at C. B. Fry, or 'Hello, Willie!' at W. G. Quaife. Art or high skill refined these cricketers out of the tracks of simple comprehension. Tyldesley was even cleverer than these two batsmen, but his play had in it no austerities, no alienating refinements.

His was batsmanship of a sort the average man would cultivate if he could. Technically, of course, Tyldesley's cricket touched an excellence rare even amongst the masters; it is the spirit of his play that is being discussed at the moment, and that was democratic enough— his was batsmanship 'a fellow could understand'.

A cricket bat, indeed, can look an entirely different instrument in different hands. With Grace it was a rod of correction, for to him bad bowling was a deviation from moral order; Ranjitsinhji turned a bat into a wand, passing it before the eyes of the foe till they followed him in a trance along his processional way; George Hirst's bat looked like a stout cudgel belabouring all men not born in Yorkshire; Macartney used his bat all for our bedazzlement, as Sergeant Troy used his blade for the bedazzlement of Bathsheba—it was a bat that seemed everywhere at once, yet nowhere specially. And for Tyldesley a bat was an honest broadsword—a broadsword drawn in no service but the service of Lancashire. This last sentence is not intended as a rhetorical flourish. If we are not to go wrong over the character of Tyldesley we need to know that for him batsmanship was first and last a means to a workmanlike end, which was Lancashire's welfare. The brilliance of his play often blinded us to Tyldesley the canny utilitarian. Art for art's sake was not his cry; his play took the senses by assault, inflamed the imagination, but certain it is he never set himself deliberately to do this. To say the truth, we are at liberty to remark of this wonderful cricketer, who was perhaps the most skilful, the most audaciously inventive batsman of his time, that his philosophy is contained in: 'Be good in service and let who will be clever.' He shed glory over the field unwittingly. A bird that is attending to the hard utilitarian job of building a nest will move us to the artist's delight by poise of swift curving flight. And an innings by Tyldesley, though moving on wings and enrapturing the senses, was always attending to the utilitarian job of building the Lancashire nest. What was an innings of a hundred to Tyldesley if victory did not come to Lancashire along with it?—the man was mocked; the taste of ashes was in his mouth. This, of course, is not the way of the artist. *He* can thrive on an individual achievement because of the wonder in it. He lights his fire that he and others may be ravished by colour and fine flame; he does not insist that it be capable of boiling the pot. Tyldesley was certainly not an artist in this deliberate, proud, selfish way. Remember his dourness as he stood over his bat ready for the bowler's attack. He was the image of antagonism, vigilant and shrewd. Tyldesley never seemed, even in his most sparkling innings, to be toying with the bowlers in the manner of the virtuoso, merely to amuse himself and us; he most plainly was checkmating them by courage and opportunism. If he was audacious that was because audacity 'paid'—offence was his best means of defence. He improvised strokes never seen before on the cricket field, not out of the artist's love of doing things in a new way, but because inimical circumstances could not be thrust aside by the old expedients. When he tried a fresh stroke he asked if it 'worked', not if it was 'artistic'. We all recollect his slash stroke, that uppercut over the slips' heads. It was not beautiful to see, but immensely fruitful of runs. Had it happened in an innings by Spooner it would have looked like a flaw in a delicate piece of porcelain. But how in keeping the stroke was with the punitive game of Tyldesley!

Again, take his on-driving: he had no objections to lofting the ball, so long as it was lofted profitably. The batsman who is an artist before he is a cricketer has a fastidiousness which is set all on edge, so to say, at the very sight of a stroke 'off the carpet'. Tyldesley had no such compunction. Nor is his lofty on-driving to be taken as evidence that after all he was more than the canny utilitarian, that he liked now and then to live dangerously for the good of his spirit. No; when Tyldesley sent the ball into the air he knew exactly what he was doing; he was not snapping fingers at Providence, nor indulging in quixotry. It is doubtful whether Tyldesley ever hit in the air during a big match out of sheer high spirits. Perhaps the field was set inconveniently for ground hits; very well then, they must go over the heads of the scouts. He could place the ball almost to a nicety. So with his famous cut from the middle stump. Surely, you might object, this stroke was a piece of coxcombry—a display of skill for skill's sake, or, at any rate, a display of skill intended to astound us. Why should it have been? The cut was Tyldesley's master-stroke; he had it under perfect control. 'But,' you may still object, 'why from the middle stump?—nothing canny about an adventure like that.' You may be sure Tyldesley did not cut from the middle stump without a good workmanlike reason. Bowlers knew that he would cut to ribbons anything on the off-side at all short, and they would in consequence keep on or near Tyldesley's wicket. Was Tyldesley then going to let his cut go into disuse? Was his most productive hit to run to waste? Why should he not cut a short ball on the middle stump? Let him only get into position for it—his foot-play was quicker than the eye could follow—and it was much the same as a ball on the off-side, made for cutting. Of course if he missed it the chances were that he would be out. Well, he weighed the chances against his marvellous ability at the cut, and the risk was not palpably greater than the risk a cricketer takes in playing any straight ball—either defensively or offensively.

Macartney used to cut from the middle stump—but for a reason different from Tyldesley's. Macartney would exploit the hit even when it was in his power to make another and safer and even more profitable stroke. For Macartney, though a good antagonist, was a better artist; the spoils of war became in time cheap and tawdry to him. Often did one see disillusion on his face at the end of an opulent innings. Then would he find the challenge of the best bowler irksome: he would throw discretion to the winds in a way that a sound tactician like Tyldesley never did. To refresh his spirit, to save himself from the stale and the flat, Macartney was ready to risk the profitable—to indulge in some impossibly fanciful play of the bat. In this hot quixotic mood his wicket would go to the simplest ball. 'Macartney gets himself out,' was a common saying. How seldom one heard that much said of Tyldesley. A bowler had to work for the wicket of Tyldesley. You might baffle him by skill, inveigle him into a false step; never could you hope that he would give himself away. He wore the happy-go-lucky colours of the care-free soldier of fortune, but they were as borrowed plumes: in the flesh Tyldesley was a stern Ironside, with a Cause—the cause of Lancashire—so sacred that it demanded that a man cast the vanities of art and self-glorification to the wind. This most dazzling of all Lancashire batsmen was, forsooth, a Puritan—a conscript of conscience even, trusting in Lancashire but keeping his powder dry!

There lived not a bowler in his time that did not suffer the scourge intolerable from Tyldesley's bat. Rarely was he to be found not 'ware and waking—on a sticky wicket he was as formidable as on a dry one. At the Oval, or at Edgbaston, his happy hunting-ground, the bowler all too soon would behold Tyldesley's wicket as a wicket a long way distant, his bat a sword of fire guarding it. 'Heaven help me!' the sweaty toiler would appeal to the sky. 'If only he would let one go! I don't ask for his wicket—I've been flogged out of vanity like that—but merciful power can surely grant me a maiden over now and then.' Maiden over, indeed, with Tyldesley in form! He would plunder the six most virgin deliveries you ever saw. It was hard even to pitch a decent length to him. For he knew, unlike the modern batsman, that length is not absolute, but relative to a batsman's reach. And though Tyldesley was a little man, his feet had the dancing master's lightness and rapidity of motion. He covered a larger floor space as he made his hits than any batsman playing today—not even excepting Hobbs. What a disdain he must have in these times for the excuse of timid batsmen that they must needs practise patience till bad bowling comes to them! How long would Tyldesley have required to wait for half-volleys from J. T. Hearne, Trumble, Blythe, Noble, and the rest? He turned the well-pitched bowling of these masters into the length a punishing hit asks for by swift foot-play. He would jump a yard out of his ground to make a half-volley; he would dart back to the wicket's base to make a long-hop. Two old cricketers once discussed an innings by Tyldesley after the day's cricket was over in something like this language: 'Tha's a reight bowler, Tom. What's thi analysis today—after Johnny'd done wi' thi?' 'Nay, Bill, be fair—tha can't deny I bowl'd well. It wer' t' wicket were too good; I couldn't get any spin on t' ball.' 'Spin, eh? I likes that. Spin on t' ball? Why, I never saw thi hit t' floor all t' afternoon.'

He was in possession of all known strokes, and, as we have seen, he improvised strokes of his own when circumstances challenged him to do so. His square-cut was powerful, and the action of it has been vividly described by C. B. Fry: 'He threw the bat at the ball without letting go of the handle.' Many a day-dreaming point—they needed a point, very deep, to Tyldesley—has been seen hopping agitatedly after the advent of the Tyldesley cut. Sometimes he went on his toe-points to make this stroke. His driving was accomplished by a vehement swing of the bat and a most gallant follow-through. There was no saying whether forward or back play was the mark of his style, he combined the two so thoroughly. He was perhaps the best batsman of all time on a bad wicket. P. F. Warner is never tired of singing the praises of Tyldesley's innings of 62 made on a 'glue-pot' at Melbourne in 1904. England's total was then 103, and Relf was the only other batsman to get double figures.

A great batsman is to be estimated, of course, not merely by his scores, or even by his technique, but also by taking into account the quality of the bowling he had to tackle in his day, and the quality of the grounds he mainly played on. When Tyldesley came to greatness English bowling was in a classic period; he had to face men like Lohmann, Richardson, Peel, J. T. Hearne, Noble, Jones. But not only did he take his whack out of some of the best of our classical bowlers; he was also one of the first batsmen to master the new googly bowling. He passed, in fact, through all the manifold changes in fashion which came over bowling between 1903 and 1919. And whether it was J. T. Hearne or R. O. Schwarz, Rhodes or D. W. Carr, Tyldesley was always the same brilliant and punitive Tyldesley.

Then let us bear in mind as we do honour to his genius that half of Tyldesley's cricket was played at Old Trafford, where in his time the wickets were not above suspicion. What would Tyldesley's record have been had he played mainly on the hard, beautiful wickets of Kennington Oval? But Tyldesley himself never would worry his head over the averages and records, nor need we. His service was all for England and his county—given in happy devoted heart. Think of him as brilliant if you like, but also think of him as modest —if you would keep the idea of the real Tyldesley in mind. The man is by nature as discreet and modest as few geniuses ever are, and that modesty and discretion, as one tried to show, came out even in his most flashing play. Once, in the days when cricketers were asked by a London newspaper to write reports, Tyldesley was the historian of the Lancashire XI. And he wrote his accounts very much in this style: 'Yesterday we had the good luck to get Worcestershire out cheaply, thanks to some good bowling by Mr Brearley and Dean. When we went in the wicket was faster, and Mr Maclaren and Mr Spooner, batting finely, gave us a good start. Sharp did well too, and Mr Poidevin had the misfortune to play on after a promising beginning. I also managed to get a few.' And turning to the scores you would read:

A. C. Maclaren, b Wilson	41
R. H. Spooner, c Arnold, b Wilson	31
Tyldesley, not out	200
L. O. S. Poidevin, b Arnold	16
Sharp, b Burrows	20
Extras	10
Total (for 4 wickets)	318

The real Tyldesley peeped out in his cricket writings—and he never played an innings that was untrue to his nature.

A REQUEST FOR CRICKET

AFTER a ten-year interruption, we shall this summer see Test matches between England and Australia. It is to be hoped that they will add to the gaiety of the nation. None of us wants to suffer again the Oval boredom of 1938. Our cricketers will perhaps lend an ear to the hint that if they should still be intent on breaking records by hard Spartan labour, there is nowadays another avenue for them, another opportunity. They might transfer their zeal to record-breaking in, say, the coal-mining industry.

A fair case can be argued in these times against day-by-day sport absorbing 'man power' in plenty. This case will considerably be strengthened if Test matches should lapse back to the old dreary penurious stalemate, with over-production of runs at the expenditure of hours of unsmiling manual labour, and an increase of depression amongst thousands of people who pay at the gates in the hope of receiving some elevation of spirits by good, free and tolerably happy sport.

This is not to clamour for indiscriminate hitting, and sixes every over. Let us be reasonable. There are occasions, especially during the more crucial periods of a Lancashire and Yorkshire match, when a drive to the boundary (before lunch) is vulgar, or at least, lacking in due reticence. But we have a right, in an age of rations, to ask cricketers to give themselves generously to the game itself, to draw inspiration from its promptings as it goes through its own lovely changes and hazards. There is a time to drive and a time to restrain from driving; a time to use the bat with a challenging flourish, and a time to turn it into a locked door severely guarding the wicket.

Cricket is wearisome and sterile only when the minds of the players are wearisome and sterile, or when the prize, the aggregates and records, render impulses of sport null and void. Thou shalt not covet thy colleague's average. On the other hand, the true cricketer has no use for the cant pretending that the other side is as much entitled to victory, or any sort of prowess, as his own. 'May the best team win.' 'Certainly,' said the Hon. F. S. Jackson, a Yorkshireman, 'but our team is the best.'

Between 1920 and 1938 the greatest of all cricket matches in this country was the least active and animated as far as the score-board was concerned. I refer, of course, to the Lancashire and Yorkshire match in the heyday of Rhodes, Robinson and Makepeace. No sight more humorous could be witnessed, in the most humorous places of our land—Sheffield for instance—than Rhodes bowling so cannily, determined not to give the ghost of a run away; bowling with all his skill and shrewdness outside Makepeace's off-stump, while Makepeace, crouching low, his eyes bright with suspicion, was obviously not going to lift his bat an inch from the base of his stumps, not on his life, not if somebody were to come and present him with a full-toss on a silver salver.

Character, unselfconscious character—that's where the fun

23

comes in. Nerve, wit, muscle and skill, all absorbed, sucked dry by passion for cricket: these things have made Lancashire and York-shire matches grand and historical.

I am not, I hope, spoiling the case I set out in this article to argue, if I cast my mind back to cricket in which austerity was indeed a virtue. Times are different; besides, Lancashire and Yorkshire are inimitable places of the North of England, with ideas of their own about *joie de vivre*.

Test matches at the present day are part of our means of national rest and refreshment. The players are fortunate that, week after week, their occupation takes them into the open air, and that they will fail us only if they do not succeed in enjoying themselves.

THE SORCERER'S APPRENTICE

WHEN the Australian match began against Middlesex the edge of the field became the schoolboys' opportunity and fairground. Only the coconuts were wanting: there was orange peel enough.

On an easy wicket Middlesex began indifferently, for Robertson allowed Johnston to bowl him behind his back or his legs, which amounted to the same thing.

Lindwall now and again switched on his faster pace, but on the whole he allowed the batsmen to perform a stroke rationally intended in the first place. When he retired to his sweater—and what a season for sweaters it is, and as Betsy Trotwood might well ask, 'Why in the name of Heaven, sweater?'—Johnston seemed to be the Australians' only really antagonistic bowler.

Brown played well and confidently; Edrich moved very confidently to the bowling and repeatedly struck it strongly to the fieldsmen's hands along the grass.

Again we could believe that the Australians' attack is not penetrating after the new ball has waned and Johnston is resting.

With much composure, Brown and Edrich scored 65 together. Lindwall tried again, still not prestissimo, McCool could sometimes not hit the floor, and during several overs I noticed that he pitched on the off: hardly ever did he spin his leg break from the leg stump.

When all appeared set fair for the county, Edrich snicked to Tallon from a ball swinging past his left side, and with lunch imminent, Brown closed a most promising innings by a lazy stroke to extra cover.

Then, after the interval, Dewes was unable to avoid playing a quicker ball from Johnston, and Tallon caught him swiftly, while all the Australians near the wicket threw up their arms and emitted onomatopoeia at the umpire. Johnston now had taken three for 20 , in 13 overs. He swings his left arm and body powerfully and purposefully, and usually he demands to be played as the ball comes in with his arm.

Middlesex, 92 for four, were not happily placed. Mann came in, and Compton was at the other end, the cynosure of all eyes, his every stroke punctuated by small boys choiring like the cherubim. No cricketer has even meant as much to schoolboys—and schoolgirls, if it comes to that—as Compton. He is, of course, himself a schoolboy in excelsis, a schoolboy with the technique of maturity. As he executes a stroke we can admire the bloom and vintage of years of the game's long culture; none the less. Compton himself remains young. He is a wiser sort of sorcerer's apprentice.

He was at his best and easiest and most winning; he made his many strokes with time to spare, leaning over for his lissom square drives, and turning to leg as comfortably as a man in one of those chairs that swing round. He has the art—and the leisure—to play Lindwall back from the region of his left breast bone.

By private arrangement he made a monopoly of the bowling, so that for a long time Mann was not the least admiring spectator on the ground. But Mann reminded us that he was engaged actively in the game by an off-drive from Johnston so excellent that the small boys unanimously put the four down to Compton in their rather desultorily-kept scoring books.

When Lindwall bowls at any batsman other than Compton he looks to be yards faster. The Australian fielding was beautiful: a pick up by Brown at long leg thrilled eyesight, blood and body alike. Compton's strokes rippled and flickered everywhere, so that the pigeons could find no place of rest, and the grass and air were a seascape of wings.

Loxton now bowled really well, and not only struck Compton on the knee painfully but clean bowled him a few overs afterwards. Lindwall caught L. Compton at cover from a good stroke; Lindwall's capital fielding is possibly not altogether approved by the Union of Fast Bowlers.

Jim Sims failed to do himself justice as batsman, and McCool after all took two wickets.

JESSOP THE CROUCHER

IT is the grossest error to think of Gilbert Jessop (who died yesterday at 80) as a rude primitive hitter: it is almost blasphemous to
describe him as a 'slogger'. In first-class cricket during a period
when bowling was at its best, often on natural wickets, he scored
29,930 runs, average 32, with 54 innings of three figures. No
cricketer lacking science could maintain Jessop's pace and prodigality.

The secret of his swift aggression was his command of the cut,
which was quick and powerful. Because of this stroke in Jessop's
armoury bowlers were afraid to pitch short: and as soon as they
tossed the ball into the air Jessop leapt panther-like to the kill. The
'slogger' can be tamed by the length that is just too short: he has no
wrists, no footwork. Jessop was one of the finest cutters the game
has known: also he was a driver on quick feet—so what could the
poor bowlers do if he happened to find his form?

The 'poor bowlers' included all the masters of accurate length and
direction—J. T. Hearne, Mead, Trumble, Noble, Relf, Hirst.
Among them were classical fast bowlers—Richardson, Lockwood,
Mold, Bestwick, Kortright, Brearley. Superb spin bowlers suffered
under Jessop too—Rhodes, Blythe, Haigh. All of them were put to
the sword.

On four occasions he made two separate centuries in a match:
104 and 139 in the match between Gloucestershire and Yorkshire at
Bradford in 1900. He scored his 104 out of 153 in 70 minutes and his
139 out of 182 in 95 minutes with at least a quarter of an hour
wasted while the ball was brought back from places adjacent.
Against Hampshire at Bristol in 1909 he made 161 and 129. The
innings of 161, scored out of 199, was cut and driven in 95 minutes.
The highest score of his career, 286 against Sussex at Hove in 1903,
was a whirlwind lasting five minutes under three hours: the first 50
came in half an hour, 100 in 70 minutes, and 200 in two hours.
Against the Players of the South in 1907 he scored 191 in 90 minutes.

But even Jessop never performed a miracle more staggering to
mind, imagination, and mental arithmetic than his 104 for England
at Kennington Oval in 1902. On a nasty wicket England were
apparently doomed: they needed 263 and five wickets fell for 48.
The cream of English batsmanship, MacLaren, Palairet, Tyldesley,
Hayward, Braund, all out to a triumphant Australian attack—
Trumble, Saunders, Noble, Armstrong. Jessop now went out to

bat, square of shoulder, square of chin. He at once attacked. Before he had come to the wicket the Australian field had seemed a ruthless machine, every man in a ravenous place, every ball dropping on a vicious spot. In a short space of time the Australian ranks were more or less a rabble running here and there. The bowlers recoiled, helpless in the teeth of the cyclone. And at the centre of the cyclone was a calm pivotal spot. Jessop's eye and brain were always un-ruffled and discerning while he scattered far and wide the best of balls, crashed them against sightscreens, through windows of pavilions, into the bottles and glasses of bars, on the roofs of houses in the vicinity. At Kennington Oval, on that August afternoon, Jessop scored 50 in 55 minutes, then another 54 in twenty minutes.

A hit counting six had to go out of the ground in those days, not merely into the crowd but out of the premises, so to say. At Scar-borough against Kent in 1913, playing for an England Eleven, he made 116 in an hour. In one over he drove D. W. Carr (a 'googly' bowler) for 26—4, 6, 6, 4, 6. One of those blows landed the ball in Trafalgar Square, and years afterwards when the deed was related to an old lady in London, a friend of Jessop's and fond of cricket, she is reported to have asked. 'And was Gilbert playing at Lord's or at Kennington Oval?'

Against South Africa at Lord's in 1917, he scored 93 in an hour and a quarter: and Kotze, one of the fastest of all bowlers, was obliged and grateful to place four men to guard the boundary.

The sight of Jessop going forth to bat would cause a cricket crowd today to wonder what on earth was about to happen to the game. Before he had walked menacingly half-way to the crease four of five fielders would be seen journeying to far-flung positions, going there as though by instinct for self-preservation, not by official direction.

Jessop played for Gloucestershire from 1894 to 1914. He was in the Cambridge University Eleven in the seasons of 1896–9. He played for England in eighteen Test matches. He was one of the matchless England team which took the field at Birmingham in 1902—A. C. MacLaren, C. B. Fry, K. S. Ranjitsinhji, F. S. Jackson, J. T. Tyldesley, A. A. Lilley, G. H. Hirst, G. L. Jessop, L. C. Braund, W. H. Lockwood, and W. Rhodes. Of these cricketers only Fry and Rhodes remain with us now.

Jessop, besides his cutting and driving, found time to take 878 wickets, average 22. In 1900 he scored 2,210 runs and helped him-self to 104 wickets. Needless to say he bowled fast. Also he was a cover-point rapid and comprehensive, with a shattering throw-in, rattling the stumps with sounds terrible to hear by panting and deceived batsmen. He was a force of nature, not to be accounted for in terms of cricketing talent. Nature breaks the mould in which her wonders are made. There will be no second of G. L Jessop, the 'Croucher'.

GHOSTS FROM THE PAST

YORKSHIRE batted so imperceptibly at Leeds today that a Yorkshire crowd was impelled to clap hands at defensive strokes of a Yorkshire player, Halliday, while he was travelling in the nineties of his innings. As I shall hope to show in this message, the match had the form but not the genius of Lancashire and Yorkshire battles long ago.

Lancashire bowled ably, but it was as well to forget Walter Brearley, who in 14 Lancashire and Yorkshire matches took 125 wickets; and Briggs and Parkin; and the piercing, silent speed and destruction of McDonald.

This was a cricket match of competent bat and ball, not a bone of contention gnawed by Lancashire and Yorkshire teeth and jawbone—wits pitted against wits, thrust and temper and humour the source of every move, with fair cheating all round.

Where, oh where, was Emmott Robinson?

It is many years since I repaired to the matches of these Northern folk, but I watched and wrote upon every one of them between 1919 and 1939, and though old ghosts from the past came distractingly today between present actuality, yet the setting was the same, the crowd vast enough, the scene far from pastoral under a gloomy sky and the red and white roses on the caps of the cricketers, some of whom were perhaps rather too young really to know what they were doing, in a feud a hundred years old and murmurous with tradition.

These innocents could at least claim indulgence and benefit under a sort of First Offenders' Act, and very soon in the day's proceedings a young man needed almost the benefit of clergy to condone an error not altogether his own.

From the third ball, bowled by Pollard, Hutton went for a single pushed by himself in front of the wicket. Whether his call was audible I am unable to say, but Lowson remained stationary and Hutton could not turn quickly enough to regain his crease. He was run out.

The stroke or push did not go far, the direction was towards forward or close mid-on, and a batsman of Hutton's greatness needed surely to be in no such reckless hurry to open his score on an occasion so momentous. Lowson's immobility though it added to Hutton's strangely precipitate action, was understandable. But I go hot and cold to imagine Sutcliffe being run out third ball in a Yorkshire and Lancashire match from a stroke of his own in front of the wicket.

The Yorkshire heavens would have wept.

It is a sign of the times that the Headingley crowd witnessed this downfall of Hutton for a duck in a respectful silence: there was no blasphemy, no necessity for reference to the Riot Act. And it was to be noted that at half-past one, Lowson returned to the pavilion for his lunch, and didn't stay in the field and have it brought to him.

Halliday, who batted after Hutton, was nearly caught at first slip in the same first over of Pollard, also for nothing. While the ball remained new, Pollard persuaded it to rise once or twice wrist-high, but only from a shortish length: the wicket was easy, almost apathetic.

So changed is this match in character and blood pressure that not until ten minutes past twelve did we hear an appeal of authentic temper, and it was emitted from the throat and lungs of Pollard, who is recognizably a grand survival from other years: he thought he had got Halliday caught at the wicket.

In the same over Pollard broke through Halliday's defence, striking his pads, and he looked for justice to the sky above. Why didn't everybody appeal now, square leg and third man? As Richard Tyldesley said, 'There's no harm in askin', and it costs nowt.'

Pollard bowled excellently for nearly an hour, and at half-past twelve Yorkshire were 43 for 1. Lowson 18, Halliday 20. Obviously the young men are being brought up to the game, even if a boundary to the on by Lowson and another to the off by Halliday might have been deemed out of order during the period when, in Lancashire and Yorkshire matches no fours were hit before lunch, on principle.

When Ikin took part in the attack, he struck Halliday's pad second ball and appealed; but, like Pollard, he appealed alone, with no body of opinion behind him. Once on a time, in such matches, appeals were unanimous, with only the umpire occasionally a dissentient.

Though slow and pedestrian, without majesty or the nature which commands, Lowson and Halliday played pleasantly enough, always performing good professional strokes, Lowson with some hint of style, Halliday with a nose-on-the-ball kind of opportunism and broad shoulders ready to attend to loose stuff.

Only imagination was wanted to transform utility into a better and more purposeful and creative world.

The Lancashire attack, especially the flight of Berry, was calculated to keep down runs against batsmen unwilling to chance a full unchecked swing of the bat.

Yorkshire's second wicket fell after lunch when Lowson was leg before to the deserving Pollard. Lowson and Halliday added 105 in roughly two hours, and in this period Halliday reached 50.

Berry pleased me by the curved flight of his left-handed bowling, but the wicket was all against him. Of course, no attempt was made to hit him or Ikin on quick feet, and so the game became rather null and void, not to say invisible. It was one thing, in the old days, to watch Rhodes bowling at Makepeace, maiden after maiden, the two old soldiers at work undermining, so to say, Sappers of suspicion. But the spectacle of Wilson putting a bolted door of a bat before Ikin's off-breaks was not an inspiration of heroic poetry or humour.

A sudden cut to the boundary by Wilson off Berry was quite electrical, and when Halliday at 77 mishit a ball from Pollard over the slips, the crowd broke silence.

Not that the batting of Halliday and Wilson was without skill and appeal; it simply fell short of the power to dictate and bend good but not difficult bowling to its will.

Ikin bowled Halliday just before tea. He was on view nearly four hours and the crowd watched him return to the pavilion with only a formal show of regret that he had missed a century by so few. Yet there had been capability in his innings: the trouble about most of our county batsmen nowadays is that the longer they stay in, the more slowly they score their runs. They seem positively reluctant to free and enjoy themselves, poor fellows.

Rain fell after tea, and though it was not heavy and though an hour and more's cricket might well be possible, the crowd dispersed.

The game resumed almost in camera, and then Wilson was bowled by Greenwood, who has possibilities with his off spin. At the close Yorkshire, in four hours 55 minutes had scored 211 for four, and it seemed slower than that to the naked eye.

30

GEORGE HIRST—THE COMPLETE YORKSHIREMAN

G EORGE HIRST was one of the greatest of cricketers, and nobody in the North of England will think the less of him if the fact is remembered that he gave his best for Yorkshire and less than his best for England.

In his career he scored 36,196 runs (average, 34) and took 2,723 wickets (average, 18·75). But against Australia his batting worked out at only 24 an innings for 746 runs, and he took not more than 49 wickets (average, 24·86).

The skill and power of Hirst were Yorkshire's perquisite in years when Yorkshire held the county championship almost as a matter of nature, and he was equal to taking five wickets for nine when the Australians were bowled out at Leeds for 23 in 1902, his victims being the incomparable Trumper, Duff, Darling, Noble, and Armstrong.

He was more than a great Yorkshire cricketer; he was a truly representative Yorkshireman. No other county, and none other but his period, could have produced him. He belonged to the era of the amateur, when professional players such as Hirst, Hayward, and Shrewsbury would raise their hats if they met their captains and say, 'Good morning, sir,' not losing but gaining dignity by doing so. In Yorkshire's pomp, the professionals enjoyed the privilege of addressing their captain as 'Y'r Lardship'; for Yorkshire cricket at this time was as much dominated by Lord Hawke as Kent's was by Lord Harris.

'And all the Gentlemen are players and all the Players gentlemen,' wrote the poet Craig, in the jingles he sold to the crowd at Kennington Oval. Hirst was certainly a gentleman, kind and courteous, with a twinkle in his eyes, and an incomprehensible accent. He was 5 ft. 6 in. in height and weighed fourteen stones and more; but in his prime he was a splendid example of strength and elasticity. He bowled with a hop, skip, and a bounce, and became a deadly taker of wickets as soon as he discovered, not by abstract thought, the trick of a swerve.

How innocent cricketers of the early 1900s were of 'swing' and seam may be deduced from the following comment in 'Wisden':

'As in the case of other bowlers who have possessed the same peculiarity, he could not keep up this swerve through a long innings,

31

but while it lasted he was irresistible and quite independent of the condition of the ground.'

During the seasons under notice only one ball was used in an innings. As John Gunn once put it, 'We went on wi' t'old 'un till they was all out or till it come in two.' Hirst's swerve, bowled left hand and fast, has been described vividly by C. B. Fry; it came to the batsman like a lightning throw-in from cover point.

He was the terror of all schoolboys born in Lancashire. He would open the Yorkshire attack with Rhodes—yes, a slow and a quick bowler on at once, whatever the state of the pitch—and he would roll up the sleeve of his bowling arm, which resembled a Yorkshire ham. I would tremble as I saw him ready to hurl red-hot swervers into the wickets protected by my beloved 'Reggie' Spooner. And I would hate the sight of him. Impressions from my infancy and youth have nearly persuaded me that Hirst and Rhodes year after year rubbed Lancashire noses in the dust, but on consulting calm, impartial history I find that on several Bank Holidays Hirst, and also Rhodes were held back, if not mastered, by MacLaren, Spooner, Tyldesley, and Sharp.

The truth is that an indelible mark was made on my memory one Whitsuntide when George Hirst rolled up his left sleeve at Old Trafford to the tune of seven for 23, and Lancashire were all out for 44. I have seldom since seen a bowler bouncing to attack with Hirst's confident, almost affable, ferocity that day. The point of Hirst's power of destruction with both bat and ball is that it was wreaked so genially on the just and unjust alike that his skill resembled his nature and the benefactory sun. He was at his best for Yorkshire or England at moments of crisis. Then the smile and twinkle might go for a while and the sturdy face and figure stiffen. Not for long, though. A thaw began as soon as he went down on his left knee and pulled a ball prodigiously round from the offside over the square-leg boundary. A stroke as big as his own heart, which was as big as Ilkley Moor. He once clean bowled P. F. Warner at Lord's, bringing to an end a superb innings. Now Sir Pelham suffered much from illness in his cricketing days, and when he passed Hirst on this occasion on the way back to the pavilion, George said: 'Well played, sir—if God had given you a proper stomach you'd 'a been a champion, Mester Warner.'

People who believe that all truth is factual, discredit the story that when England wanted fifteen to win at Kennington Oval in 1902, Hirst said to Rhodes: 'Wilfred, we'll get 'em in ones.' For my part, I am certain that Hirst gave advice much to this effect: and I am equally satisfied that he added: 'And, Wilfred, if tha gets out Ah shall warm thee.'

When he made the highest score of his career—341 against Leicestershire—he was alleged to have been out lbw before he had scored. I questioned him years afterwards on this matter. 'Nay,' he replied. 'Nay, Ah'm saying nowt. It's not for me to ursurp t'territory o' the umpire.' There was the savour and sweetness of a Yorkshire sort of Shakespeare character about him.

With Rhodes and Haigh he made a wonderful triumvirate—a terrible one in my young eyes. In those years the Lancashire and Yorkshire match was the most brilliant and gripping to the imagination of all matches: how could it well be anything else with such cricketers as the following in action, all challengers and eager to be challenged?: MacLaren, Lord Hawke, R. H. Spooner, F. S. Jackson ('the Hon.'), Hirst, Tyldesley, Denton, Sharp, Rhodes, Walter Brearley, H. G. Garnett, David Hunter, Haigh, J. T. Brown. You could pick from such a company an eleven of Lancashire and Yorkshire players capable of reducing our best contemporary England team to mincemeat, especially if we claimed, as by right of his birth we could, Hutton. And none of them would be greater than George Hirst.

He took part in 601 matches for Yorkshire, and Yorkshire won 325 of them and lost only 76. While he was one of the eleven, Yorkshire were champions ten times and were usually in the first three. At mid-off he was impenetrable; he held 518 catches for Yorkshire, nearly all of them taken in front of the wicket. He never got W. G. Grace out, but he would say with relish, 'The old man never got me.'

Cricketers everywhere will lament that another link has been broken. Yorkshire have reason today to grieve, but also to feel proud. He lived into his eighty-third year, and now he is returned to his native soil.

THE END OF SUMMER

IN a few days, cricket will come to the end, and then for some of us there will seem nothing at all to do until we get used to it—nowhere to go in the morning and nothing to read in the newspapers, not even the skimpy reports printed nowadays, impoverished successors of the tabulated columns of old, with the report in small type telling us that 'Lockwood went on at the Nursery end vice Richardson.'

The passing of cricket is a proper theme for sentiment, because it goes out with the end of the summer. Not even the passionate supporter of football can really be melancholy when spring has come; and golf and tennis may be—and I believe are—played in some shape or form the year round. But they are not English games really.

After a few more afternoons at the Festivals we shall be separated; no other game brings so many people together for so long a time in the same place day after day for a few swift months. Cricket is founded as much on good friendship as on skill and conflict. It allows time for talk, on the field and off.

So, though we have grumbled at a wet season, and complained of many things, and written to the Press about the decline and fall of cricket, we are a sad lot today, hateful of the crowds at Highbury, Maine Road and other heathen places. And memory gets quickly to work, getting rid of the dross, leaving only impressions worth while.

There is much to add to the store of years, happiest of all the fact that the County Championship has been won by Glamorgan. As a nation we always admire the vanquishing of the big by the little bantam Pertinacity. Glamorgan have played with spirit, and have boasted no fancy men, no mighty names. Here we have the popular consummation—the success of average merit, plus enthusiasm and team-work.

All together, boys, indeed. But certain names may be honoured as we make our congratulations. Wooller, the captain, has led and stimulated his men by precept and example. Honour must also be done to the work of pioneers in Welsh cricket, reaching to the days of Riches, not to forget the heroic toilers Creber and Nash. Then, most inspiring of all in recent times, Maurice Turnbull; and J. C. Clay, who in disheartening years declined to give up, but played his best in a cause nearly lost.

Bravo, Glamorgan.

The Australians have lifted the season to historical levels. The year of the centenary of Grace has seen the farewell of Bradman. New stars have risen, old ones are waning—but one of them is setting in some splendour, if such language can be applied to the veteran Jim Sims, of Middlesex and Lord's; with his smile and his conversation, his roll to the wicket ('I'll give 'em the old "googly", skipper'), and his wetting of the finger for every ball.

He has enjoyed wonderful weeks since the half-way stage, wickets against Australians, a century, a match-winning innings at the Oval. What is more, he has shown himself on his day still as good a leg-spinner as any in the land.

In the North, the big battalions are gathering again. It is only a matter of time for Yorkshire once more to dominate and destroy. Lancashire, too, are moving ahead, with an amateur batsman likely to go to the top, and wear the cap with the lovely red rose as proudly as it was worn by Spooner, Maclaren or Garnett.

Time heals wounds, and it is natural that our cricket should be a little 'down', needing a little more time for convalescence. Nottinghamshire and Sussex in their lowly places will revive by remembering their traditions. Somerset had their hour: a moral win against Yorkshire, and Gimblett's mighty triple-hundred. Worcestershire found Palmer and a gifted player who has not yet caught the general eye—Outschoorn.

There is no space to render just tribute to everybody, in Kent, in Hampshire, in Essex, in Leicestershire, in Surrey, in Northamptonshire, in Derbyshire, in Gloucestershire, in Warwickshire, and in Worcestershire. All in all they have, in favourable or unfavourable hours, played the game heart and soul, and have deserved the applause of the splendid crowds that have flocked to see.

There is not much that is wrong with English cricket that cannot be cured by time and patience. The great thing is that the people of England hold cricket as closely as ever before in their affections.

DULEEPSINHJI

K. S. DULEEPSINHJI, former Sussex and England cricketer and one of the world's most attractive batsmen, died in his sleep of a heart attack at Bombay on Saturday. He was 54. He was forced to give up active cricket at the height of his power in 1933 because of ill-health. Later he devoted much of his time to acting as coach, adviser, and selector of English and Indian teams.

In 1949 he joined the Indian Foreign Office, and a year later was appointed India's High Commissioner in Australia and New Zealand. He returned to India in 1953 and in 1954 was appointed chairman of the public service commission in Saurashtra.

Kumar Shri Duleepsinhji was an accomplished and beautiful batsman during a period of handsome stroke players, a breed now fairly extinct. He came to cricket in 1925, when critics only middle-aged remembered his uncle—'Ranji'—and therefore he had to face a severe, indeed an unreasonable comparison. He at once revealed kin not only of race but of style with the batsman described by George Giffen, the Australian captain, as a 'so-and-so conjuror'. But 'Duleep's' cricket was more definable in terms of English traditions than that of his uncle. He was as supple of wrist without the oriental jugglery, the Ranjitsinhji legerdemain. He was a brilliant schoolboy at Cheltenham College, where he was taught to play like an English gentleman, though he added to a quite classic technique the Indian swiftness of eye and of feet. Indian cricket had not yet fallen under the utilitarian paralysis which afflicts nearly all Test-match performance of the present time.

Duleepsinhji drove brilliantly, without apparent effort. At first he was limited in strokes to the offside, but soon developed easefully in that and every other direction. It was not necessary for the spectator to keep his eye on the score board to identify 'Duleep' at the wicket. Take away the score board from most important games to-day and the cricket would mean nothing.

He scored 75 in the university match of 1925. A year later, now qualified for Sussex, he scored 97 against Leicestershire in his first county match (nearly equalling 'Ranji's' feat of scoring a century in his first). In 1929, at the age of 24, he was one of the elect, the cynosure of the connoisseurs' eyes, in a period when standards of strokeplay were established by Hammond, Woolley, Bowley of Sussex, Percy Holmes, Sandham, to name a few. He took his place sixth in the batting averages with 2,545 runs, average 53·02. For Sussex v. Middlesex, at Hastings in this summer of 1929, he scored 115 and 246 not out in the same match; his 115 was rippled over the field in 100 minutes; his 246, scored in three hours and a quarter, contained five sixes and 31 fours.

In 1930 he played for England; India was not then in the international Test cycle. At Lord's he adorned the perfect Test match, the Test match of the cricketers' dreams, with all the talents in it, every kind of batsman and bowler, brilliant and steady, fast and slow, and medium pace, leg and off-spin, cricket in apotheosis, played in four days of heavenly sunshine. England went in first and amassed 425 and were not all out until 12.30 on the second day. With only four days available for a decision England surely were safe. But Australia scored 729 for six and declared . . . and though England retaliated with 375 Australia won by seven wickets.

On the first day 'Duleep' enchanted a vast crowd. Though Hobbs, Woolley, and Hammond fell for only 105, 'Duleep' stroked the ball here, there, and everywhere with elegance and charm. His late cutting left even Australian slips standing. His cricket was as though part of the afternoon's sunshine; it gleams in my mind even as I write these lines, more than 29 years after. 'Duleep' scored 173 in four hours and three-quarters. Thinking that England's position was safe enough at a quarter to six, with the total 387 in a four-day engagement, he hit too soon and was caught Bradman, bowled Grimmett. His uncle was present, watching from a box. 'Duleep', after removing his pads, went into the presence. And 'Ranji' greeted him with a severe 'My boy, that was a very careless stroke.'

In the 1930 rubber against Australia, 'Duleep's' innings, measured statistically, amounted to 173, 48, 35, 10, 54, 50, and 46. This was his wonderful year; he scored a century in both innings for the Gentlemen *v.* the Players at Lord's—125 in two and a half hours, and 103 not out in two hours five minutes, against Larwood, Tate, Freeman, Geary, Woolley, and Leyland (who, by the way, took nine wickets for 130 in the match!).

His cricket was doomed to a brief span; pulmonary disease cruelly stole from the game a precious possession while he had many summers of radiance unspent. He played his last match in 1932, when as captain of Sussex he led the county to the second place in the championship table. Illness prevented him from accepting an invitation to join the England team sailing for Australia that autumn. He was only 27 years old when he put away his bat for the last time.

He scored 49 hundreds, four in consecutive innings. In 1930 he cut and drove and glanced 333 against Northamptonshire at Brighton—in five and a half hours. Like 'Ranji' himself, he was a swift and lovely slip fieldsman; again like 'Ranji', he was a modest, charming personality. As a batsman, he played close to the line of the ball—he would not have been 'Ranji's' nephew if he had not. There is a curious notion circulating among cricketers today that the great stroke players of the past lacked solid defences. I put this point to Larwood, the last time I saw him. He bluntly replied: 'Ah never noticed it myself when ah had to bowl at 'em.'

A CENTURY FOR THE CONNOISSEUR

MIDDLESEX, who are already sure of sharing County Championship honours, and will win them outright if Yorkshire fail to beat Glamorgan, were in dire straits against New Zealand before lunch at Lord's today. A valiant stand by Dewes lent aid to Compton whose innings, in spite of actual disasters and threats of further wrath to come, began in a mood so effortless as to suggest that he had omitted to look at the score-board or could not add up correctly. After Brown, Edrich and Robertson had departed in Indian file for next to nothing. Compton and Dewes, in a fourth-wicket stand, scored 210. Dewes, as we shall read hereafter, enjoyed some luck, and subsequently proved he had deserved it.

It is a pity Middlesex and Yorkshire cannot play and fight out the issue between them before the end of this wonderful season of sunshine. Admittedly, Middlesex received a drubbing from Yorkshire when they challenged them several years ago, in a match improvised at the Oval. I refer to this match now solely to protect myself from reminders of it, delivered post-haste, even if sometimes unstamped, from Leeds, Pudsey, Laisterdyke and such places.

It was a perfect morning, made a little melancholy by a faint autumn mist. This same mist encouraged the new ball to swing, and the wicket, though good enough for good batsmanship, was not of the kind consistently depressing to good bowlers.

Cowie thumped Robertson's thigh straightaway; then Reid, whose first ball swung so prodigiously that it was denounced by Umpire Hills as a wide, bowled Brown in the same over with a superb swerve which veered from leg. A few moments later Reid, with another leg swinger, thoroughly defeated Edrich and Middlesex were now 3 for 2—a state of things which suggested we were going through the horrors of Friday morning again, in a nightmare.

Next Cowie delivered an out-swinger—the first ball from him which moved that way—and Robertson fell to a catch at the wicket.

With the total at 21, Dewes was missed behind the stumps by Mooney, who, to the accompaniment of general appeal, dropped a difficult low chance after he had apparently got a fair hold on it.

Compton, who came in as though his great innings of Friday was still in being, played so easily that his bat seemed to make lovely strokes by some habit of its own. He drove, or rather the bat drove (entirely with Compton's charming if casual consent), a 4 to the off from Reid; then an in-swinger from the same bowler was flicked, against the rules maybe, to long-on.

But even Compton, in this mood, could not at once play the New Zealand attack without a certain watchfulness. Reid, in his spell with the new ball, was really dangerous, and for 75 minutes Cowie, from the pavilion end, kept up a steady fire, an in-swinger from time to time calling for prompt attention, and an off-break from the pitch preventing that beatific somnambulism in which many centuries are scored nowadays.

Dewes was sensible enough to embrace his second opportunity, not with passion at first, but always with tenacity. He is a very sensible batsman, chock-full of cricket, vigilant and usually over the line of the ball, in personal touch with it, his bat endowed with eyesight, antennae, cat's whiskers.

He actually kept his score for a while more or less level with Compton's, and Middlesex emerged yet again from a grave, not to say ridiculous, state of affairs. At lunch they were 88 for three, and immediately afterwards, Dewes, in quick sequence, hit 4's to leg and square leg, each a muscular blow, with a swing of stimulating vehemence.

At 20 minutes to three, Compton reached 50. The cricket was in tune with the mellow afternoon and the gentle wane of the sun of this vintage summer. But Compton here and there would recall the first careless rapture of May by running out of his ground at Cowie, whose persistence at the pavilion end threatened to bring him under the notice of the Fast Bowlers' Union for an infringement of the '20-over day'.

Compton made strokes with so much leisure, so much time to spare, that he might well himself have been watching them and admiring them like the rest of us. One day he will drop his bat and applaud a hit of his own, and join in the cheers of the schoolboys and modestly ask himself for his own autograph.

An off drive by Dewes was classic in its strength and ease. He is a batsman of rare possibilities; we shall hear much more of him, and so, I fancy, will the Australians some day. And now Compton showed us how to hit a full toss, from Burke, for a lusty four.

A square drive by Compton, off Rabone, called back the brilliance of June; he was at his best, his happiest, his most winning, masterful yet courtly, not belabouring the bowlers with his strokes but engaging them in an ideal afternoon's cricket. His century, one of his most felicitous and enjoyable for a long time past, was made out of 179, and could have been played only by one who is a charming man as well as a great cricketer.

When he was 86, Dewes provoked quite hectic excitement and controversy. He cut Cowie to Reid, at first slip, shoulder high and Reid caught the ball—in some people's opinion, left-handed—but he then dropped it, and Dewes was adjudged not out. But poetic justice was immediately done to New Zealand, and possibly to Dewes, who eight short of his century, sent a similar chance to Reid's left hand, at slip off Cowie.

Dewes, not for the only time these last few days, served Middlesex faithfully, skilfully and well, in a period of impending bankruptcy.

After tea Compton performed all manner of strokes—some of them he had apparently only just thought of—but all of them were redolent of Compton.

He exhausted his repertoire, then got out. An innings of champagne for the connoisseur, with a little ginger 'pop' for the children. The New Zealand bowlers and fieldsmen stuck to their task gamely, and, with Compton not there, they advanced once more.

Sharp, Mann and Leslie Compton were dismissed processionally, so Young arrived at the wicket, and hit a fine and savage 4, as good a stroke as any seen all day. But he became suddenly clean bowled, ninth out at 271.

The innings ended with a grand and diverting display by Sims, mostly at the expense of Cowie and Burtt.

With time left for only two overs at the long day's end, New Zealand opened with Sutcliffe and Scott, and in one stroke, a drive to the off from Edrich, Sutcliffe announced his class and pedigree.

LEYLAND, A LOVABLE FIGHTER

MAURICE LEYLAND, who died yesterday aged 66, was a Yorkshire cricketer from a vintage period. Incidentally, he performed prodigies of courage, obstinacy and skill for England. I use the word 'incidentally' advisedly in relation to the career and outlook of Maurice Leyland because, for him, Yorkshire always came first.

At Sydney, the Australian 'Hill' once barracked him for his

obstinacy in a dour hour during an England innings. Afterwards he said to me, 'Didst hear 'em makin' a row on t' "Hill"? They should coom to Sheffield on Bank Holiday and hear crowd there. Why, compared to them, these folk on t' "Hill" sounded to me as 'armonious as Huddersfield Choral Society.'

He was a left-handed batsman, with strong forearms like Yorkshire hams. His position at the wicket told of mingled composure and watchfulness. Though he stood wide of the blockhole, gripping his bat rather high up the handle, the right hand came down determinedly enough, should the ball keep at all low.

He was of that rare and almost obsolete species of batsman (in this country) of whom you could say that it was difficult to point out where offensive methods ended and defensive methods began. He could drive the fastest bowling on the rise, scarcely moving any part of his body, excepting his arms, as he did so; for his judgment was so quick and sure that he could get his feet into position a split-second before the ball pitched. He would drive far to long-off, then, standing still as a pillar, put a hand to his eyes, as though shading them, as he contemplated the destination of the ball.

In Test matches, he amassed 2,764 runs, average 46·06, with seven centuries against Australia, between 1928 and 1938. He scored 187 in the Test match *v*. Australia in 1938, when England's total was piled up to 903 for 7 (declared). Hutton 364. This aggregate was made with a terribly deliberate slowness. Leyland solemnly, but humorously, resisted the Australian attack for more than six hours, stonewalling even as England's total stood at 500 for 3. He had been left out of the England XI in the preceding Tests of this 1938 season—he who for years had been England's anchor in any stormy sea. I chided him that day at The Oval at the tea interval: 'Even you, Maurice,' I complained, 'even you are perpetuating this stonewall game.' 'Hey,' he replied, 'hey, but Mester Cardus, tha must remember as I'm playing for mi place in team.'

He was superb in Australia for G. O. Allen's 1936–37 plucky and unlucky England XI, the first batsman to take the measure of W. J. O'Reilly, then the first of spin bowlers in the world. One morning outside the Belle Vue Hotel in Brisbane, an hour or two before the beginning of the first match of this 1936–37 rubber, he openly said to O'Reilly, 'Well Bill, destiny of this rubber's in lap of gods. But I can tell thi one thing already, for certain—I've got thee taped, and tha knows it.' He wasn't boasting; he was simply stating a fact. He proceeded to the ground forthwith, to score 126.

It was during this game at Brisbane that an appeal against the light was turned down, even though in the Press Box we could not easily see to write. But after a few more overs, during which Voce bowled Fingleton, the umpires decided to put an end to the proceedings. As the players were walking off the field, Leyland engaged one of the umpires in conversation. 'Tha's got reight good eyesight,' he said. 'Now, Maurice,' replied the umpire, 'none of your sarcasm.' 'Ah'm not being sarcastic. Ah'm only sayin' tha's got good eyesight.' He paused, put his hand to his eyes, and gazed hard ahead. 'Tell me,' he asked, 'wheer's dressin' room?'

He enjoyed, in his career, scoring 33,660 runs, average 40·50, with eighty centuries. Also he liked to bowl left-hand spin, his trump-card the 'Chinaman'—whenever the ball 'hit floor'. This kind of bowling was not approved of in the Yorkshire XI. There has seldom been his equal as a resolute batsman in a crisis. In August 1924, he scored a century at Old Trafford for Yorkshire against Lancashire, facing Macdonald with equanimity. Later, in a discussion among cricketers about fast bowling and 'bouncers', he summed-up and settled the argument by saying. 'The fact is that *none* of us likes fast bowlin', but some of us doesn't let on.'

My most beloved story of this lovable Yorkshireman is about a Lancashire *v.* Yorkshire match at Old Trafford in 1933. The wicket at one end began to crumble on the first afternoon, but nobody in the Press Box was aware of this fact. Arthur Mitchell stonewalled bitterly for hours—six hours for 121. I wrote an ironical column, describing this Spartan innings. Next day I met Maurice before the game's resumption. 'Tha's written a funny article in *Guardian* this mornin',' he said. 'Thank you, Maurice,' I replied, 'I'm glad you liked it.' 'Aye,' he said, 'and tha'll have to write a funnier one for tomorrow.' George Macaulay bowled Lancashire out twice, for 93 and 92, on that Bank Holiday at Old Trafford long ago.

Ripe character and natural skill and Yorkshire passion, Yorkshire character at that. We won't many times know the like of Maurice Leyland. Myself, I grieve at the loss of a friend who, seldom met over many years, has remained warm in memory.

ENTER THE BOY TRUEMAN

MIDDLESEX, in this important match, walked up the hill in the morning and down in the afternoon. A first wicket worth 198 set the stage perfectly for Compton and Edrich. The Yorkshire retaliation retold an old, old story, and as a consequence of it the game is in an enticing position, promising a battle with no quarter given or asked on Monday.

Middlesex batted first on a wicket that looked good for runs, though after the toss had been lost by Yorkshire one of the Yorkshire players was heard to say in the pavilion that it 'looked a bit green'—but no doubt that was propaganda. Robertson and Brown, at any rate, seemed satisfied with the conditions, for before lunch they scored 112 for nil, and each completed 50.

During this time not a single appeal for leg-before was heard, nor was there excuse for one, not even from behind the stumps, let alone from square-leg. Robertson hit three 4's in the game's first overs from the boy Trueman, who bowled fast and well for these days in English cricket. There is promise here.

Trueman recalls Lindwall in certain of his physical movements. He shows his left side to the batsmen, the back foot acts as a strong, flexible stanchion, and as the arm swings over the boy's energy goes naturally into it.

When Middlesex were 94 the Yorkshire attack was shared by a bowler answering to the ominous name of Robinson, but even with this advantage behind him, he did not appeal for leg-before when he struck Robertson on the pads.

Robertson played at his best, easefully, the bat steered by supple wrists, the style pretty and upright, worth watching whether he was scoring or not, Brown, if more utilitarian, kept pace with Robertson and at quarter to three on a sunny if not tropical afternoon he was 76, Robertson 80, and the total 159 for 0.

The Lord's crowd was happy and contented, the Yorkshiremen in it silent as the grave.

Mason, slow to slow-medium left-hand, hinted of ability, but so secure and long-tenanted did Robertson and Brown seem to be that when Brown sliced an outswinger or off-side ball from Yardley through the slips, the fieldsmen there leaped about like monkeys snatching at bars and poles and perches in their cages.

Close came on at the pavilion end instead of Robinson. Naturally

43

he is an off spinner, but he is employed now and then to perform the 'new ball' mumbo-jumboism, and Robertson cracked him like artillery, arriving at a century in two-and-three-quarter hours, whereat Trueman beat him by pace and a ball that came through scandalously low. Here was a splendid over.

The partnership was ended abruptly at 198. Without due warning, Brown sent a rapid catch to the off-side, not far away from old-fashioned point. Trueman well and truly deserved the wicket. The boy was bowling with all his heart, and at the pace which compels the spasmodic, not to say agitated, stroke.

Brown's 88 was the reward of some three hours' recognizably professional ability, unaffected with no frills. The Yorkshire fielding showed more than a little of the old keenness and organization.

Edrich took time to draw widespread attention to his presence at the wicket, and Robertson also lapsed into masterly inactivity, so that ironic applause was provoked. Edrich then called for a new bat, and on receiving it sarcastically pointed it at the scoffers in the crowd, and then swung it mightily at a ball of his own imagining, driving an entirely hypothetical six over the Paddock. But the third ball sent to him, when he really began again with his new bat, clean bowled him. It is very hard to be funny sometimes.

A few overs later all of this merriment was changed to ashes in the mouth. A ball of lovely length by Yardley drew Compton forward. Apparently it 'came up the hill', and it bowled him comprehensively. Yardley has a knack of overthrowing old and young masters, and so admirably and simply does he achieve the dethronement that eyesight can scarcely be believed.

At tea, Yorkshire had taken three wickets for 227 and were making a match of it. They were being faithful to Macaulay, Rhodes and Emmott, 'after their fashion'.

The tea interval had no sooner been taken, and a bathbun run to earth, than Yardley caused Mann to play on, and Brennan dramatically and vividly stumped Robertson. Now Middlesex were 227 for five. Robertson's innings declined in resourcefulness just when we had reason to look for absolute mastery. The bowling undoubtedly gained in steadiness.

None the less, a complete batsman in form should dictate length, not bow before it, once he has passed his 100. Like many of our leading cricketers today, Robertson gives us batting which contains rather more of skill than character.

Yet again there was no appeal or attempt at one when Yardley struck a pad. Why this decline in the Yorkshire morale? But I have only just completed that sentence and a tolerably audible general appeal for leg-before has been granted to Mason against Sharp; but I often heard louder when George Macaulay was merely consulting the umpire and not himself delivering judgment.

Middlesex 198 for one, Middlesex 233 for six—a Yorkshireman in the crowd might reasonably have called it a volte face. The Middlesex innings fell into a green sickness, and it was a curious sight to behold Yardley bowling to the 'tail-end' batsmen with no fieldsman out far behind him. But Thompson drove Mason for a strong, swift 4 to the off and looked like a batsman. Then L. Compton hit a full toss from Trueman straight to the hands of mid-on.

The next man in was Sims, who had possibly not thought he would be called upon during the day. A late-cut of indeterminate direction was certainly not in keeping with his usual style but he recovered touch with a sweeping drive for 4. Close now bowled round the wicket. Sims drove him to the on for 4, the ball dropping in front of Lester as he ran in, but Sims expressed no apprehension. And when he was caught and bowled in the same over, he seemed as much surprised as anything else. A lovable cricketer.

Thompson, ninth out to a nimble catch by Watson, qualified for promotion to an earlier place in the batting order of Middlesex, if one can be found for him. At 6.20 his side were all out for 316 and nine wickets had fallen for 118, after Brown got out. Probably some Yorkshireman near the Tavern profoundly remarked 'it's a foony game, cricket.'

CRICKET LAWS AND FACTS

IT is unlikely that we shall see at Lord's this week-end such strange carryings-on as occurred far away from the centre of things—namely at Manchester, where a pitch was allowed to behave according to nature and so horribly that only round about a thousand runs were scored in three days and a bit, with Hutton playing a great innings one-handed and Evans rising above his Kentish stature to the extent of a century, and Stollmeyer so much at ease that his bat performed the lovely curves of R. H. Spooner. At Lord's we are usually privileged to watch, or overlook, the game in the throne-room, so to say; yet there was a time, within living memory too, when the turf at Lord's was not a sort of processional red carpet laid down for a run-getter's grand parade. As a rule, indeed, the Lord's wicket does justice both to skill of bowler and skill of bat—which is only to be expected in the place where the traditions and history of the game are one and indivisible.

And right and proper is it that Col. R. S. Rait Kerr, secretary of the M.C.C., should have written the best book extant on the laws of cricket, so that it is already a classic and as fascinating as it is comprehensive of fact and precedent. There is nothing musty or academic about Col. Rait Kerr as he tells us of the changes that have occurred in legislation. For the constitution of cricket, like the British Constitution, was not made but has grown—and that is saying much. A foreigner (say from Göttingen) might suppose that three stumps were agreed upon out of some respect of that order of English Trinitarianism symbolized by Three Feathers, Three Balls, the Three Card Trick—and so on. But no; at first two stumps sufficed until, in a fierce game between Hambledon and Kent in 1775, John Small went in last and 'fetched 14 runs', and won the victory. 'Lumpy' Stevens, who was the bowler, several times beat Small, but the ball went through the wide gate of only two stumps. By pressure of circumstance and justice, a third was added. Contemporary critics of slow play might be heartened to learn that when John Small 'fetched' those fourteen runs he batted two-and-a-quarter hours.

You will quickly discover how much the laws of cricket crystallize actual and personal experience in the field of play if you try to expound them to somebody who has never had a bat in his hand in his life. A few years ago Professor Schneevoigt, the musical conductor of music, was taken to the Sydney cricket-ground to see Bradman. The game was explained to him in some detail, and he listened with apparent intelligence. 'So,' he said, 'I oonderstandt. Der badsman is before the wickeds. If der wickeds are 'it mit der ball, the badsman is oudt. Oondt if der badsman stroke the ball and 'e is caught, also 'e is oudt. I oonderstandt. It is very simple. Now I vatch.' After a while Bradman was out to a sudden catch on the leg-side. Thousands of voices lamented as he began to leave the wicket. 'Why does he go avay?' asked Schneevoigt. 'But, Professor —I have explained. He is caught . . .' 'Ach, so,' replied Schneevoigt genially. 'I oonderstandt. 'E is oudt. So 'e goes avay. So. Does 'e come back?' 'But no, Professor; as I told you——' 'I oonderstandt. 'E doesn't come back. Very goodt. I do not like eem.' Whether this was a technical or personal criticism remains in doubt.

If an umpire at Lord's this week-end and subsequent days raises his arms to announce a six (and I fancy that Worrell will give him cause for this signal), how many in the crowd, or on the pavilion sitting next to you, will name the stroke a sixer if it hits the top of a sight-screen, standing just within the field, first bounce? And when was six runs first allowed for a hit into the crowd over the rails? When I was a boy a sixer was a stroke out of the ground; that is, out of the premises. Hereby hangs a tale; I have never seen a comment upon it in print. In 1902 England lost the match and the rubber at Old Trafford by three runs. The finish was agonizing. 'With fifteen needed Rhodes [number 10] joined Lilley, and in three hits, one of them a big drive over the ring by Rhodes, the score was carried to 116, or only eight to win.' (I quote *Wisden*.) Lilley was then marvellously caught by Hill at deep-square leg. Tate, last man in, snicked a four, and Saunders bowled him fourth ball. I have been told that he threw it—but that is by the way. The important point is that the score-card states that Rhodes was not out four. A hit over the rails did not in 1902 count as six. So, in modern reckoning, England lost this dreadful day by one run. 'Ranji', in the crisis, faltered for once in his life; he was, to our dismay, hypnotized by Trumble—l.b.w. nought. He was promptly dropped from the England XI. When he sat in the amateurs' dressing-room, waiting to go to the wicket, he carved, with a penknife, the initials 'K. S. R.' on the wooden ledge of the window. Time, or bomb, has erased this moving human document.

In the current Laws of Cricket a note to law 20 says: 'In deciding on the allowances to be made for boundaries the umpires will be guided by the prevailing custom of the ground.' And during this same year of 1902, of Tate's martyrdom at Old Trafford, G. L. Jessop scored 109 at Hastings in rather less than 80 minutes. According to *Wisden* he struck 17 fours. Nothing is said, inexplicably, of those of his hits which fell first bounce in, or adjacent to, St. Leonards.

A passage in Col. Rait Kerr's book very apt at the moment runs as follows: 'As a result of the Findlay Commission [1938] . . . Counties unanimously accepted a proposal put forward by the M.C.C. that all groundsmen should be instructed 'that the ideal pitch is one which makes the conditions equal as between batsman and bowler without being dangerous, and that under no circumstances should pitches be prepared so as to favour the batsman unduly".' The operative words there are 'without being dangerous'. Was the Old Trafford wicket for the Test Match the other week described by anybody as 'dangerous'? In 1901, admittedly, the Old Trafford wicket, because of a mishap of preparation in the winter, was denounced by Sydney Pardon (that master of understatement) as 'absolutely dangerous' for the not very fast bowling of Jack Sharp. And that summer, J. T. Tyldesley, batting half his innings at Old Trafford, scored 2,605 runs for Lancashire, average 60.

One of the several charming illustrations in Col. Rait Kerr's beautifully-printed classic depicts William Davies of Brighton sitting at a little round table taking the score. A full bottle of wine stands by the side of the book; an empty one has been discarded and lies on the ground. I can find nothing in the written Constitution of cricket which discountenances such a procedure, or precaution, on a scorer's part. Precedent, in fact, is three-parts of cricket's Common Law.

SOME THOUGHTS

ENGLAND *v* AUSTRALIA

1948

NO REASON FOR TEST PESSIMISM

THE labours of the Cricket Selection Committee today should not be heavy, for there is an obvious nucleus—Hutton, Washbrook, Compton, Wright, Evans and Edrich—and the remaining players of the England team can be found without too much discrimination from 20 or 30 other honest artisans now engaged in county cricket.

The names might as well be drawn from a hat containing Young, Howorth, Pollard, Woodhead, Robertson, Simpson, Hardstaff, Fagg, Barnett, Bedser, Cranston, Fishlock, Palmer—the technical product will remain much the same. From these supernumeraries, temperament will probably be taken into account, and whether any one individual talent is likely to mingle with the whole.

But the nucleus is so good that no England captain could ask for much better. It may not approach the combined excellence of Hobbs, Sutcliffe, Hammond, Woolley, Hendren, Chapman, Larwood and Robins—the first eight in the order of going in of the England XI at Nottingham in 1930, a wonderful company. None the less, an England captain commanding Hutton, Washbrook, Compton, Edrich, Wright and Evans need not, even if a student of Schopenhauer, feel pessimistic at Trent Bridge next Thursday.

Wright is potentially the most dangerous bowler of the present day, though much dependent on shrewd leadership. He has the sensitive moods of an artist, and thrives on encouragement and the wheedlings of suggestion.

In Australia in the 1946–1947 rubber, it was apparent that he bowled at his best when he was given two slips and refrained from cheapening his 'googly'. A well-tossed ball, with flight and some syncopation in the air, followed by the spin that leaves the bat—this is the trick, if any there be, to checkmate Australian batsmen in general and Bradman in particular, failing a Larwood.

Wright tends to exploit his 'googly', in and out of season with a short-leg field, an offensive sight whenever an expert leg-spinner is at work. To bowl a 'googly' persistently is as though a detective were to go about constantly and day by day wearing a false moustache.

At all costs the England attack should avoid pitching a short-length to the Australians—but this is to instruct the Selection Committee in the rudiments of their office and function.

The England captain's responsibility this year seems rather heavier than usual. His main duty is to dispel the possibility of self-doubt from his ranks, any sense of inferiority provoked by gloomy prophecy which has perceived invincibility in Bradman and his men before the firing of the first shot. In a rainy period, in fact, England might even be said to have a chance of starting favourites.

And those of us who would like to see Robins in charge are not disloyal to Yardley. Robins happens to be in form: his natural gifts for tenacious leadership have been known and admired for years. He is our best match for Bradman: they are friends, and they know one another, which is good for the rigour of the game.

There is no reason in the world why the Australians should be allowed to use an attacking field while England's field waits patiently for opportunities and chances to come by favour of fortune.

Hutton and Washbrook are masterful enough. Compton possesses genius. Edrich, though under a cloud, must feel that the law of averages is on his side. Hardstaff, by his century against the Australians on his native heath last week, deserves a recall, and given a fast wicket there is little in Bradman's attack to ruffle as fine a forward method as any on view anywhere.

Hardstaff's only trouble is the sudden myopia that sometimes visits him when he is faced by slow spin, compelling him to bend interrogatively over his crease like a man peering downstairs in the dark, suspecting a burglar. I would go far to see Hardstaff and Barnett on a true, fast Trent Bridge turf, in full swing next week—and so would the Australian fieldsmen.

The Selection Committee will receive much help by telepathy today. Up and down the land, recumbent on beds and sofas, semi-erect in smoke-rooms and upright in public bars, men will variously choose the team, sometimes absent-mindedly, omitting the wicket-keeper.

Hutton, Washbrook, Compton, Edrich, Hardstaff, Barnett, Robins or Yardley, Evans, Bedser, Wright and Young—this is an 'obvious' selection. Barnett would do as well with the new ball as most bowlers, though the attack does not look too comprehensive for a damp wicket.

Inspiration might descend upon the appointed judges, leading them to that finishing touch, a name chosen by intuition, not extraordinary in itself, but brilliant in a context and company, making all the difference.

FIRST TEST
3rd Day, Trent Bridge
Nottingham, Saturday

ENGLAND

First Innings: 165 (J. C. Laker 63, Johnston 5-36, Miller 3-38).

Second Innings

L. Hutton, not out	63
C. Washbrook, c Tallon, b Miller	1
W. J. Edrich, c Tallon, b Johnson	13
D. Compton, not out	36
Extras (b 1, lb 6, nb 1)	8
Total (2 wickets)	121

BOWLING (to date)

	O.	M.	R.	W.		O.	M.	R.	W.
Miller	12	5	34	1	Toshack	8	3	22	0
Johnston	13	5	31	0	Barnes	4	1	11	0
Johnson	14	5	15	1					

AUSTRALIA—First Innings

S. G. Barnes, c Evans, b Laker	62
A. R. Morris, b Laker	31
D. G. Bradman, c Hutton, b Bedser	138
K. R. Miller, c Edrich, b Laker	0
W. A. Brown, lbw, b Yardley	17
A. L. Hassett, b Bedser	137
I. W. Johnson, b Laker	21
D. Tallon, c and b Young	10
R. R. Lindwall, c Evans, b Yardley	42
W. A. Johnston, not out	17
E. R. H. Toshack, lbw, b Bedser	19
Extras (b 9, lb 4, w 1, nb 1)	15
Total	509

BOWLING

	O.	M.	R.	W.		O.	M.	R.	W.
Edrich	18	1	72	0	Laker	55	14	138	4
Bedser	44·2	12	113	3	Compton	5	0	24	0
Barnett	17	5	36	0	Yardley	17	6	32	2
Young	60	28	79	1					

THOUGH England are in a pretty hopeless way, a beautiful innings by Hutton and plenty of composure by Compton in their second innings here this afternoon revealed limitations in Australia's attack with Lindwall not one of the spearheads. So there should be scope for rendering honour to the style and spirit of English cricket, no matter what the competitive result may be, or whatever heavens or stars should fall.

Australia took their first innings to 509, and with a total of 121 for two to add to our first innings of 165, England are still 223 behind.

On a glorious morning the England eleven went into the field again, galley slaves to their oars, while the crowd assembled in thousands and endeavoured to work themselves into irrelevant and rather distracting excitement. Maybe they were stimulated by the fact that Bradman, after showing signs of havoc was caught at short leg off Bedser, bowling to an attacking field. Edrich also galvanized the ball with all his superb energy, risking physical strain and bursting buttons.

A little of such gusto and vehemence on Friday, following the dismissal of Barnes especially, might conceivably have led to a positive and prosperous afternoon for Yardley and his men in a dubious situation. Any batsman prefers not to be assaulted for hours with intent towards destruction of his stumps, and challenged to his capacity for reflex action.

Bradman's long innings was masterful if onerous; again he was Australia's spinal column, and when he has passed from cricket England's chances should become more reconcilable with equality. He was applauded when he completed a thousand runs. But what are an additional thousand runs to Bradman? They are as a legacy of £100 for a millionaire.

Yardley's policy was constructive this morning; he called on Compton for his change, and whatever and however Compton bowls, his ideas are not negative. Unfortunately he could not pitch a length, and had soon to retire to his place in the field, where he wiped his hands on the turf and seemed to chastize himself. It is to be doubted whether his experiments with the googly or chinaman are calculated to develop his inborn gift for left-hand slow spin. After all, he is not by nature a man of dark and devious ways. He should study and follow the classics—Wilfred Rhodes, for example.

Ian Johnson made several ominous and strong hits before Laker defeated him. Laker was England's best bowler by far; he kept a nicely flighted length from round the wicket, and turned inwards a little. If he could command the out-swinger he would be indeed dangerous. Hassett tried persistently to drive him, and though at last he hit for six to the on, the reward came after much investment of will and watchfulness.

Young also was hard to get away through Yardley's protective cordon. Young missed a hard catching and bowling chance from Tallon, but shortly afterwards held another return wide to the off-side from him. So once again England momentarily thrust aside the menace of sweat and fruitless toil; for in two hours to lunch three Australian wickets were taken for 92 runs, the interval total being 385 for 7.

Hassett, not out 84, was comfortable on the whole in his dapper compact method, but obviously restricted by bowling and fielding much more concentrated on antagonism than yesterday. Hassett sometimes suggests champagne in the bottle locked in ice, waiting for the cork to be drawn, and the sparkle and fizz and foam.

The trouble with an Australian innings is that until the swarthy Toshack is seen emerging from the pavilion, there is really no end in sight, except in far-reaching perspective. Any stranger to cricket arriving after lunch at Trent Bridge today might have imagined that Australia's innings had just begun, if he had caught only one glimpse of Lindwall driving Laker stylishly through the covers—as lovely a stroke as could be desired or dreamed of on a sunny cricket field.

Hassett had to wait nearly five hours for his century; the champagne was in the bucket a little too long for the good of the true vintage. But he was always making strokes of precise deportment; fastidious and unsmutched as an old engraving.

Lindwall reached 40 with a snick for four off Yardley, which was the first sign that the seventh Australian wicket had fallen; the eighth wicket had now added 100, and the batting was suddenly struck with brilliance against the new ball. But Hassett now tried to cut off the stumps a quick ball from Bedser, and was bowled; and 25,000 stood up and stretched themselves. Australia 8 for 472, and at last Toshack was buckling his pads, which was a comforting thought.

A catch at the wicket finished Lindwall's admirable innings. Then Toshack complete with sweater came forth, a pleasing sight in the circumstances. Obliged by slow bowling by Young and Laker he severely combined defence and offence, and played his part in a last wicket stand which carried the score from 476 to beyond the 500 total which is regarded by Australia as their rightful inheritance on a good pitch.

When England went in again Miller bowled a great over to Hutton, which was greatly played. The red ball flashed from the ground with a life and velocity which came out of the splendid spirit and muscles of the handsomest young cricketer in the game at the present time. To stop a vicious in-swinger Hutton needed to assemble suddenly all his skill, eyesight, sinew and nerve in a convulsion of defence. And in Miller's next over Washbrook was caught at the wicket desperately trying to get rid of another spiteful ball that bounced upwards, electric with Australian antagonism. England 5 for 1—trouble, trouble, trouble.

Lindwall could not bowl because of a strain, and after Miller took a rest and the new ball faded, Johnston and Johnson were not more than good bowlers, excellent of length and purpose, but within the resources of Test match batsmanship to deal with, on a wicket fit for Reggie Spooner or Palairet.

But Hutton and Edrich could not dispel the mood of England's travail and at 39 Edrich, after much setting of his teeth and several determined thrusts, succumbed to Ian Johnson, caught at the wicket, a real stumper's opportunity.

Yet even now, with two wickets down for 39 and the crowd beginning to wax ironic in the Trent Bridge manner, I could see no reason why some English hero of our county cricket, poised opulently at the peak of the averages, should not take root and decline to discern in the Australians more than eleven men in green caps, while Miller was out of action and Lindwall denied the chance to open fire.

This is not to underrate Johnson, Johnston and Toshack; none save an exceptional bowler could hope to get many quick wickets in conditions adverse to anything but killing speed off the pitch.

Still, Ian Johnson, by his persistent accuracy, found the edge of Compton's bat more than once, and it was clear he was putting spin on the ball whether the turf took it or not—which is what a slow-medium bowler should always do, if only for art's sake. Twice Hutton sent the ball to the on-side after batting to the off, a proof of off-break.

Compton at length found the middle of his blade, if enchained by the state of things, and Hutton remained resolute, so the evil hour was delayed until another day. It need not come too soon; the Australians should be compelled to work hard for their spoils; at any rate, not assisted or aided and abetted.

54

NO DRASTIC TEST TEAM CHANGES NEEDED

Trent Bridge was not a total loss for England. Much salvage was achieved. After eight wickets had been lost on that dreadful first afternoon, England, in fact, shared competitive spoils more or less. To battle from a hopeless position to a fifth day, giving a third innings a total of beyond 400, was an act of retaliation as strong as any in the Test Match annals.

Bradman's victory did not come to him open-armed; as he contemplated his bowling resources in England's second innings he might well have remembered the Duke of Wellington's remark, after an inspection of his troops for the Peninsular campaign: 'I don't know what effect these fellows will have on the enemy, but by God, they frighten me!'

Without a new ball, Australia's attack at Nottingham was steady, persistent, but not at all dangerous. Maybe no other Test match this year will be played on a wicket as sleepy and easy as Trent Bridge's on Monday and Tuesday, until a rain-shower enlivened it. Ian Johnson probably put so much spin on the ball that after the match he needed the aids and consolations of a chiropodist. But the Trent Bridge turf did not receive the spin hungrily, turning it over on the palate, so to say, like a dog mouthing a lump of bread after anticipating meat.

Johnson's offbreaks, even combined with beautiful length and flight, remained in the circumstances without power of penetration.

W. A. Johnston is a hard-working quick left-hander; and hard work should usually be his portion, if our batsmen will only keep eyes on the ball and remember their reputations; and, what is more, remember that the bulk of this Australian team, compared with the stalwarts of England, are more or less green in experience of the day-by-day ordeals of first-class cricket.

If Lindwall's injury doesn't mend, Bradman is certain to call on one of his leg spinners: he will scarcely risk another long trial to his philosophy such as he obviously suffered at Trent Bridge, when the Australian attack, as far as the disposal of England's best batsmen was concerned, depended utterly on Miller and the new ball.

So there can be comfort drawn from the reflection that not all the Test match worries this year will be the prerogative and perquisite of our own Selection Committee. As we glance back on Trent Bridge, we can, with a little imagination, see that the issue was by no means as one-sided as the score-sheet would suggest, even following the inexplicable collapse that began it—for it *was* inexplicable, and open to no technical explanation.

If Lindwall had been got rid of as a batsman after Australia's seventh wicket fell, the total need not have reached 400; and here is a point which requires stressing. There is no moment in a Test match against Australia when an England XI can afford to relax, either in physical or mental strain. The Australian never rests; if a situation becomes 'unstuck' as they say, the whole game is begun once more.

We can hardly indulge the romanticism of counting on an English victory if conditions favour each side fairly. You can't beat a cricket team that possesses the greatest batsman of his day, and the greatest all-rounder, and nine others all fighting fit, except if fortune smiles on you—and she is ready to look the other way any minute.

But there is no reason why England should not confidently aim at a draw, not by slow play but realistic batting that perceives a bad ball in a green cap; and by determined bowling that attacks over by over. The services of Wright, if fit, will be necessary at Lord's; a contemporary Test match XI without a leg break or a fast bowler is like a contemporary navy without submarine and aircraft.

The Selection Committee is under no obligation to make drastic changes today, in spite of a letter I have received from a reverend gentleman in Bath, who, after a preliminary 'Now, sir,' says the Selection Committee should begin by 'abolishing' itself—for reasons not stated, Compton, Hutton, Washbrook and Edrich are our most seasoned Test match batsmen; they cannot be bettered in knowledge of the Australians' methods. So it would be idiotic to drop any one of them at any time because of some temporary and peculiar loss of form.

If Barnett is recalled yet again, he should be sent in to open the innings. If a fresh mind to the onerous job is wanted, maybe Robertson, Crapp or Dollery will provide it: but on a good wicket wouldn't any Australian prefer to bowl at any of these rather than at Hardstaff?

Apart from the possibility of eccentric speculations and suggestions taking force, the following team might represent our best resources of skill and character—Hutton, Washbrook, Edrich, Compton, Hardstaff or Robertson, Crapp or Dollery, Yardley, Evans, Laker, Wright and Bedser, with Young at hand in case of the prospect of floods.

He bowled wonderfully well to keep the runs down at Nottingham, but now that the Australians are one up, there should be no more negation in the English strategy.

SECOND TEST 1948
3rd Day, Lords

AUSTRALIA

First Innings.—350 (A. R. Morris 105, D. Tallon 53, Bedser 4–100, Yardley 2–35).

Second Innings	
S. G. Barnes, c Washbrook, b Yardley	141
A. R. Morris, b Wright	62
D. G. Bradman, c Edrich, b Bedser	89
A. L. Hassett, b Yardley	0
K. R. Miller, not out	22
W. A. Brown, not out	7
Extras (b 17, lb 4, nb 1)	22
Total (4 wkts.)	343

To BAT: I. W. Johnson, D. Tallon, R. R. Lindwall, W. A. Johnston and E. R. H. Toshack.

BOWLING (to date)

	O.	M.	R.	W.		O.	M.	R.	W.
Bedser	21	5	51	1	Wright	19	4	69	1
Coxon	19	3	47	0	Laker	28	6	96	0
Yardley	13	4	36	2	Compton	3	0	11	0
Edrich	2	0	11	0					

ENGLAND

First Innings

L. Hutton, b Johnson	20
C. Washbrook, c Tallon, b Lindwall	8
W. J. Edrich, b Lindwall	5
D. Compton, c Miller, b Johnston	53
H. E. Dollery, b Lindwall	0
N. W. D. Yardley, b Lindwall	44
A. Coxon, c and b Johnson	19
T. G. Evans, c Miller, b Johnston	9
J. C. Laker, c Tallon, b Johnson	28
A. V. Bedser, b Lindwall	9
D. V. P. Wright, not out	13
Extras (lb 3, nb 4)	7
Total	215

BOWLING

	O.	M.	R.	W.		O.	M.	R.	W.
Lindwall	27·4	7	70	5	Johnson	35	13	72	3
Johnston	22	4	43	2	Toshack	18	11	23	0

As I saw the crowd gathering at Lord's for the third day of the Test Match, I remembered a passage in the diary of Pepys, describing how he went to Charing Cross to see Major-General Harrison hanged, drawn and quartered 'which was done there; he looked as cheerful as any man could do in that condition'. The crowd was certainly commendably cheerful and hopeful considering England's condition after an inglorious first innings against splendid fast bowling which might have enjoyed less prosperity and success against the forward method of, say, Tom Hayward or Morris, the contemporary Australian.

Possibly the warm sunshine contributed towards the spirit of the multitude; in the troublous universe of the present there are few better places than Lord's in June to go for rest and friendliness and the restoration that comes from living for a while in a place traditional and evergreen.

The Australians made no mistake this time. They rubbed the English bowlers in the dust—a metaphorical dust so far; but there might be real dust enough in the pitch during England's second innings. Morris alleviated the ruthlessness of it all by an appeal to the aesthetic senses, but Barnes and Bradman for long put such childishness behind them and not until five o'clock did Barnes revert to original type.

He was once a natural stroke player, and now, after completing the century he planned while voyaging to England, he assaulted the weary bowling with a thunderous and mightily swinging bat.

Bradman, of course, did not waste the golden opportunity, though his innings was not gilt-edged; at times, in fact, he batted rather like a millionaire in slightly reduced circumstances. But the total of 343 for 4 leaves Australia already 478 ahead.

At five minutes to twelve today, Lindwall sent a sudden quicker and shorter ball which Bedser stabbed into his wicket. The off-stump was knocked out of the ground, putting an end to a quite monumental essay in batsmanship by England's heroic bowler.

So, after a second rolling of the pitch in 40 or so minutes, leading by 135, with royal weather blessing the scene, and the uncertainties of a changeable climate over the week-end providing a possible ally, Australia went in again in circumstances happier than any cricket team could well imagine. The state of the game and everything else suggested a bed of roses for Bradman and his men.

Barnes could not walk to the wicket quickly enough; he seemed afraid that somebody would come and roll it up and carry it away before he was able to bask and revel on it. He avoided spectacles at once, but it was Morris who hit the first boundary, in Coxon's first over from one of the half-volleys which Coxon is prone to bowl while the ball is new and he is trying to get enough flight for the swing.

Barnes, when eight, survived an appeal for leg before to Coxon, addressed mainly by the spectators on the grass near the Nursery, led by a cluster of schoolboys. Another lovely four by Morris, to the off from Yardley, who quickly came on in place of Bedser, sounded a resonant note of confidence in the Australian ranks.

At lunch, Australia were 88 for none and only from some absence of mind did it seem possible that anybody would get out, though Barnes when 18 apparently gave an extremely difficult chance of stumping. He tried to sweep an off-break square from Laker, and no doubt Evans was unsighted. Had Barnes lost his wicket this way we could scarcely have said that he was technically defeated. Just before lunch Morris, at 40, drove a ball into the air and Yardley touched it one-handed, a ghost of a chance.

Morris reached an almost immaculate 50 out of 92. Barnes continued to inspect the bowling minutely, quite willing to wait all day for an appointment with a century. A magnificent pull for four off Wright reminded us that though a man of patience he is a quick opportunist and a superb cricketer.

The heat of the afternoon increased, and it was a mercy for the English that scoreboards in this country do not openly announce the name of the batsmen to come in, especially when they are Bradman, Hassett, Miller and the rest, not excepting Toshack. A spinner from Wright puzzled Barnes when he was 35; but here again this was but a faint indication of a very deep-seated possibility of mortal error.

Barnes reached 50 after 2 hours, out of a total of 122, by means of a great square cut from Laker. It is in keeping with this highly individual character that for all his distrust of romanticism he invests often in a cut, which Wilfred Rhodes once said was 'no business stroke'.

When Australia were 257 in front with ten wickets in hand the accident happened. Morris received a short, easyish ball from Wright and missed it as he sought to pull the spin comfortably to leg. He was bowled behind his back, so to say, a gift for England welcomed by noisy gratitude amongst thousands.

Morris played pedigree cricket; blue-blood aristocracy. Debrett in Australia. Without hinting of effort he drove with the speed of light across the grass. He appeared certain to score two hundreds in the same Test, as he did at Adelaide against Hammond's team.

Morris's 62 was woven in two hours, an innings of the purest texture, rendering honour to Lord's.

Bradman had scored 13 when Laker, put on at last at the Nursery end, from where Ian Johnson had spun his off-breaks for 35 overs, baffled him entirely four times in six balls, drawing him forward with the light of speculation in his eyes. There was hysteria in the crowd when Bradman was caught from a 'dolly' catch off his boot by Evans. The great man was hereabouts as unhappy as on Thursday, and the onlookers rejoiced because of some relief from the general scourge.

The English attack revived during this encouragement, Laker especially causing close attention by reason of his flight and off-break, from round the wicket. And when the new ball was used at 159 for one, Bedser twice beat Bradman, who in the same over snicked a four of little design and no dignity.

The Australian innings seemed unnecessarily careworn just now, but Barnes did not share Bradman's psychological complexes, and he forced Bedser, new ball and all, strongly to the on boundary, rapid and flexible in the wrists and forearms. A half-volley from Coxon restored Bradman like oxygen. Bedser bowled to trap Bradman at short leg again, and Bradman was willing to allow his pads to be thumped—not a majestic retaliation, and proof that Bradman is definitely human, ready when necessary to defer and stoop to conquer.

He got over his early vicissitudes much as rich relatives given up by the doctor survive to an old age and frustrate the expectations of many. He arrived at 50 in 95 minutes.

After tea Barnes, having batted four hours for 100, attacked Laker without fair warning, and in five consecutive balls hit or plundered him for 2, 2, 4, 6, 6, each six a most masculine drive to the on. Laker was bowling from the end opposite to the one from which he had worried Bradman severely.

Barnes, going for another six over the tavern, was grandly caught on the edge of the field by Washbrook from a really glorious drive. Washbrook split his hand and had to leave the field. The next ball, also by Yardley, clean bowled Hassett. An alarming collapse all of a sudden, after Barnes and Bradman had scored 174 for the second wicket. Australia were three down and only 431 ahead, and Yardley given a chance to do the 'hat trick'. Miller contrived to prevent it with difficulty, but the crowd wallowed in any sort of downfall of an Australian batsman at this time of the long day.

TEST SELECTORS MAY CALL ON POLLARD

When the Selection Committee meet again today to choose the England team to play the Australians at Manchester, at least three ways of approach to their task will perhaps help them to stimulating conclusions.

They can argue that as the rubber is already more or less beyond our reach, and must be counted a dead loss, the future policy in Tests should encourage young blood, and begin at once to build and train our international cricketers of tomorrow.

Or the Selection Committee can with equal justification decide that it is their job to pick the best England XI of the moment strictly on form, and that it is no part of their job or function to apply themselves to the joint responsibilities of schoolmastering and prophecy.

Or, as a last resort, they might, for the period of the Manchester Test match only, resign in a body, giving as a reason that usually it rains at Old Trafford at the first mention of England *v.* Australia and that not a ball was bowled in the engagement of 1938.

The likelihood is that few alterations will be made or risked today. We live in the age of youth, no doubt; but for the purposes of Test cricket experience of fast bowling is more our need than the first fine careless rapture, if any such rapture there be. It would be a peculiar sort of generalship that preferred to send a young man unaccustomed both to Test matches and to Lindwall into action next or any other week.

No doubt a certain satisfaction comes from the cry of 'Sack the lot!' in moments as gloomy as the one which saw England's weakhearted collapse at Lord's on the closing day. And it is true that one or two of our responsible batsmen revealed much too openly a reluctance to stand firm to the line of a perfectly fair and beautifully classic fast bowler.

I think it was Maurice Leyland who, speaking of fast bowling said, 'None of us likes it, but some of us shows it more than others.' There is nothing of intimidation about the attack of Lindwall. To refer back to 1921 and Gregory and Macdonald is irrelevant: the onslaught of Gregory was as far-removed from Lindwall's style and tactics as the atom bomb from spear and lance.

The Selection Committee and England's captain have a right to expect, after a player has received the honour of an invitation to play for England that he will not defeat himself by want of nerve or concentration at the pinch.

The failure at Lord's was not the bowlers' fault. Lockwood and

Richardson themselves could not have done better on an easy wicket than to account for seven contemporary Australian batsmen in a day for 250. All the same, the England attack at Lord's will probably be strengthened at Old Trafford by the inclusion of Pollard for Coxon. Coxon contributed manfully at the first chance, but he frequently wasted the new ball in a way Emmott Robinson would have thought un-Christian.

Pollard is accurate and keeps the batsmen playing. The other week, at Trent Bridge, Sidney Barnes, one of the greatest, if not the greatest of all bowlers, broke silence after watching the cricket for an hour or so and wondered why bowlers today so often allow batsmen to 'leave them alone'. 'I never liked to give a batsman any rest at all,' said Barnes.

Most of us are resigned to the temporary passing-over of W. J. Edrich. For my part, if I were captain, I should still want to have him with me at Old Trafford. I can never forget his splendid isolation in Australia for a while, when he batted almost alone during a period in which expectations aroused by others were being sadly disappointed. He proved his character then. But if he is out of touch, as they say in Australia, we cannot risk him again at the moment. A good player, on the other hand, comes as quickly back to form as he falls away from it—and Edrich got his hundred yesterday.

Dollery in his second innings at Lord's, showed self-reliance as well as cultivated skill, and presumably he will be given a second opportunity.

There is a constant possibility of usefulness in Cranston of Lancashire: and Robertson of Middlesex also has his thousands of admirers and advocates.

There is no need for the present writer or any other to add to the advice now being directed at the Selection Committee. We—that is those of us who are writers past and present—are ourselves the objects or receptacles of voluminous correspondence urging us to 'action'. A rightly furious Welshman points out in several pages that not a single player in the champion county—meaning Glamorganshire—has been asked, 'up to the moment of writing,' to play for England. Others, notably from Derbyshire, ask 'What about Gladwin and Pope?'

Maybe the question will be answered in the statement which the Selection Committee will publish today. It will, I fancy, be a judicious statement, undisturbed by the agitations that overwhelmed our councils of war in the Armstrong campaign of twenty-seven years ago.

THIRD TEST 1948
3rd Day Old Trafford

ENGLAND

First Innings.—363 (Compton 145 not out, Lindwall 4–99, Johnston 3–67).

Second Innings

C. Washbrook, not out	85
G. M. Emmett, c Tallon, b Lindwall	0
W. J. Edrich, run out	53
D. Compton, c Miller, b Toshack	0
J. F. Crapp, not out	19
Extras (b 9, lb 7, w 1)	17
Total (3 wkts.)	174

BOWLING (to date)

	O.	M.	R.	W.		O.	M.	R.	W.
Lindwall	14	4	37	1	Loxton	8	1	29	0
Miller	14	7	15	0	Toshack	12	5	26	1
Johnston	14	3	34	0	Johnson	7	3	16	0

AUSTRALIA

First Innings

A. R. Morris, c Compton, b Bedser	51
I. W. Johnson, c Evans, b Bedser	1
D. G. Bradman, lbw b Pollard	7
A. L. Hassett, c Washbrook, b Young	38
K. R. Miller, lbw b Pollard	31
S. G. Barnes, retired hurt	1
S. J. E. Loxton, b Pollard	36
D. Tallon, c Evans, b Edrich	18
R. R. Lindwall, c Washbrook, b Bedser	23
W. A. Johnston, c Crapp, b Bedser	3
E. R. H. Toshack, not out	0
Extras (b 5, lb 4, nb 3)	12
Total	221

BOWLING

	O.	M.	R.	W.		O.	M.	R.	W.
Bedser	36	12	81	4	Yardley	4	0	12	0
Pollard	32	9	53	3	Young	14	5	36	1
Edrich	7	3	27	1					

Whether England win or lose or draw this match—and as a philosopher in a bowler hat observed in the pavilion bar, 'it isn't over yet'—our cricketers have lavishly polished the escutcheon and dispelled self doubt. What is more they have exposed a seat of mortal error in the Australian ranks. 'As stiff a cove as ever I see,' said the Game Chicken, 'but within the resources of science to double up with one blow in the bread basket.'

England bowled and fielded with admirable spirit, and as a result are 316 runs ahead with seven second innings wickets in hand.

Pollard and Bedser clenched teeth, Pollard undisguisedly, Bedser striking intermittent sparks from the slow fires of his temperament. In two hours before lunch Australia could score only 76 for the loss or Morris, Miller and Tallon. They were dismissed early in the afternoon for 221, and without in the slightest belittling England's magnificent rally, the fact must be stated that the batting was as poor as any committed by England in the rubber so far.

The disaster to Barnes clearly put the Australian machine out of gear. A day by day smooth mechanism does not readily respond to improvization.

The startling recovery of England created the wildest enthusiasm from the vast crowd. For long we have been waiting for the turning of the tide, and it is a comforting thought that all tides sooner or later do turn.

The attack of the Australian fast bowlers at the outset of England's second innings had something of desperation about it. Miller endeavoured to assail by pace alone, and his unruly direction wasted the new ball. Lindwall was unlucky to see Washbrook missed twice at long leg after he had played upon Washbrook's love of a hit round to that direction. Hassett dropped the ball in a way I do not recollect ever having seen before in an Australian fielding side during a Test match.

Washbrook was under an obligation to thank his stars. So was England, for had the first chance been taken England would have been only 28 for 2.

As welcome as Washbrook's subsequent skill was the rejuvenation of Edrich, who has recently seemed to be going about in some sort of disguise. He remembered his powers of driving, and a straight six off Toshack cracked like a gunshot into the Australian battleship so calmly voyaging in prosperous seas only a few days ago.

England began the day catching for the first time since Melbourne during the Hammond campaign a glimpse of victory in the far distance. The sun shone for the occasion, and Old Trafford took off its mackintosh but sat upon it, in case of accidents.

Yardley claimed the new ball at once. Bedser thumped the pads of Miller noisily and the crowd gave him out to a man and a small boy, but Umpire Chester deemed differently.

Pollard, red of hair and redder of countenance, bowled his heart out at the other end: everybody was trying, the rope of the match was strained and taut as in a tug of war. Pollard flashed the ball past Morris's elbows, a sign of life and antagonism. Bedser again beat Miller's bat, and made him toss his hair and champ his feet like a young horse.

The pitch appeared to have gained a little of pace, or perhaps the bowling was more highly tempered than Friday's: it was still a true pitch, full of runs.

When he was 29, Miller snicked Pollard through the slips without foreknowledge, and the next ball came swiftly from the earth, an outswinger that straightened, and trapped Miller leg before, leaving him with nothing to do about it whatever. And now Barnes came in, acclaimed by the crowd as a hero home to the wars.

Pollard at the top of his form, next nearly got Morris caught at the wicket, and a few minutes later compelled him to slice impulsively at a brilliant outswinger; the stroke only just failed to carry like greased lightning to the slips.

This was exciting cricket, hot with effort, vivid with skill.

Morris required 40 minutes to take his Friday evening's score from 48 to 51, and several times Pollard compelled him to play balls he would obviously have preferred to leave alone. So goaded was he that he suddenly swept Bedser loftily to long leg, where Compton waited and held a catch with the loveliest cupping of the hands, and a gracious and grateful bowing of the body.

Australia 139 for five, an astonishing and enlivening situation. A resurrection for England from the mortifying limbo of Thursday. And at this boiling point of crisis, Barnes collapsed to the grass and the English players rushed to his aid. Bradman ran into the field, and Barnes again was taken to the pavilion, walking slowly and warmly applauded for his brave but unavailing effort.

Loxton showed teeth in his forward action. With Tallon his companion a stand threatened, one of the traditional Australian acts of retaliation. As Pollard and Bedser needed rest, there seemed little left in the English attack piercing enough to force the issue to a quick end.

Yardley called on Edrich, who at risk of breaking his backbone, hurled a shortish ball at Tallon, who edged it, and was caught by Evans in a way he might himself have applauded in different circumstances. Edrich proceeded to give Lindwall a slight taste of

C   65

his own medicine in a series of bumpers, not exactly a tactful lack of deference due to a fast bowler of Lindwall's pedigree.

Lindwall and Loxton were not out at lunch, when Australia were 202 for 6, and immediately afterwards Pollard shook Old Trafford once more to its generous foundations by clean bowling the dangerous Loxton.

There was only Lindwall left now to do something towards diminishing Australia's deficit, and he could get runs only at cost of drawing on reserves of energy which would be wanted to bowl England out again. So when he was caught from a skier, Bradman maybe derived some consolation from the fall of his wicket.

The gloves were off when England went in again. Miller bowled with Lindwall, and a wonderful one-handed catch by Tallon, low on the off-side, dismissed Emmett, only one run scored.

Miller bumped savagely, Lindwall tried to bowl on all his cylinders. The multitude roared and rooted when Washbrook slashed with a bat changed to a sabre, and then drove a no-ball from Lindwall to the on for four.

The match was vehement, the antagonism uncompromising. Daggers were in the air.

Washbrook, when he was 21 and England 28, pulled Lindwall round to long-leg, straight into the hands of Hassett, who dropped the ball amid shouts and explosions of joy. It was a change to feel that the ironic gods were for once in a while making sport of Bradman and his men.

The onslaught of Miller and Lindwall was as gusty, as stormy, and it was weathered by strong nerve. A great cut by Washbrook off Johnston broke the cordon; the English city was no longer beleaguered.

Washbrook, after his escape, was palpably under the impression that the match was by this time safe as houses for England, and the moment ripe for virtuoso strokeplay: he cut Ian Johnson clean as a guillotine.

Next over from Loxton he drove thrice for 11 in the over, each hit easy to the point of leisureliness. In the same over Edrich cut square for four all the way.

The cheering and whistling when Washbrook reached 50 in 70 minutes, out of a total of 80, was probably heard half a mile away. This was not balm for English cricket, it was elixir.

Edrich renewed his proper form and resemblance, so that at the tea interval England were nearly 250 ahead with nine wickets left.

After Edrich had driven Toshack straight into the crowd he ran himself out, which was a shame, for he was set and in full swing. But he and Washbrook had added 124 and enjoyed themselves while they were at it.

The sunshine and glitter of the England innings was abruptly dimmed. Compton sliced Toshack, Miller took the slip catch with a gesture of happy dispatch, and Compton found himself on that long and lonely way back to the pavilion which must be travelled by all who get out for nothing at cricket.

Washbrook hit his second chance to Hassett when he was 78, and this repetition of error in a very safe fieldsman was as remarkable and as diverting as anything else in a day of exhilarating play.

HUTTON CERTAIN TO BE BACK FOR LEEDS

Today our cricket Selection Committee will meet again, this time with not a little confidence, and possibly with even a wink, after the manner of the ancient augurs as they passed one another in the public streets.

Something we had not suspected was revealed at Old Trafford, the Australians are not entirely mechanically precise in the field; moreover, they are subject, like the rest of us, to the ups-and-downs of the human spirit. They are not kings and victors by divine right; they are under the necessity of having to win by sheer technique and hard work upon the field of play.

Yet while making the most of consolations derived from the disappointing end at Old Trafford, we must bear in mind the extent of the loss sustained by the accident to Barnes. He is the pivot of the Australian XI, a great opening batsman, the most reliable in the world, and a character and psychological force beyond estimation.

If I were picking the present Australian XI, Barnes would be my first choice. If he had batted at Manchester the chances are that he would have stayed with Morris until the 100 was scored; then the usual harmony, with its substantial ground-bass, would have been established, also the rhythm and the traditional atmosphere.

I do not think that English cricket today can find anywhere a technical *ensemble* equal to Australia's. But the difference in skill between the two teams is not so vast that an ascendancy of the spirit might not easily turn the scale. Here is England's opportunity. The Australians are not as inured as we to the idea of defeat.

At Old Trafford, during the Saturday afternoon's dramatic tension the Australians were perceptibly rattled in mind and body: catches were rather outrageously dropped and fieldsmen were inclined to become hasty and uncertain of direction. It was a team with only a surface resemblance to the one that had won so affably at Lord's.

As I watched them while Washbrook and Edrich dealt with the fast bumpers, I remembered the story of the unlettered Lancashire man who when he saw the sculpture of 'Victory' for the first time said: 'Well, if that's "Vict'ry", ah'd like to see other feller!'

Little as possible should be done to disturb the mood and technical balance of the England XI as we saw it at the crisis at Old Trafford. Hutton will of course be recalled. Nobody will wish him to be passed over at Leeds—except, possibly, Bradman. We did not need his splendid innings for the Players to confirm his greatness.

Edrich has rehabilitated himself, and Crapp has suggested calmness and solidity. The batting nucleus is thus Hutton, Washbrook, Edrich, Compton and Crapp. But there is need of another bowler who must be able to bat to the length of 50 in a Test Match. Pollard and Bedser, with Young or some other spin-bowler, are not enough.

I would support the claims of Cranston if it were not for the fact that a new ball cannot well be shared and exploited by three bowlers. Cranston has enjoyed a splendid season. He is always 'in the game'. He is capable of making 50 and taking three or four wickets any day. And if a cricketer contrived to get rid of, say, Morris and Hassett and also scored 40 or 50, the service contributed would equal the century which Dollery is expected to give us one fine day.

Before the rubber is over we may also hear more of Whitcombe.

The eclipse of Wright is sad. He has recently seemed to harbour a desire to succeed to the noble if at present attenuated line of England's fast bowlers. If only he would be satisfied with the leg-breaker's slowish pace and alluring flight, and bowl to two slips —but a man cannot change a habit in the throes of a rubber.

For, though we cannot win it now, we can, by a single victory, bring to an end the long, long Australian dominance on the cricket field and give a lead for the future. So that if the next historian of the game should be Max Beerbohm's great and glittering T. Fenning Dodworth the final chapter might be entitled '1948—And After' with a proper and characteristic aptness.

FOURTH TEST 1948

3rd Day Leeds

ENGLAND

First Innings.—496 (C. Washbrook 143, W. J. Edrich 111, L. Hutton 81, A. V. Bedser 79, Loxton 3 for 55).

AUSTRALIA

First Innings

A. R. Morris, c Cranston, b Bedser	6
A. L. Hassett, c Crapp, b Pollard	13
D. G. Bradman, b Pollard	33
K. R. Miller, c Edrich, b Yardley	58
R. N. Harvey, b Laker	112
S. J. E. Loxton, b Yardley	93
I. W. Johnson, c Cranston, b Laker	10
R. R. Lindwall, not out	76
R. A. Saggers, st Evans, b Laker	5
W. A. Johnston, c Edrich, b Bedser	13
E. R. H. Toshack, not out	12
Extras (b 9, lb 14, nb 3)	26
	—
Total (9 wkts)	457

Fall of the wickets:

1	2	3	4	5	6	7	8	9
13	65	68	189	291	329	344	355	403

BOWLING (to date)

	O.	M.	R.	W.		O.	M.	R.	W.
Bedser	31	4	92	2	Laker	30	8	113	3
Pollard	37	6	103	2	Yardley	17	6	38	2
Cranston	14	1	51	0	Compton	3	0	15	0
Edrich	3	0	19	0					

The wicket subsided to docility after a brief period at the day's beginning, during which rain in the night enabled a ball here and there to bounce a little and come off the turf with alacrity. In this time there were alarums and excursions. Bradman and Hassett both succumbed. England caught a glimpse of victory, and the crowd was loud and voracious.

As a fact, Miller and Harvey waved crisis aside almost condescendingly, and not only held back the advancing bowlers but scored 121 together in an hour and a half.

A fortuitous ending of Miller's innings probably robbed us of a most inflammatory display of batsmanship, for he was obviously happy, and in the mood to apply the sword all over the field and out of the field.

His cricket had savagery, litheness and rapid power, and Harvey, a mere youth, scored a century in his first Test Match against England, even as not long ago he scored a century in his second Test against India.

Loxton failed by seven only to make a magnificent century, and he smote so many sixes that they were becoming quite vulgar in a Test Match.

When Harvey was bowled, Australia were 294 for five and 344 for six when Loxton lost his wicket going for another six. His downfall was providential for England, who may be said to have had a narrow escape.

Yardley by putting on Laker after tea, frittered runs away and Lindwall was able to enjoy a few encouraging and easy hits.

I imagined for a while that Pollard and Bedser were being held in reserve to dispose of Toshack with the new ball. When Toshack did come in, crippled somewhat and needing a runner, he defended exasperatingly and he and Lindwall held the tenth wicket so long that thousands turned away before the end of a long and, for England, trying afternoon of disappointment at the pinch.

The morning began eventfully. After Bradman had struck a no-ball from Bedser for two to square leg rather hungrily, like an urchin snatching at a thrown coin, he was hit between wind and water. Pollard then bowled, and from a good length ball that popped up to the shoulder of the bat, Hassett was caught easily in the slips.

Miller drove his first ball for three and now, before the crowd had recovered after one complete exhaustion of breath, Pollard clean bowled Bradman, the off stump falling to earth with an inertness really awful.

The sight of it, this sudden removal of Bradman from a position threatening restoration of old power, caused a roar of exultation such as is heard nowhere except in Yorkshire at cricket or football matches.

From my position in the Press box it was difficult to describe how Bradman faltered: he played rather late, and maybe the ball came across sharply, a little low. He missed, as a man misses his footing on the safest stairs, and he came back to the pavilion deep in thought.

On Friday he had made the blue print for a century. Pollard's over, fatal to two batsmen of their eminence, will go down in the game's history as one of the most momentous ever achieved by an Englishman born in Lancashire.

In an hour of severe challenge young Harvey began his first innings in a Test match against England as coolly as a veteran, with perfect footwork. Miller, his companion, showed fight and pulled a great six as soon as Laker came on.

Harvey's strokes were thoroughly cultivated on the whole, though Laker quickly beat him with a superb off-spinner; very nasty for a left-hander. Though Pollard also beat Harvey, the boy was not at all downcast.

Here is a great and beautiful batsman in the making. He watched Laker carefully, and at the first chance pulled him three times for fours, each stroke invested with some grandeur. But when an off-spin bowler permits a left-handed batsman to hit him square to the on, the offence is more than offence—it is anathema.

Miller who has been out of form, now was nearly at his best. Nobody drives a six like him: he swings all his tall, supple strength vehemently, yet there is a thrilling grace as well as elemental punitive power in his drive.

He seems to try to send a ball as far as a cricket ball can ever travel, and still there is ease in the glorious swing of his bat.

He sent a half-volley from Laker soaring straight for six, and when Yardley came on he drove for four to the off and four to the on. A leonine blow. Then, as he tried a mighty sweep to leg, he only just touched a bad ball and it somehow collided with Evans's or his own pads whence it bounced into the air, and Edrich held a grand catch near the wicket, full stretch on the grass.

Lucky for England, and an irreparable loss to the glamour of the match. Australia were now 189 for four, and Harvey had reached 50 in 80 minutes. In one over from Cranston he cut and pulled two fours and a three: the boy was showing us real cricket in a Test Match.

Like all Australian batsmen he is strong on the on-side, but has a pretty square cut, and when he was 88 he had made 32 by means of this neglected stroke.

Harvey reached one of the most valiant centuries in all the history of Test cricket at 25 minutes past three, after three-hours' extraordinarily resolute play for one so young. The Leeds crowd cheered him long and generously, and Loxton ran down the pitch to shake him by the hand.

This same Loxton had not been negligent: he punished a loose ball at sight, as though livid with scorn. He mistimed once or twice, while going forward, but he had immense confidence and completed his 50 with a gigantic straight six off Cranston; the ball went so high that I got a crick in the neck watching its course.

The Australian batting, in spite of the early catastrophe of Bradman and Hassett, caused England's effort on Thursday and Friday to appear, in retrospect, laborious and acquisitive.

Harvey was bowled by Laker at 294, and was fifth out, he and Loxton adding 105 in an hour and a half.

Another six by Loxton off Laker, over the square-leg boundary, was massive. And in Laker's next over Loxton drove yet another six to the on. The Australian is a very naughty animal: when it is attacked it defends itself.

Yardley who is always breaking a partnership when he puts himself on belatedly, bowled Loxton just when the game was eluding England's grasp altogether. Loxton lambasted his 93 in some two hours and a quarter. On the stroke of tea, Saggers was stumped, eighth out for 355, and so England could breathe again.

After tea the Australian Lindwall enjoyed one or two excellent and free fours from Laker, so Pollard was put on, possibly as a protest against levity at a moment when England's lead was coming down as Montague Tigg might say, to the ridiculous sum of less than 50.

For an hour Lindwall and Johnston held the ninth wicket, a most irritating resistance to the rather impatient multitude: and when Johnston was caught at 403 and did not leave the field, everybody got excited and outraged. But Johnston was merely remaining there to run for lame Toshack; so sensation, having smacked its lips, subsided regretfully.

Lindwall, by diversified cricket, compiled 50 and more. Toshack, limping badly, could not do justice to his strokes.

Still, in the end and after all, Australia were only a mere bagatelle behind, and the crowd went home disillusioned and dusty.

FIFTH TEST 1948
3rd Day Oval

ENGLAND
First innings

L. Hutton c Tallon, b Lindwall	30
J. G. Dewes, b Miller	1
W. J. Edrich, c Hassett, b Johnston	3
D. Compton, c Morris, b Lindwall	4
J. F. Crapp, c Tallon, b Miller	0
N. W. D. Yardley, b Lindwall	7
A. Watkins, lbw b Johnston	0
T. G. Evans, b Lindwall	1
A. V. Bedser, b Lindwall	0
J. A. Young, b Lindwall	0
W. E. Hollies, not out	0
Extras (b 6)	6
Total	52

BOWLING

	O.	M.	R.	W.		O.	M.	R.	W.
Lindwall	16·1	5	20	6	Johnston	16	4	20	2
Miller	8	5	5	2	Loxton	2	1	1	0

Fall of the wickets

1	2	3	4	5	6	7	8	9	10
1	10	17	23	35	42	45	45	47	52

AUSTRALIA
First Innings

S. G. Barnes, c Evans, b Hollies	61
A. R. Morris, not out	77
D. G. Bradman, b Hollies	0
A. L. Hassett, not out	10
Extras (b 3, nb 2)	5
Total (2 wkts.)	153

To bat: K. R. Miller, R. N. Harvey, S. J. E. Loxton, D. Tallon, R. R. Lindwall, W. A. Johnston and D. Ring.

BOWLING (to date)

	O	M	R	W		O	M	R	W
Bedser	15	4	35	0	Hollies	32	7	50	2
Watkins	4	1	19	0	Compton	2	0	6	0
Young	19	6	38	0					

Fall of the wickets:
(to date)

1	2
117	117

73

England's innings at the Oval yesterday struck rock bottom on a wicket not consistently difficult, if it could not be described as easy. As a fact, the Australians perhaps got the worst of it, for the ball could be turned quite awkwardly at times after tea, especially by Hollies.

The England breakdown was the consequence of beautiful class bowling by Lindwall, aided and abetted by an opposition with no apparent policy. Hutton, in splendid isolation, nearly carried out his bat; his was the tenth wicket to fall and our admiration for his polished defence was qualified only because he could not discover enough chance, to push along the score.

To seek again explanations for this latest lapse of our chosen cricketers would be tedious and end in no obvious judgment or verdict—they are not good enough, not properly instructed, and, because of the war, out of touch with and not reverent or emulative of the traditional technical methods and the traditional mental approach.

We will spare ourselves an abstract analysis of the horrid details, and stress them no more in this account than is necessary to present a fair report of the day's doings.

To the general surprise play began at noon, and Yardley, having again won the toss, decided England should take first innings. It is certain that Bradman would have done the same had he guessed accurately.

The wicket, to begin with, was sluggish: not until 1.0 p.m. did a ball rear nastily, and Johnston bowled it. By this time the back of England's batting had been broken by irresolute, irrational, or incompetent play.

Dewes was bowled in Miller's first over; he missed an inswinger, simply missed it. Edrich pulled a short, dubious-length ball from Johnston, striking precipitately, for the ball lost something of pace on the heavy turf, and Hassett held a superb catch at short square-leg above his head as the ball was leaving him.

Compton received a rising one from Lindwall on his glove, sending it high over the slips, and his bat was knocked out of his hands. He lost time as he picked it up, but Hassett, at third man, declined to throw at the opposite wicket and try to run him out. Chivalry in a Test match, open and unashamed.

In the same over Compton hooked another rising, short length ball. He hit hard and Morris caught him wonderfully, with no time for thought, quick as impulse. A grand stroke, grand fieldsmanship, and extraordinary eyesight.

Then Crapp gave a copybook example of how to get caught at

the wicket by letting his bat touch an outswinger going into the line of Lindwall's pace as a moth into the flame.

At lunch, after 90 minutes' play, England were 29 for 4, Hutton not out 17—an innings of quite noble loneliness, not active in stroke play enough, maybe, considering the need for runs at any cost before the pitch quickened, as quicken it did indeed for Lindwall, after the interval.

Now we witnessed one of the finest pieces of fast bowling of our time, against batsmen unworthy of the compliment.

Lindwall kept a good length, usually of the sort that invites a forward stroke, but only Hutton seemed able to remember the fundamentals. The others were without visible means of support, except that each was at least bowled, caught or leg-before standing more or less erect on foot, and not actually prone or prostrate physically.

Yardley was so late as to be virtually retrospective; Evans possibly played on, which, if he did establish contact with Lindwall, was at any rate, something. Bedser and Young heard the rattle of stumps behind them, the first and only intimation.

Watkins, a little distraught, received speed fatally on his pads, and they emitted the sound of carpet-beating. And Hutton, last out, fell to another brilliant catch by Tallon, low to the earth left-handed. Hutton, with a magnificent drive to the off from Lindwall, achieved the only boundary of the innings, which perished at 10 minutes past three, after a very mortal tenure of two hours 10 minutes.

Charitable talk about a 'sticky' pitch was, or should have been, knocked on the head by the way Bradman placed his field, always for pace.

Lindwall before lunch seemed so robbed of edge and power of penetration that Bradman deserves high praise for the foresight that persuaded him to keep Lindwall in action and mood; no doubt he was encouraged by the unconvincing, almost improvizatory methods exploited by the England batsmen.

Even Hutton for too long performed unproductive hits of formal beauty, as though playing in a sort of classic void; the situation called for a dash of that outmoded romanticism contumaciously exhibited in the past by say A. C. Maclaren, or the mettlesome timbre of J. T. Tyldesley, who used to resent the very presence of fast bowling, especially on a wicket of yesterday's nature—a wicket which, on the whole during England's innings, was not likely to be approved of by batsmen or bowlers.

Lindwall, by pace not alarming, and of a length that hit the stumps, once again demonstrated that English batsmanship at the present time is as unaccustomed to, and nervous of, velocity, as old folks once were afraid of crossing the roads when the freewheel was in its first and empirical stage of development.

It was an innings seen as though in a bad dream. The match, in fact, had an air of unreality. As I contemplated the English casualties I was reminded of those pathetically superfluous battles that are fought at frontiers remote from the centre of things, after an armistice has been declared, and before the news of it has percolated universally.

The pale sunshine assisted the impression of a disembodied Test match. The procession of the English batsmen to and from the wicket was ghostly; there was no speculation in the eyes. But this was not to belittle Lindwall's glorious and most opportunist attack, and the quite vehement Australian fielding.

They dismissed their victims contemptuously, as though to say, 'You have told us so often that you wanted to play on a wicket natural to a wet English season. So here you are.' And here we identically were.

Barnes and Morris passed the English score easefully in rather less than an hour, watched silently by the crowd whose humour was not improved when Barnes, with his score 29, pretended to walk from the wicket after Hollies had beaten him and nearly had him stumped. This was adding insult or ribaldry to humiliation.

The wicket was taking spin more than a little at this point, and whenever Hollies found a length he prompted second thoughts in the mind of the striker. But too many short or over-tossed balls were bowled both by Hollies and Young, and the Australian batsmen do not miss scoring from anything at all inaccurate.

But Hollies certainly deserved to prosper. The most watchful skill of Morris and Barnes was needed to cope with him, and most watchful and skilful they were.

The atmosphere of the Australian innings and the *sound* of it, was far removed from England's unpoliced sequence of reflex action and self-doubt. Barnes and Morris passed the 100 with unhurried craft; there was no reckless hitting round to square-leg and no timid respect paid to the occasional faltering length.

But Hollies at last received due reward; Barnes was caught at the wicket off him, the total 117 and the time of day 10 minutes to six.

Then Bradman came in, cheered generously by thousands who had more than ceremonial reasons for acclamation when Hollies defeated him second ball, as he played forward at a 'googly' which came back and bowled him neck and crop all the way.

With mixed feelings we saw the many spinning deliveries of Hollies; for they would have won the match for England at Leeds on the dusty earth of the fifth day.

The value of Barnes to Australia was more than ever emphasized in the first wicket stand with Morris; had he failed England might have retrieved substantially their ruinous innings, for, as I say, the wicket became something of an ally to spin.

Morris once more was beyond praise—masterful, stylish, imperturbable, sure in defence, quick and handsome in stroke play. His batting is true to himself, charming and good mannered, but reliant and thoughtful.

Seldom does he spare a ball of suspicious character, yet he is never palpably acquisitive, never brutal. He plunders bowlers tastefully, and changes rubbish to cultured art. I never tire of watching him.

WOOLLEY: AN APPRECIATION

YOU must see Woolley batting on one of Kent's cricket fields to enjoy thoroughly the charm of his delightful art. Of course Woolley can spread beauty about him wherever he goes, but at Bramall Lane—even at Old Trafford—one thinks of him as one thinks of a butterfly in a city street on a summer's day. The writer once saw Woolley the batsman set ideally, and never will he forget it. It was while an August afternoon turned to evening in Kent. The tumult and the shouting of the day were over, and now we all sat in quiet, just waiting for stumps to be drawn while Kent played out time in the calm light. Woolley made gentle movements with his bat. His body would fall a little forward as he flicked a ball to the off-side; there seemed no weight in him when he negligently trotted down the pitch. And as the sun shone more and more aslant, the light seemed to put this batsmanship of Woolley's under a glass; we had cool and polished contours given to it, the hard outlines of reality were lost in soft shades. Woolley's batting is frequently called 'brilliant'; it is the wrong word for his art at any time.

Brilliance hints at a self-conscious gesture, of some flaunting of ability. And nobody ever has seen the touch of the braggart, or even of the coxcomb, in Woolley. The condition whereby grace has its being is a perfect unawareness of the fact that it is graceful. In grace there is always a sense of modesty; the arrogance that masterfulness breeds does not go with grace, which is one of the gentler virtues.

This is not to hint that in Woolley's batsmanship there lurks a timid spirit. We all know that Woolley is one of the world's greatest match-winning batsmen. One wishes to establish nothing more than that a batsman so winsome as Woolley is not properly to be called 'brilliant'. The word's very mention fills the mind with lurid colour. In Woolley's batsmanship there is radiance, but never a light that is garish. Even when he drives in front of the wicket the softest splendour falls over the field. None of us of these times has seen a left-handed cricketer play a handsomer game than Woolley's. To describe his forward hits one is tempted to borrow Nyren's words about Silver Billy Beldham: 'One of the most beautiful sights that can be imagined, and which would have delighted an artist, was to see him make himself up to hit a ball.' Yet the phrase will not quite fit Woolley. 'Make himself up' is too strong a term; it denotes a sudden accumulation of energy to be seen by the eye —an act of violence. Woolley has not been known to look violent or to seem stung suddenly into effort. He does not, like, say, a K. L. Hutchings or a Hirst, use a bat as a rod of punishment and flog boundaries by force out of bowlers. Rather a bat is a wand in Woolley's hand; he makes enchanting passes with it.

Woolley causes batting to appear the easiest pastime in the world. A fast bowler, pounding heavily to the crease, bowling at Woolley with the loud grunts of unloosened energy, working himself to death in the hot sun in quest of Woolley's wicket—and Woolley, all restful curves, making his easy opposition! What a contrast, and what a nice irony in it! Woolley hardly ever seems to hit a ball; of him you can really say that his strokes are *strokes*. Surely he just caresses the ball with a bat of velvet surface. One day an assertion of some primitive nature left somewhere in Woolley will impel him to smite once with all his might, and then the ball will pass far beyond the fields of Kent. For the force even of his caresses is strong enough; the secret of his motive power is timing. He gives us the lyrical in batsmanship, just as Trumper gave us the dramatic. When Trumper batted, he met the onslaught of the bowler with an onslaught of his own as vehement. There was a conflict of will and skill when Trumper and a fast bowler were face to face, and so we had the dramatic, which thrives on conflict. As we have seen, Woolley does not look to be in stern opposition against a furious attack; he meets it effortlessly. And because drama cannot be felt unless we are made to understand that conflict hot and bitter is present, we get no drama from Woolley. He just goes his own sweet ways. While other batsmen turn the wicket into a battle-ground, the bowlers into an enemy to be plundered for runs, Woolley makes a soothing music that lures everybody after him, bowlers and all, as he moves along his happy track. He does not bat for his runs; he bats a serene course to them. So easeful and natural does a long innings strike you, when Woolley passes through one, that you well might think of some act blessedly predestinate. And it is likewise when Woolley fails; you are not outraged, you are not made to think that here ambition and skill have been frustrated. In Woolley's failures there is no jar that hurts you—they are as becoming as his conquests. Grace, one has already said, is modest, and has the air of fragility always. Rude human nature, such as Hirst showed us in his pulls to the on-boundary, never peeps out of Woolley. His batsmanship has been through a purifying fire; refinement one day came to Woolley

'And whipped the offending Adam out of him. . . .'

The point for technical men about Woolley's batting is important; he achieves his style mainly by back play—and have we not been told time after time by the dons of the game that if a batsman would own a beautiful style he must cultivate the forward method? In Woolley you find working to perfection the modern principle: 'Play back if you cannot drive'. How many times in a long innings does Woolley exploit the forward lunge, made from a rigid back foot? The writer does not recollect having seen Woolley use this stroke. Woolley has a great height and consequently a wide swing for all his hits—so wide that in the curve of one full swing are included the three points at which a half-volley, a good-length ball, and a rather short one may be struck. Woolley, then, does not need to move his feet extensively; he has only to 'time' accurately his swing down as the three different lengths come to him—which three lengths, of course, are the common lengths of bowling. Granted the slightest readjustment of the feet, Woolley's swing will serve in itself for a strong hit from any of these lengths. His height, then, makes grace hard to miss by one so naturally willowy (let us

overlook the faint suggestion of gawkiness in him); the small batsman—a Bobby Abel—is compelled to nip backwards and forwards
on his feet, as the varying lengths come along, and though his
animation is often thrilling, it must of necessity let the graceful go
hang. Woolley has all the strokes; his leg glances, with his tall
body half turning and drooping ever so slightly over to the on-side,
are not magical like Ranji's were, but they are, in a quieter way,
as precious. But discussion of Woolley in terms of technique is
abominable. Who would talk of the *Mona Lisa* in the painter's
jargon? And speaking of the *Mona Lisa*, is there not always about
Woolley's dark face an inscrutable hint of a smile held back, like
that we get from the lady sitting among the rocks?

Woolley's bowling was fashioned by the Tonbridge nursery, and
Blythe served as the model. But the way of Nature after she has
turned out a masterpiece is to break the mould. She does not let
her best things get common: a solitary Blythe was enough for her;
she made him once and for all. Woolley as a bowler is excellent on
doubtful wickets, but he is plainly a bowler who is happier with a
bat in his hands. He first trod a county cricket field at Old Trafford in Whit Week, 1906. And some of us that were in the crowd
thought we had seen the beginning and the end of this tall,
pale boy's experience in big cricket. It was the match in which
J. T. Tyldesley cut and drove the Kent bowling for 295 not out.
On the first day Woolley missed two catches; his bowling analysis
when 'J.T.T.' had finished with it was 1 wicket for 103; and in
Kent's first innings Cuttell bowled him first ball. On the last day,
though, he hit 64, and discerning men on the ground said the
innings heralded a new glory coming into Kent cricket. Woolley
is the most stylish professional batsman in the country; his style
carries the Tonbridge stamp. Kent have rarely, in fact, had an
uncultivated professional batsman. They consider in Kent that a
boy needs to be taught to use his blade in the way that a boy with
music in him is taught in other places to use a violin; batsmanship
at Tonbridge, in short, is regarded as an art and a science and
therefore a matter for culture.

AN INNINGS FROM YARDLEY

The cricket at Lord's yesterday seemed for a period to reflect the greyness of the sky. On a pitch willing to take spin, though not avidly, the Yorkshire innings proceeded conscientiously, and until afternoon the only positively vigorous strokes occurred when Compton pitched a long hop and occasionally a polyhop, a ball so easy to pull for four that the family pride of a county batsman was definitely challenged.

In two hours before lunch 87 runs arrested the attention of the official scorers, and Hutton reached 50 without entirely finding true form and touch. It was difficult to fix the cause of his want of the usual precision, and after close inspection of his technique, I was obliged to conclude that Hutton was probably playing in the wrong boots, or something—which indeed turned out to be an accurate conjecture.

The spirit of Hutton was here, obviously, but in a strange body. Edrich troubled him at the outset, and hit him on the legs with a splendid break-back, or late in-swinger when he was 18; Edrich during his first onslaught bowled well.

Halliday, after much introspection and stumbling in his crease, like a man coping with a non-existent stair, was caught at forward mid-off from an amiable and obliging little push. Wilson then put his bat ornamentally to the generally steady bowling for 25 minutes. No fieldsman was discernible in the straight deep, yet the temptation to drive to that quarter was successfully resisted. But Wilson was willing to chance getting out leg before wicket, and Compton trapped him that way.

After lunch the rhythm of Yorkshire's innings, became more securely controlled and accentuated. Another long hop from Compton was the means of removing some impediment or foreign body from Yardley's style and mechanism, and he emerged with a sequence of brilliant hits, pulls or forcing shots to the on boundaries one after the other, rapid and powerful and cracking.

He put Hutton into a shade impersonal if not anonymous. He pulled Gray for six, threatening breakages in the Tavern. Yardley's innings broke and snapped a month's shackles and regained freedom of limb for a gallant and gifted cricketer. The crowd revelled in the liberation; they sensed a good omen for England.

Hutton was 45 when Yardley's innings began, and Yardley was 90 and Hutton 95, when he trod on his wicket pulling Compton for four, a royal stroke which hit the boundary rail at a rare velocity. This was a simple end, but nothing could be done about it; law must be administered even though justice occasionally be outraged. Yardley batted an hour and three-quarters, and he hit 13 fours. A captain's innings—and for once in a way this old saying is not a cliche, but perhaps a prophecy.

Hutton, serene and masterful now, reached his century in just under three hours forty-five minutes, and the sun came out for the occasion.

Hutton at last was out to a brilliant catch by Sims, who held a sharp, low return from his own bowling and combined agility with elegance. Then, a few minutes later, Lester was caught beautifully at deep mid-on off Sims by Robins from a swinging pull.

BILL WORSLEY STRAIGHT FROM THE PITS

Bill Worsley belonged to the hinterland of the county where existence is carried on near to the knuckle, where cobbled streets go up and down hill, where in the pitch-black of cold winter mornings mills' sirens or 'buzzers' awakened the dead, and the rattle of clogs was like the sound of a sort of Last Day or Resurrection. From one of the pits of Lancashire emerged this Bill Worsley, who kept wicket for the county in the great high noon of Maclaren's reign. He got his chance unexpectedly. The Lancashire Eleven was touring the West of England and the regular wicket-keeper received an injury to the hand which rendered him a casualty for the rest of the summer. A telegram was sent for reinforcements and was received by Bill Worsley on his back in a seam of a coal-mine. He was brought to the surface, where he blinked his eyes to get accustomed to the light of day. After he had slowly read the telegram he said, without emotion: 'It's signed A. C. Maccle-aren'—he always pronounced it that way—'and it ses Ah've to pack oop and go to Edgbaston, Birmingham, and keep wickets for Lankysheer.' He scratched his head and added: 'Ah'm non so sure as Ah rightly knows where Edgbaston is.' But his proud and admiring friends saw him to the train and bought the correct railway ticket, and Bill departed, with a farewell message as he leaned out of the carriage window: 'Ah reckon Ah'll be back wi' thee all in a day or two. Look after mi whippets.'

He duly arrived at the cricket ground of Edgbaston. Lancashire were about to play Warwickshire. Bill stripped and sat in a corner in the dressing-room. Nobody spoke to him and he, as he afterwards said, kept himself to 'hisself'. He was discerned by Walter Brearley, the fast bowler and an 'amateur', meaning a 'gentleman'. Brearley, the kindest man and the friendliest in the world, hailed the new-comer. 'You are Worsley, aren't you; wicket-keeper for us to-day?'

'Yes, sir,' replied Bill.

'Come and have a drink,' said Brearley: 'We'll just have *one*, to baptize your first appearance for the county. This is your oppor-tunity Bill; just you keep a decent wicket and you can say good-bye to the pit, and have a grand life up and down the country. Come on, Bill—this way.' Brearley led Bill to the bar in the members' enclosure. When they reached the counter, Brearley smote Bill on the back and said: 'Now, Bill; what'll you have to celebrate this famous day in your life?'

'Well,' responded Bill politely, 'if you don't mind, Maister Brearley, Ah'll 'ave a Creem de month.'

Brearley was rather taken aback. 'A what?' he said. And Bill repeated with equal politeness: 'A Creem de month, if you please, Maister Brearley.'

Brearley concealed his astonishment and gave the order, including a can of beer for himself, which he picked up and drained at a draught. 'There's luck to you, Bill,' he gulped. Whereupon Bill drank his green fluid and said: 'The same to you, Maister Brearley, and many of 'em.'

Lancashire lost the toss, and Maclaren led his team into the field. When he reached the middle he as usual spent some time distributing his forces, waving men here and there, while Brearley measured his run and swung his arms and prepared to attack. The two opening Warwickshire batsmen came to the wicket, and Kinneir took his guard. All was ready. Then Maclaren at first-slip withdrew his attention from the bowler and the precise position to an inch of cover-point; he saw Bill Worsley 'standing up', an inch or so from the stumps. 'Worsley,' he said, 'get back a bit—Mr Brearley happens to be pretty quick.' 'Just as you like, Maister Maccle-aren,' said Bill, retreating exactly four inches.

'Farther back still,' shouted Maclaren impatiently: 'he's fast, I'm telling you.'

'Just as you please, Maister Maccle-aren,' reiterated Bill, retreat-ing another four inches. To himself Maclaren said: 'Well, if he wants his so-and-so head knocked off, very well.'

The match began. Bill 'stood up' to Brearley. Kinneir, a left-hander and a most obstinate batsman on a good wicket, was in form. He scored ten in a quarter of an hour—rapid work for him. Then he moved gently over to the off-side and beautifully glanced at a fine angle to leg. Worsley also moved across, made a brilliant catch, and without a change of action or pause, sent the ball high into the air with a one-handed jerk behind his back.

'What the . . . what the . . .' expostulated Maclaren. But Brearley said, behind his hand, 'Hush, Archie; you'll put him off! Marvellous catch!'

So Maclaren held his peace and the game was resumed. The next batsman was the formidable W. G. Quaife, most notorious of stone-wallers, almost beyond the powers of known science to get out on a hard wicket under six hours. He, too, began well and he, too, presently moved gently across his wickets and glanced exquisitely off his pads, fine to leg. And again did Worsley swoop on the ball, catch it, and with one comprehensive and encircling action jerk it sky-high behind his back.

This was too much for Maclaren. In spite of Brearley's muffled, 'Shush, Archie; you'll only put him off. Marvellous catch!'—in spite of Brearley's kind admonitions, Maclaren approached Bill. 'Well caught, Worsley,' he said, 'but damn it all, what's the idea of this behind-the-back foolery?'

'Well, Maister Maccle-aren,' replied Bill, 'we allus does it in t'Saturday afternoon league—a little bit o' 'fluence, tha knows, sir.'

'You can't do it here,' said Maclaren, 'in front of all these people. Bless my soul. Now, Bill, get on with your job. You're doing splendidly. But no more bits o' 'fluence, if you don't mind.'

As it happened, one or two Warwickshire batsmen took root, and Lancashire spent a long day in the field. But Bill acquitted himself well, though he did not get any more chances to make a catch. When they all came to the pavilion at close of play, it was discovered that Bill had been wearing primitive gloves. His hands were swollen and black. A pair of scissors was needed to cut his gloves away from his wounded hands.

Brearley's heart went out to Bill. He took him to the bar, the same bar where at the beginning of the day they had drunk to Bill's first appearance for Lancashire.

'Come, Bill,' said Brearley, 'you've won your colours. You'll come with us on the whole tour now. No more pit for you, my lad. You've done "gradely". But for God's sake, get some proper gloves —and drop all that behind-the-back business. Can't do it at Lord's

—Heaven help us. . . . Well, here's to you, Bill. Let's celebrate the occasion properly now. What'll you have?' And Bill replied, polite as ever: 'Well, if you don't mind, Maister Brearley, Ah'll have a Creem de month.'

AN INNINGS FROM HUTTON

ENGLAND

First Innings

L. Hutton, c Sutcliffe, b Cowie	101
C. Washbrook, c Sutcliffe, b Cowie	10
W. J. Edrich, c Donnelly, b Cowie	36
D. Compton, not out	103
A. Wharton, lbw b Cowie	7
F. G. Mann, c Scott, b Burtt	38
T. E. Bailey, not out	6
Extras (b2 lb4)	6
Total (5 wkts)	307

To Bat: T. G. Evans, A. V. Bedser, J. A. Young, and W. E. Hollies.

Fall of the wickets:

1	2	3	4	5
17	92	194	214	273

Bowling (to date)

	O.	M.	R.	W.		O.	M.	R.	W.
Cowie	36	6	104	4	Rabone	18	7	56	0
Cave	27	5	85	0	Burtt	33	15	56	1

England has today performed not more than moderately, occasionally not a little depressingly, in the first Test Match here. Only at intervals could runs be scored at the pace likely to bring victory in a three-day match, and too seldom were they scored with the gesture we expect from an England eleven playing New Zealand cricketers.

Hutton's century was flawless in form, aspect, and execution, but even Compton lapsed into competence scarcely worth observation by a connoisseur, a curious experience for him and for the rest of us.

At the afternoon's fall some aggression entered the England

innings, and Mann set the example and tempo, but by this time the New Zealand attack, not perilous at its freshest was tiring. All in all, New Zealand must be allowed at least a half share in the honours up to the moment of writing.

New Zealand had the misfortune to lose the toss on a pleasant pitch, and very soon a long stand by Hutton and Washbrook seemed as certain as the growing burgeoning in the sun of a plant that takes to soil by nature.

Cowie is not the fast bowler who once knocked Hammond's leg-stump flying at Lord's; and Cave, who used the new ball with Cowie, is definitely medium-paced and rather dependent on his right arm. But he is steady, just short of a length.

Yet once again an England opening partnership was nipped in the bud, for after performing one great hit, a drive to the on, quite late, with his feet suddenly concentrated to a forceful stance over an inswinger from Cowie, Washbrook was brilliantly caught at short leg by Sutcliffe, low down to the earth, from a rapid stroke to another inswinger by Cowie.

England 17 for one, and Sutcliffe already a contributor of some 50 runs at least, a sort of re-insurance against the possibility of a continuance of the poor and untrue batting form that has dogged him recently.

A lovely thrust to leg by Hutton off Cowie suggested consummate ease. Rabone bowled at Cave's end, and Cave crossed over to allow Cowie a rest. The attack remained much the same, the more it was changed.

Another on drive, this time by Hutton, was a model of timing, effortless and even leisurely. The ball sped to the boundary quick as light. Edrich somehow managed to miss a ball or two to begin with, but a straight drive by him off Cave was positively voracious.

The New Zealand bowling badly needed leg spin and the flight which asks questions. It was excellent of its rather unvariable kind. But Cave was guilty of a half-volley to the off, after he had gone round the wicket to a field containing three short legs. Hutton struck it for four, and England reached 52 in 85 minutes.

For too long England could not jump to a golden chance. Edrich, when 27, played Cowie to the slips without freedom of will and was missed. Hutton though always immaculate in technique, remained academic until lunch. So far the England batting had been of the kind that has lost us more than one rubber against Australia in living memory. The score was 82, less than a run a minute, Hutton not out 42.

I ventured some criticism of him to a Yorkshireman and he talked back at me throughout the interval so that I could not know what I was eating.

Immediately after lunch, Edrich slashed at the pitch of Cowie and was caught cleverly on the wing by Donnelly, in the gulley— 95 for 2. The situation for England would become intriguing if Hutton or Compton were to fail.

A dazzling off-drive from Cowie by Hutton completed his 50 to the multitudes' mighty satisfaction. His cricket was perfectly organized, an encyclopedia of batsmanship. An onslaught upon the New Zealand bowling was coming at last I felt certain. A four to the on, off Burtt by Compton, defied pursuit, but it was beautifully chased. The running of the New Zealand fieldsmen gave constant delight: they made fielding an art and a source of personal enjoyment changing it from mere utility and toil.

A cover drive by Hutton from Rabone, left foot across, the swing of the bat all rhythm and balance, calm but strong was a ray of glory from the past. Next over another off-side drive by Hutton, square with the wicket, can be said to have rendered honour to Rabone, the bowler: to collaborate in the creation of such beauty at cricket is a privilege.

Hutton was at his best now, senior in poise and authority of stroke to Compton, whose cricket, contrasted to Hutton's seemed useful, for all its natural genius. Hutton's strokes are conceived: the style of them in plan and idea rendered objective. Compton's strokes often are improvizatory: their swiftness defies classification and category. On the one hand we have the order and fulfilment of science; on the other the imagination and overtones of temperament.

Even at four o'clock no holocaust of runs had accrued, though all the time apparently pending. The New Zealand bowlers were tenacious, runs would not come themselves, and neither Hutton nor Compton seemed able to dictate or consume, in spite of technical mastery in the main, always good to look at. Cowie for a man 37 years old, sustained a speed which demanded lively attention if it was not devastating. Compton missed three widish balls on the leg side, errors of mistiming never committed by Hobbs in all my experience of the master of them all.

Hutton reached his 100 after nearly four hours' copybook cricket, but the England total was then only 193, not 50 an hour. Compton was curiously sketchy, not sure of touch. I cannot imagine that in such circumstances Australia, by tea, would have scored with so much respect to such industrious admirable, but not formidable opposition.

A few overs following tea Hutton made his first major mistake, sending a quick ball round to short leg, where Sutcliffe once more held an agile catch.

Wharton, who has a bad habit of bringing his back shoulder round and moving across his stumps, succumbed leg before to Cowie at 214, after Compton had reached 50 more or less anonymously for him.

The crowd tended to go home when Hutton got out, but two fours from consecutive balls by Burtt drew attention to the presence at the wicket of the England captain. Mann, in fact, achieved one of the grandest hits of the day, a square drive from Cowie, the bat sending forth a most martial sound. He improves in his batting match by match; but he was twice very lucky against Cowie, who at half past five was attacking as determinedly and almost as vitally as at noon.

Mann's busy and likeable innings was ended by a ladylike catch at mid-on off Burtt, whose bowling is not without a wrinkle or two of humour and slyness.

Cowie actually renewed effort at 6 o'clock, and Compton hit him twice for fours, both strokes of the rapid and vibrant kind only to be made off bowling that contains something hostile and combustible. Before stumps were drawn Compton was himself, and with so much charm in his score that the weary New Zealand attack might well have thought him irresistible and courteous.

McCABE—BATSMAN OF POISE AND CHIVALRY

Stan McCabe was one of the most chivalrous of batsmen, in the line and succession of Victor Trumper. He was not a cliff-jawed killer, like Macartney or Bradman. He came by his runs with the courtesy of an eighteenth century highwayman, a Claude Duval, holding up a stagecoach containing elegant ladies. His runs were trinkets, gems of purest degree, extracted from bowlers with manners and poise.

At Trent Bridge, in 1938, he scored a double-century in face of an overwhelming total by England. The last man in—Australia's first innings—was, I seem to remember, Fleetwood Smith. Some seventy runs bedazzled the Trent Bridge grass in half-an-hour or so, nearly all from McCabe's knightly bat.

But I hear the modern seamer scientists saying, 'we could have kept him quiet; we'd have placed a close surrounding leg-side field to him and concentrated, with short-of-a-length stuff, on his leg stump.' At Trent Bridge, in that far-off summer, England's fast bowler was Kenneth Farnes, in the class of Statham and Trueman, among fast bowlers of recent renown. At Melbourne, in 1937, on a flawless wicket and against Bradman at his most rapacious, Farnes took five wickets for 90 in spite of Australia's total of 600. At Trent Bridge, on the occasion preserved by memory, Farnes and the England fieldsmen exploited every familiar device to check the glorious flow of McCabe's strokes. In vain.

We should not forget, also, McCabe's wonderful 187 in the teeth of Larwood and 'bodyline' at Sydney. Compared with the pace of Larwood, that of Snow and Brown might fairly be described as amiably lethargic. That afternoon, at Sydney, Larwood aimed his terrific pace to bounce nearly shoulder high, supported by a leg-side field of six or seven. Yet McCabe hooked and pulled Larwood's nuclear attack—dangerous to limb, cranium and thorax—with a proud nonchalance never to be forgotten. Larwood himself was the first to applaud.

McCabe could not be described either as a front-or-backfooted batsman. Like any other master of the bat, he played from the front or from the back foot according to the length of the ball he had politely to receive. His treatment of the really difficult ball was classically straight and sound. But, again in the manner of any great batsman, he could frequently 'make his own length', by quick, sure and easy footwork. I have seen Larwood bowling to McCabe with a fieldsman at deep long-on.

He could be on view with Bradman at the other end of the wicket and not suffer diminution by contrast. In fact, the difference between the technique and mechanism of motion of McCabe and Bradman was the difference between the technique and mechanism of a swallow and a jet plane. McCabe's style and technique were rational and correct; but he gave the impression that his batsmanship was instinctive, unstaled by routine. I can't state, in this tribute to him, the amount of runs he amassed in his career as cricketer—or his average.

I would no more try to assess McCabe's quality by adding up his runs than I'd assess Schubert by adding up his notes. McCabe, indeed, appealed as much to my musical sensibility as to my love of cricket. Nearly all his innings were those of a cricketing 'Musen-sohn', a son of the game's presiding muses. In his hands, Kreisler's violin was enchanted into a bat; he played for us the easily recognizable music of the willow. I make no apologies for writing of McCabe in this purpled sort of prose. It was inspired, or, at any rate, provoked, by his gallant and lovable cricket.

AN INNINGS FROM BAILEY

ENGLAND
First Innings

L. Hutton, b Burtt	23
J. D. Robertson, c Mooney, b Cowie	26
W. J. Edrich, c Donnelly, b Cowie	9
D. Compton, c Sutcliffe, b Burtt	116
A. Watkins, c Wallace, b Burtt	6
F. G. Mann, b Cave	18
T. E. Bailey, c Sutcliffe, b Rabone	93
T. G. Evans, b Burtt	5
C. Gladwin, run out	5
J. A. Young, not out	1
Extras (b 9, lb 2)	11

Total (for 9 wkts dec.)   313
W. E. Hollies did not bat.

Fall of the wickets:

1	2	3	4	5	6	7	8	9
48	59	72	83	112	301	307	307	313

BOWLING

	O.	M.	R.	W.		O.	M.	R.	W.
Cowie	26·1	5	64	2	Burtt	37	7	102	4
Cave	27	2	79	1	Sutcliffe	1	0	1	0
Rabone	14	5	56	1					

NEW ZEALAND
First Innings

B. Sutcliffe, not out	12
V. J. Scott, not out	8
Extras	0

Total (for no wkts)   20

To bat: W. A. Hadlee, W. M. Wallace, M. P. Donnelly, F. B. Smith, G. O. Rabone, F. L. H. Mooney, T. B. Burtt, H. B. Cave and J. Cowie.

England's innings in the second Test Match against New Zealand here today suggested a broken back shortly after lunch, if indeed it could be said to have been vertebrate at all so far. Five wickets were taken for 112, and our batsmen had made heavy weather of it against the enthusiastic and likeable New Zealanders, who in their own country are content to regard themselves as Saturday afternoon cricketers playing for the fun and love of the game. Compton, occasionally at his best, and a splendid innings by Bailey, skilful and unafraid, pulled England from the hole.

One or two mistakes of Bailey at the outset were smiled upon by fortune, and he deserved to thrive and go his way. But though the stand came as a relief to the crowd, creating immense jubilation, some of us viewed it with mixed feelings—appreciation of batting, of cleverness and temper; disappointment that the match as a swaying tug-of-war was gradually being spoiled.

Many lovers of the game would like to see New Zealand encouraged by a possibility, always round the corner, of defeating England, or at any rate, of running a close race to a short head. New Zealand now will be obliged to fight uphill again for it is not likely that the Lord's wicket will improve in a fourth innings.

Again the toss was won by England. The wicket, though good enough for good batsmanship, did not discourage a capable bowler; at the Nursery end of it, in particular, a quick ball here and there rapped a knuckle, always a source of innocent amusement for onlookers.

The New Zealand attack was steady, and that was enough to cause much acute introspection in England's innings. Hutton and Robertson were studiously empirical, glad to get runs at the rate of 30 an hour. In spite of a few clean strokes, Robertson seemed uncertain and a little untidy, rather like a man who, usually fastidious about his personal appearance, has forgotten to tie his bootlaces.

But Hutton was clearly planning a long and possibly austerely masterful innings when he became suddenly bowled by a ball of pretty length by Burtt, which he tried to push forward, only to play over it. His wicket fell at 48.

Then, after Edrich had assumed an attitude confidently indicative of self-defence and belligerence, he was persuaded into an unconditioned reflex action as a short ball from Cowie reared without fair warning and discovered the top edge of his bat. A perpendicular catch to the slips was inevitable.

Next, Robertson, after some percussion upon the slice of his bat, waved the full and complete weapon at Cowie, and gave a catch to the wicket-keeper, a stroke lacking freedom of the will.

Just before half-past one Watkins played out at Burtt trustfully, if not hopefully, and got sufficiently into touch with the ball's circumference to send it to forward short leg's grip. So England, and the rest of us, were expected to take lunch with four out for 84. Much logic, Jevonian and almost Hegelian, was practised during the interval to account for this latest of England's cricket delinquencies. But it had been merely a matter of keen bowling, accurately directed, and batting not governed by opportunism, character, or considerable skill. Edrich, at any rate, had used his feet and envisaged attack.

When the game was resumed, Compton at the Nursery end, suffered a sharp knock on the gloves—another sign that the pitch was not consistently as decorous as it should have been on an occasion so solemn. At the Pavilion end, too, a ball kept low, compelling Compton into a startled genuflexion and snick. We were, indeed, looking again at a sportive cricket match masquerading as a Test match.

Some beautiful hits by Compton were as cool winds filling England's sails, taking the ship out of the doldrums; but Mann, after at least one strong blow, drove across a length well up to him, and now five wickets were down for 112, and the New Zealanders gathered round and sent one another catches as like any Australians as ever you see.

Two fours to leg in rapid succession by Bailey off Cave provoked such tumultuous applause that anybody coming into the ground at this moment might well have imagined that some batsman had completed his 10,000th run or the second edition of his latest book. And a four to leg from Burtt by Compton—a spacious sweep, rhythmical as a scythe and as decisive—awoke the welkin.

The New Zealand fielding was swift and sure; a ball that went for four byes was almost out of order—a solecism. England 147 for five at 3.20; the match was in the balance, and New Zealand's bowlers taxed nerve and muscle highly, even for these days.

Bailey snicked Cowie involuntarily, and second slip flung himself flat to the ground, full-length, boneless, in vain. A square drive by Compton was as power of swing and forearm changed to light and velocity, all the more handsome because Compton himself appeared unaware of its handsomeness. He is never rhetorical or self-conscious; he bats poetry without knowing it.

Bailey was no mere accessory to this important stand. He played his own part, sensible in defence, near the line of the ball, and vigilant for the short one to crack to leg.

England reached 200 for five at five minutes to four. This resourceful stand only extended New Zealand to sterner and more strenuous efforts. It was grand to see them doing battle, tackling the assembled strength and reputation of English cricket like cubs of the lioness that had begot them.

In an hour after Bailey joined Compton 95 runs were scored; Bailey reached 50 in 67 minutes and an innings of better spirit, begun in a searching moment, could not reasonably be desired.

At this crucial turn of the tide, Hadlee must have longed for some accomplished leg-spin.

After tea Bailey pulled Burtt round for a really magnificent four, and an over or two later Compton arrived at his century and all Lord's rejoiced.

Burtt and Cave sought to check the rate of scoring, and both were persistent and not unduly pessimistic, though the attack had lost the morning's offensive intent and demeanour.

At this time of the afternoon, with the score 287 for five, the onus was, of course, on England to push the game ahead. Frankly the pace was not quite quick or politic enough, mainly because Bailey was nearing his 100 and took more than half of the bowling during several overs.

Eventually Compton, unable to dictate his terms to Burtt, was caught off him in an effort to do something really punitive. He batted three hours 40 minutes and was sixth out at 301—a good authentic Compton innings, but not, so to say, de luxe.

Bailey, almost before Compton could have removed his pads, was deprived of his first Test match century on the very doorstep. He snicked a quicker one from Rabone to the wicketkeeper's pads, and it bounced thence to second slip, who held it. Bailey expressed mortification, but he had 16 4's.

Evans was emphatically bowled at 307, so England's innings yet again declined from sovereignty. It entered the slapstick stage when Gladwin came in and hit his boot with a drive of lofty aim, and Young fell flat on his stomach playing defensively.

Gladwin was missed from a skier by Hadlee on the off side, not at all to Gladwin's embarrassment, for he is a man who regards as potential runs every moment of contact he achieves between bat and ball. His innings ended through excess of enterprise and want of swiftness in transit.

Then Mann declared, submitting New Zealand to the ordeal hated by all cricketers—a quarter of an hour's batting with something possibly to lose, nothing possibly to gain, at the long day's end. Sutcliffe and Scott faced the music cheerfully, and seemed sorry when they had to stop and go home.

GREATEST OF ALL CRICKETERS

Every day a new 'record' is set up in cricket. Batsmen are the darlings of the hour; the groundsmen nurse them solicitously; they are securely rocked to sleep in the cradle of a perfect wicket. The imagination sees the daily store of runs mounting higher and higher, like a dump. The shovel of Bradman is perpetually casting its load. But imagination also sees a mighty figure which no amount of digging and heaving can conceal. The pile of contemporary cricket, the heaping together of all the booty of many a year, cannot submerge W. G. Grace, cannot overwhelm his stature, cannot hide his broad bat, cannot get anywhere near his whiskers. Those whiskers were crucial, they created the sense of authority. The present age has yielded much by taking to the razor; heavens, what a collossus Bradman would seem to us now if he wore the whiskers of a Grace!

'W. G.' was more than a cricketer, though, more than the father of all modern batsmanship. In a delightful little book about W. G. Grace, Mr. Bernard Darwin tells us about a photograph of 'W. G.' as a private person. 'He wears a black tail-coat, and waistcoat built on easy-going lines with an expanse of watch-chain, dark trousers, a little baggy at the knee, and boots made for muddy lanes. In one hand is a solid blackthorn stick with a silver band round it.'

This was the greatest cricketer of all time; with humour does Mr Darwin make the remark that future generations who see that photograph will protest that this cannot be a mighty athlete about to lead the chosen of England to victory. It must be, they will say, a jovial, middle-aged doctor discussing the price of oats with a patient or neighbour he has met in the market place.

The old cricketers were able to keep close to nature; the game had not yet been divorced by excessive specialism from the ordinary life of the country in the summer time; they were first of all players of a game in the fields; it was only by accident that they found themselves not only sportsmen but items in the public news and fit subjects for the public gaze, simply because in their gusto for cricket they acquired abnormal skill.

W. G. Grace enjoyed a renown far beyond anything achieved by the organized genius for publicity of these times. But for all that he was free to live his life as he would have lived it had he played cricket only on Saturday afternoons on the village green. It is not Larwood's fault, of course, if one of his big toes has become a matter for special editions of the evening papers; Larwood has the bad luck to be living in the age of the 'stunt'. But I cannot believe that even if 'W. G.' were alive to day it would occur to anybody to think of his big toe. Contemplating W. G. Grace, we should think that his big toe was a small matter, dwelling at the periphery of things.

At the age of sixteen he stood more than six feet high and weighed eleven stone 'with no premonition of the massive splendour to come'; he played for England against Surrey at the age of eighteen and carried out his bat for 224, his first century in first-class cricket, and he felt nervous at the beginning of it. In 1870, when he was twenty-two, he scored 66 at Lords' against George Freeman and Tom Emmett. Freeman, years afterwards, said 'it was a marvel the Doctor was not either maimed or killed outright. I often think of his pluck when I watch a modern batsman scared if a medium-paced ball hits him on the hand; he should have seen our expresses flying about W. G.'s ribs, shoulders, and head in 1870.' When Grace was in his prime for the Gentlemen, the Players were for years vanquished. 'W. G.' and ten other cricketers, no matter what their names, were equal to challenging the world.

In 1875 he fell away a little in batting; six people were above him in the averages. So he took 192 wickets, at 12 runs each, to console himself. Next year he began badly again and scored only 163 runs in eight innings; the Players smiled and said 'The old devil's gone off at last.' Heaven probably helped their ignorance; he scored his annual century against them at Lord's, then in three innings he amassed 839. He began with 344 against Kent for the M.C.C. at Canterbury (his side were 'following on'!); he broke his bat and borrowed one that was too small in the handle and hit harder than ever. He spent the next day, which was Sunday, travelling in hot weather to Bristol. He went in first for Gloucestershire in the morning, and for three hours he flogged the bowling of

Shaw, Morley, and Barnes to the tune of 177. Nottinghamshire were beaten by ten wickets, and as they were going home they met Yorkshire on the way to play Gloucestershire at Cheltenham. When they told Tom Emmett about 'W. G.'s' latest monstrosity he only laughed and said: 'Well, the big 'un can't do it three times running.'

Next day Yorkshire lost the toss and Grace went in and did not come out until his score was 318 and then he came out only because there was nobody left to stay with him. The Yorkshire bowlers were terribly upset and some of them declined to bowl when Ephraim Lockwood asked them to go on. 'Why don't you make them!' exclaimed Tom Emmett to Ephraim, 'you're t' captain, ain't you?' Then he seized the ball himself and bowled three successive and vindictive wides. In his forty-seventh year Grace made 1,000 runs in May, and his total of runs for the season was 2,346. But his most wonderful deed of all, unparalleled yet, was done in 1871, when he scored 2,390 runs, average 78·90. The next best average of the year was Daft's 37·10.

The day came when 'W. G.' threw his bat on the table of the dressing-room and said: 'I shan't play any more.' He was fifty-eight and for the Gentlemen he had just scored 74, forty-one years after he had first played for the Gentlemen. He came back to the pavilion happy and tired. 'I shan't play any more.' But he did play again; in 1908 at the Oval, on a day of bitter weather, when snow-flakes fell on his beard. He made 15 and 25 and bowled two overs for 5 runs and no wickets. Never again did he tread on a county cricket field.

That a man like 'W. G.' should have an end, and grow old, and not be able to go to Lord's and take the field and bat and bowl, and chuckle and scheme and pull at his whiskers and say, on the off-chance, 'How's that?' and talk at the batsman on the other side who won't get out, and fret at the time that must pass before the next innings! In those far-off Junes and Julys the Champion must have got up on brilliant mornings feeling somewhere in him an inexhaustible energy, inexhaustible years to be lived to the brim. He died in 1915 and the air raids upset him badly. 'You can't be frightened by aeroplanes,' said a friend, 'you old man, who had Ernest Jones bowling through your beard.' 'That was different,' answered the Old Man, 'I could see that Jones and see what he was at. I can't see the aeroplanes.' 'W. G.', who went to Lord's and Bristol countless times in a hansom-cab tinkling gently on a summer morning in the peaceful Victorian days, went there and played cricket to his heart's content, and then went home in the afternoon's soft light, again in a hansom-cab; he lived till the age of aeroplanes, and they hastened his end.

MARTIN DONNELLY A PEDIGREE BATSMAN

NEW ZEALAND
First Innings

B. Sutcliffe, b Bailey	9
V. J. Scott, b Bailey	13
W. A. Hadlee, b Bailey	34
W. M. Wallace, c Washbrook, b Close	12
M. P. Donnelly, lbw b Bailey	75
J. R. Reid, lbw b Jackson	50
G. O. Rabone, not out	27
F. L. H. Mooney, b Jackson	5
T. B. Burtt, st Evans, b Compton	32
H. B. Cave, not out	6
Extras (b 1, lb 9, nb 3)	13
Total (for 8 wkts)	276

Fall of the wickets:

1	2	3	4	5	6	7	8
22	23	62	82	198	205	217	269

BOWLING (to date)

	O.	M.	R.	W.		O.	M.	R.	W.
Bailey	28	5	75	4	Brown	18	4	43	0
Jackson	24	10	41	2	Compton	6	0	28	1
Close	25	12	39	1	Edrich	4	1	8	0
Hollies	18	8	29	0					

ENGLAND
L. Hutton, C. Washbrook, W. J. Edrich, D. Compton, R. T. Simpson, T. E. Bailey, D. B. Close, F. R. Brown, T. G. Evans, W. E. Hollies, L. Jackson.

F. R. Brown celebrated his appointment as England's cricket captain by winning the toss at Old Trafford and sending New Zealand in to bat, a procedure not on the whole sanctioned by tradition or custom in Test Matches. It was not only a case of bold tactics, but of bolder weather prophecy, remembering where we all happened to be at the time.

The wicket, so the experts conjectured was 'green', which seemed to my comparatively old-fashioned way of looking at cricket and cricket fields, an arbitrary choice of English: for the whole of Old Trafford's expanse was a delicious green.

There was little perceptibly wrong with the pitch. England would not have asked Australia to bat first in the circumstances.

An onslaught of fast bowling by Bailey came near to breaking the back of New Zealand's innings before lunch. Scott, Sutcliffe, and Hadlee succumbed to him, and Wallace to Close for 82. Then Donnelly staked another claim to a position amongst the finest of contemporary batsmen, especially on a big and challenging occasion, and with aid from Reid, the New Zealand innings acquired some body and duration, to end the day at 276 for 8.

A really first-class spin bowler should be able to trap Reid at most times. To say the truth, England's attack, but for Bailey, wore the look of persevering competence, and on the whole it was as well that Barnes, Morris, Harvey, Loxton and Miller were not on view. We do not get appreciably nearer to a solution of the problem of how we dare hope to dismiss Australia next year in Australia ten times during the same year.

Scott scored New Zealand's first run, a drive to the on, very confident. Then Bailey from the Stretford, or Mold and Walter Brearley end, bowled a series of quick aggressive overs of which nearly every ball threatened the stumps or conjured visions of rapid slip or behind-the-wicket catches from strokes impulsive rather than rational.

An out-swinger missed Sutcliffe's bat by an inch, and in the same over Scott hit another three to the on, and Bailey's next ball necessitated a lightning snick which fell in front of Close at second slip. It was a snick not related in any way to Sutcliffe's technique or consciousness.

Sutcliffe was therefore obliged to drive Bailey for four to the off, a hit flushed with blood at high temperature. But in his next over Bailey clean bowled Sutcliffe all the way, and in his subsequent over he comprehensively and unambiguously bowled Scott, whose bat was as though deprived of length, breadth and all substance whatsoever.

In eight overs Bailey took two wickets for 19, by an attack as menacing and swift-piercing as any seen since Lindwall was with us. And now Hadlee batted like a grave and born leader. Hollies and Brown took charge of the gradually ageing ball and twice Hadlee drove Hollies with power and a swing of the bat which expressed not only purpose but command.

His colleague in responsibility, Wallace, who after scoring nearly a thousand runs in May, has suffered as long a season of negligible scores as any that has ever tried the philosophy and self-esteem of a fine player, gave himself up to a caution and concentration almost to be felt.

A flawless on-drive by him, from Brown, hinted that fortune was about to return to him, fulsome as she always is with mortals or gods: but she was again outrageously unprincipled, for she presented him with a full toss from Close and Wallace pulled it cleanly and handsomely straight to Washbrook, who held the catch knee high at deep square leg.

Just before lunch, Bailey bowled once more, and though the ball lacked some of the bounce, he produced a delivery fast enough to make an end of Hadlee's staunch and splendid little innings. Hadlee seemed willing not to play it as it sped by outside the off-stump, and it struck his knee and went thence to the wicket. Bad luck for New Zealand's captain if not altogether good judgment.

The game resumed in steaming weather, and Bailey recaptured something of the early morning's vivacity, and Reid sliced a ball from his leg stump like a man temporarily electrified and set alight.

Hollies at the other end, could not spin awkwardly on a wicket thoroughly comfortable: moreover, his length frequently dropped short. Apart from Bailey, England's attack appeared not more than steady and industrious. I doubt if it would have caused the Australians to worry in the slightest, or curb their back-footed powers of propulsion. Apart from Bailey, in a word, it was an attack rather dependent for success on the mistakes of good batsmen who are not amongst the greatest.

Donnelly, after an error of timing, settled down to his own attractive and fluent method. He and Reid protected New Zealand's fifth wicket stubbornly, but not without appeal to the eye and ear: the vast crowd watched quietly appreciating the struggle and New Zealand's need of a stand. It was strange that so many people gathered together in the same place, could be so quiet.

A 'googly' by Brown nearly betrayed Reid, his score 20. Reid then hit three loose, meandering balls from Brown to the on, using masculine shoulders. From Test Match bowlers let us have no meandering.

Two consecutive maiden overs by Close stimulated applause: he bowled ably and insisted on serious attention, but generally the scene and the action remained unspectacular.

Compton lent his left arm to the attack when New Zealand were

141 for four, and the sixth ball to which Reid had to reach forward whether he wanted or not, was edged dangerously in front of first slip. Reid drove Compton's next ball for a lovely four to the off, was beaten by the next, pulled the next gigantically for four, and played half-cock to the next, lobbing it halfway down the pitch low to the ground out of Compton's grasp.

Again Compton spun a way through Reid's bat: if only he could bowl his best ball oftener he might count among the match winners. As it is, he is usually every over sending down a difficult one spinning away, but more or less hidden in a profusion of vagrant ones.

Bailey took the new ball at a quarter to four, a little belated with it, for Brown gave all his spinners ample opportunity; and Donnelly plundered four runs from one over by Bailey, one of them behind the wicket from a high full toss, batsmanship of brilliant opportunism. Thus he passed his 50 mingling cool and artistic defence with cool and artistic attack in stroke play. If he has a superior in cricket as a left-hander today it is only Morris, who has the advantage of playing for Australia.

Reid arrived at 50, too, by a different style and psychology from Donnelly's. He is a club cricketer *in excelsis*. I do not mean that he is not endowed technically, but only that he combines with commonsense against a good ball an unashamed appetite for a brawny blow against a bad one.

Donnelly and Reid, in a bad hour for their side, and one which endangered the match as a three-day trial of strength, achieved a rally of excellent spirit and intelligence.

Just as tea was intervening the stand was broken after it had added 116. Reid endeavoured to turn a ball from Jackson, well up to him, and was leg before.

After tea Rabone joined Donnelly, whose cricket became more and more easeful and untroubled. He plays late, like all batsmen of class, and without rhetoric or show of violence or waste of muscular motion.

He can send the ball to the boundary at a speed which makes pursuit an act of faith or, as they say in Lancashire, of 'showing willing'. He is a courteous batsman, a pedigree batsman.

Still, when he was 71, his composure was ruffled by Bailey, who made him edge blindly through the slips; and to the next ball he was leg before, glancing across the line. So Bailey, though naturally less dangerous than at the day's outset, advanced England's position beyond measure at a time of some emergency.

Shortly afterwards Jackson bowled Mooney by length and 'fizz' from the pitch.

We could understand the deficiency in the bowling when nobody could come forward and sweep the New Zealand later batsmen out of the way and save waste of time. To win the match England will need to score on Monday at a speed well beyond their habit.

D. R. JARDINE

D. R. Jardine was one of the strongest-minded captains ever to command an England eleven. He asserted his character and leadership in Australia in 1932–3. Bradman at the time was at the height of his supremecy over all bowlers. So long as he remained tyrannically the master-batsman, almost certain to score a century, even a double or triple century, in every Test match, England could never hope to defeat Australia in a rubber. So the so-called 'body-linc' method of attack was put into force, to reduce Bradman to a normal prowess and efficiency.

Jardine boldly exploited this method, which could scarcely be encouraged ethically. The method involved fast bowling directed to rise shoulder or rib high, pitched on or outside the leg-stump, with some eight fieldsmen placed on the leg side, three close up round about the batsman's left trouser pocket. At the time, I described the method of body-line attack as the 'Jardinian theory': it was an attack designed to show ruthlessly that none but the fittest could hope to survive. It had the immediate effect of reducing Bradman's batting average from the nineties to the fifties. Larwood was Jardine's main executive agent, and none but a bowler of Larwood's pace and accuracy could have succeeded with the method.

Jardine stood his ground in the teeth of all Australia's rage of protest. At Adelaide, Woodfull was hit over the heart by a ball pitched on the offside to the orthodox offside field. Then according to plan already arranged, Jardine switched the field to leg. He would not allow any circumstance, not even one demanding some humane if only temporary consideration, to interfere with policy. The bruised Woodfull had now definitely to look to his ribs, not to say his cranium. The Adelaide ground, naturally enough, quickly sounded like outraged pandemonium. Even Whitehall, far away in London feared a disruption of Colonial relations.

When Jardine and Larwood returned to England they found that what was good (or bad) enough in the land of the barbarian would not do in the home of the Establishment. One or two counties at once threatened not to renew fixtures with Nottinghamshire if Larwood and Voce persisted with the 'body line' specific.

But in the English season of 1933, Jardine himself scored a century at Manchester for England against the West Indies, and treated a fast leg-theory attack of Constantine and Martindale with the loftiest disdain of which his physical height, his long nasal sniff and his Harlequin cap could express, singly and in combination.

He was born in October, 1900, in Bombay, and his father was in his day nearly equally famous for a while for a brilliant 140 in the university match of 1892. The son went to Winchester, and it must be admitted that in subsequent years he interpreted the motto, 'Manners maketh man' with uncompromising masculinity. At Oxford his cricket developed with characteristic patience, but in 1921 he scored 96 not out against Warwick Armstrong's invincible team, though Gregory bowled only ten overs in the match and McDonald did not play. Still, here were signs of the wrath to come sooner or later to the ancient enemy. In 1927 he came to the honour of a century for the Gentlemen v. the Players at Lord's, when the next highest innings on his side was 46.

It is a testimony to the dominating sense of his presence, if felt only for a moment or two, that he is now regarded part of Surrey's cricket history, as well as England's, despite that after one or two active seasons in the 1920s, his appearances at the Oval and elsewhere were comparatively few and intermittent. In one of his few full seasons for Surrey—1926—he scored 1,050 runs, average 43·75. He twice was one of the England team in Australia, first with A. P. F. Chapman's side of 1928-9, where the result was four victories to one for England, as subsequently happened when Jardine made himself notorious if not immortal. His Test match innings in Australia were registered in the score-sheet as follows: 35, 65 not out, 28 run out, 62, 33, 1, 98, 19, 0, 27, 1, 0, 3, 56, 46, 24, 18, 24. But the scorers could only indicate superficially the value of an innings by Jardine; his influence was psychological.

He was a tall hard-boned personality, having none of the unction often associated in his period with cricket. His was a realpolitik. He determined in the early 1930s to wrest back the 'ashes' from

Australia, and to put Bradman in a reasonable, if still high, place. All the howls and winds of the world would not deter him. As a batsman he was upright and unbending, strong in defence and to the onside. His bat was scrupulously straight. The fastest bowling could not hurry him. His batting, indeed, was like the man himself —calm, well-bred, not given to rhetoric, common-sensed, and imperturbable. He had, off the field, a canny wit and gifts for fellowship. On the field, even a Harlequin cap did not lighten or brighten his pervading air of relentless purpose. Against Australia he played cricket to win. He was perhaps the first to lead the reaction against Edwardian gesture and romance and the humbug of a 'may the best side win'.

FRANK WORRELL

Frank Maglinne Worrell was the most completely stylish of all West Indies batsmen. He had not the dynamic, spectacular energy of Weekes or Walcott; he was never, to my knowledge, demonstrative or spectacularly aggressive, as Sobers sometimes is, in spite of his general show of easeful mastery. Worrell's strokes were literally strokes, smooth and polished, sending the ball here and there at his sweet will and leisure, with the minimum of matter to be moved.

His cricket, in fact, expressed the man himself, engaging, companionable, lithe, effortless. I have to think as far back as R. H. Spooner to recall his like in point of wristwork; they were not wrists of iron but of finely-tempered steel. I watched his innings of 261 v. England in 1950 at Nottingham, in company of George Gunn, who looked on entranced. 'See,' said George, 'he is late-cutting the ball almost out of the wicketkeeper's gloves.' Worrell leaned over his late cuts with time enough to spare to enjoy, without offence to the bowler, his own delicacy of touch.

There was nothing in his play, as batsman, bowler or fieldsman of that hint of primitive impulse which has usually marked even the most civilized of West Indian batsmen: never a rush of blood to his head. During the past few decades, West Indies cricket has gained in a sophistication which has merged it with English and

Australian cricket, so much so, that it can now fairly be called non-racial and International. Worrell was the first fine fruit of this harvesting of refinement and poise. His method as batsman was orthodox—but he put a bloom on it. I can say of him, as I could say of Hobbs, that I never saw him make a crude or ungrammatical stroke; he would get out to the wrong right stroke, so to say, to the correct stroke applied wrongly by error of judgment.

Curiously, he began his career as a slow left-arm spin bowler. At the age of 18 he was sent in to act as 'night-watchman', near close of play, for Barbados v. Trinidad, in 1943. He scored 64 not out, and a month later, also against Trinidad, scored 188 and 68. His cricket blossomed season by season until, in 1950, he was one of the great West Indies trinity in this country, with Weekes and Walcott. One of his most superb innings was played against Australia at Melbourne in 1952, 102 in three hours and three quarters, facing Lindwall, Miller and Johnstone, and going his tranquil way in spite of a severely bruised hand caused by a blow from Miller.

We must constantly bear in mind, as we try to get at the worth of batsmen, the quality of the attack to which they have been subjected. It can safely be said that Worrell was seldom subjected to *any* bowler. At his best he gave us the impression that he could hypnotically, but in the most friendly way, draw the ball to his bat's middle. Even when scoring quickly he never looked to be in a hurry. If he hooked a short rising ball, he did so without the air of killing pugnacity and aggression which is the characteristic visual appeal of the hook. I described, years ago, how A. C. Maclaren, when he hooked, 'dismissed' the ball from his presence. Worrell was not so arrogantly magisterial; he *waved* the ball away. His bat was always sending out sounds quite musical.

Likewise with his bowling. From an easy weightless run, a loose swing of the left arm, forward shoulder classically straight, he could swing sinuously this way and that. In Test matches he scored 3,860 runs, average 49·48, and took 69 wickets, average 38·73. But he was much more than a cricketer of pedigree; he was the most inspiring captain of his time, inspiring not only his West Indies colleagues but the opposition as well. All Melbourne turned out in royal procession to hail him, after the wonderful West Indies tour in Australia in 1960–61. Then, in 1963, his best days over as a player, he was leader of the most triumphant and magnetic team ever to play Test matches, winning the rubber here three victories to one.

When Hall was about to bowl the famous last over in the drawn match at Lord's, England needed only eight to win, with eight wickets down. Worrell ran out Shackleton from the fourth ball. The injured Cowdrey, in last, fortunately hadn't to face the remaining two balls of the over; this was Allen's ordeal. Before Hall began his last assault, six runs wanted, Worrell calmly walked up to him and said: 'Be careful of no balls.' The advice of a statesman.

Worrell, in fact, was much more than a cricketer. When he took part in league matches in Lancashire, he found time to study Economics and Optics at Manchester University—Optics, indeed, a strange study for a flawless batsman! ('all the better to see you with, my dear Lindwall'). Shortly after his retirement from the game, he was knighted, and became an active influence at the University of West Indies in Jamaica, and a worker in sociology with the Trinidad Government.

In the Test match at Lord's in 1963, Worrell helped Butcher to add 110, at a most crucial point of the West Indies' second innings —on the Saturday afternoon. On the following Monday morning, the West Indies innings collapsed, the remaining five wickets going for 15. I met one of the West Indies players immediately this collapse had ended. 'Worrell must be pretty sick about this,' I said. 'No,' came the answer, with a flash of a grin, 'he's been lying on the locker fast asleep or just thinking.'

Nothing ruffled Worrell's temperament, nothing ruffled his cricket. His loss to the West Indies goes beyond cricket. He was a man of truly political sense and feeling, a federalist who, in time, would surely have served well and perspicuously the Islands he loved far above little loyalties and little jealousies. Wherever he travelled he was courtesy itself. It's a sad thing whenever a cricketer dies young enough to remain in the game, if only as a power behind the scenes. It is sad, indeed, when it is Sir Frank Worrell, at the age of 42.

THE GREAT INDIANS

IT was apt and delightful that Queen Elizabeth should have gone to Lords' on the day that saw an Indian cricketer bringing again to a Test-match the spirit of youth and adventure. This same match had been begun gloomily and parsimoniously, not to say unchivalrously, by England's new captain Hutton, abetted by the amateur Simpson. Between them they apparently dared not attack India's bowling for two hours on a perfectly easy pitch; they prodded the ball or pompously stopped it in a way which, if repeated twelve months hence, will not only be unworthy of the Coronation, but will certainly provide a psychological asset to the Australians, who seldom need anything of the kind.

On a weak side bound to lose from the bowling of the first ball, unless blessed by miracles of luck, Mankad in all that he did honoured the art and nature of cricket. In his first innings at the beginning of so solemn an occasion, he drove straight for six, and I know of no precedent of such a solecism during the first hour of a Test match. Mankad scored 72 in this first innings of his; then bowled 73 overs in England's portentous advance to 537, redeemed for pleasure only by the gameness of Evans, and Graveney's suggestions of style. Still inexhaustible and avid for relished action, Mankad went to the wicket again, and, in spite of odds and encircling gloom, sent forth from his bat those sounds which are the game's music. With sustained brilliance of stroke-play and liveliness of the sporting instinct he scored 184, the highest innings of any Indian in a Test match. His captain, Hazare, helped him in a third-wicket stand of 211. When Mankad's second innings came to an end, twenty minutes after lunch on Monday, June 24th, he had been on the field for all but three-and-a-half hours since Thursday morning, and for only ninety minutes of that time had he not been busy with bat or ball.

The secrets of cricket have so little to do with competition's values, averages and results that often I could wish for some other way than the score-board's of awarding the prize. India emerged from the Lord's Test match, thanks to Mankad and Hazare, on the side of the Angels, as far as playing the game is concerned. England, needing seventy-seven to win with eighty minutes of Monday available for getting them, again played without a single gallant gesture, scoring only forty; not only insulting tradition and art, but placing the match and victory at the mercy of the weather next day. Personally, I would have given India the match on, say, aesthetic and spiritual 'points'. And the crowd in the main would have been with me.

Mankad is now the most renowned Indian cricketer since Ranjitsinhji, and his nephew Duleepsinhji. A comparison of method and character of these three players might serve to illustrate my pet theory that cricket has a way of reflecting or indicating changes in a social, even a racial, order or psychology. The magical opulence of 'Ranji' was entirely in accordance with the India of the rajahs and principalities. He played many a Koh-i-Noor of an innings; his cricket was scintillating and of the East. He seemed to wear flannels that were more easily and beautifully rippled by the wind than the wear of other players; his bat was held lightly, and his strokes were less strokes than 'passes' of conjuration.

Ranjitsinhji was the most original genius the game has so far known, with the possible exception of Jessop. Your Bradmans, remarkable enough, are to be comprehended; their skill is rational, the sum-total of all that has for years been developing in batsmanship, just as the 'Queen Mary' is the sum-total of all that for years has been developing in the science of shipbuilding. 'Ranji' came from nowhere; his way of batting was scarcely deducible from the technique known when he first began his strange lovely flickerings and glidings. The left leg quietly put across the right to a break-back from Mold, then lo! the ball was going to the fine-leg boundary, not with the weight or ponderousness of a material object, but as a ray of energy out of 'Ranji's' sinuous blade.

Against Lancashire at Brighton in August, 1896, Sussex were apparently beaten to the world—nearly 200 behind, and three or four wickets fell in the second innings for next to nothing. 'Ranji' seemed unlikely to bat because of a damaged finger. The following morning, the third day, the Lancashire XI packed up their bags and ordered cabs so that an early train home might be caught. But 'Ranji' decided that perhaps he would be able to bat one-handed; he was also suffering from a sore throat and also—so George Lyttelton always maintains, rather rhetorically, I think—from corns. Anyway, 'Ranji' that day scored 165, and saved Sussex from defeat. The next highest score in the innings was 25. The Lancashire bowlers included Mold and Briggs and Hallam.

In this same summer of 1896 'Ranji' was in his twenty-fourth year, and at Brighton, again in August, Yorkshire made 407 and Sussex lost 2 for 23; but next day on a 'sticky' wicket against Hirst Peel, Wainwright, F. S. Jackson and Ernest Smith, 'Ranji' scored 100 out of 132 in an hour-and-a-half, and when Sussex 'followed on', he scored another century in two hours—two centuries in a day in a losing cause, and every stroke a source of wonder and delight.

The age of Victoria burgeoned for 'Ranji's' coming; the old Queen held the East in fee. It was as though 'Ranji' were one of

107

the cavalcade that journeyed from the Empire's corners to do homage in the Diamond Jubilee year of 1897. He and his kind—MacLaren, Fry, Jessop, Grace, Jackson—passed from one period of imperial magnificence and opulence to another. They lived to become Edwardians, and saw the age blaze away in a pretty lurid sunset. They were part of the time's pomp and circumstance, and we know nothing of them except by what they expressed with bat and ball. Such men would never have stood about a field in June waiting for some contemporary professional to complete a century in four-and-a-half hours; they would have preferred Ascot. They made cricket their summer pleasure—and 'Ranji' brought a light with him that never was before seen in cricket, and never will be seen again.

His nephew Duleepsinhji nearly persuaded us that nature was about to depart from custom and not break a mould after making a masterpiece. But 'Duleep', though a beautiful player, had nothing esoteric about him, no dusky enigma. His play and his nature told of the English amateur culture, and was redolent of the lawns of Cheltenham and Fenner's. In him the Indian witchery was mingled with sweet reason of the Occident. He contributed through cricket to the Georgian scene of England, after the manner born. 'He never made a Christian stroke in his life,' said 'Ted' Wainwright of 'Ranji'. Nobody dreamed of saying the same of 'Duleep'.

When English professionals were annually engaged to go to India to coach cricketers there, the 'Westernizing' work soon began to bear fruit. Impulse was subjected to discipline, and in next to no time three Indian batsmen emerged who for circumspection and craftsmanship would survive comparison with Hutton, Ponsford and Hassett: I refer to Pataudi, Merchant and Hazare. But not altogether has the magical spirit been exorcized. Only the other year we were all put under the spell of Mushtaq Ali, and there is Mankad, Oriental enough to this day, in spite of Haslingden. I remember an innings of Mushtaq Ali in a Test match at Old Trafford; he came forth with a bat apparently as finely-tempered as a scimitar. His was primitive cricket in the best sense, glowing with style of its own, and a beauty which had its own axis and balance. His off-side flashes and shooting stars of strokes were all wrong in our astronomy, but right and splendid in some other dazzling solar system. A certain English professional bowler spoke patronizingly of Mankad's batting at Lord's: 'He won't "get away" with that sort of cricket again.' But we'll remember Mankad at

Lord's for many a long day. There ought to be some other means of reckoning quality in this the best and loveliest of games; the scoreboard is an ass.

CRICKET'S CORONATION YEAR

EVERYBODY interested in cricket has been glad to see Leicestershire running for the County Championship as never before, and I suppose that as I am a Lancashire man I should be taking a grim satisfaction in Yorkshire's lowly state during Coronation year. Once on a time I would have exulted to the heart's core to know that Yorkshire cricketers were being reduced and humbled, fair means or foul. But I was then a barbarous partisan schoolboy; and Old Trafford was situated amidst green fields, and every Whitsuntide and August Bank Holiday, Yorkshire, led by Lord Hawke, would invade us, and George Hirst, after rolling up the sleeve of a left arm which looked like a smoked ham, would assault my favourite batsman, the unparalleled Reggie Spooner, with a swerving new ball, red and as red-hot in my imagination as a coal of fire.

Today, with the broadmindedness of age, I confess to feelings of sadness at the departure—only temporary, we may be sure!—of glory from Yorkshire. But consolation for unaccustomed adversity will have come to most Yorkshiremen by means of Len Hutton's success as captain of an England team that has recovered the 'Ashes' for us. But few people, even those who admire Hutton the other side of idolatry, realize how great the strain the rubber has imposed on him, physically and mentally. When Hobbs provided an England innings with its spinal column match after match, he could give the whole of his attention, as batsman, to the Australian attack of the period, free of worry about tactics, knowing that if he chanced not to get runs there were other great players to follow. Seldom in recent Test matches has Hutton been able quite to trust any of his colleagues not to get out; never has he enjoyed the position of confidence occupied once by W. G. Grace, who, when they asked him his ideas about the composition of the next England XI, simply said: 'Give me Arthur'—meaning that if Arthur

Shrewsbury were chosen to open the innings with him the names of the others didn't matter.

Pudsey, of course, has already paid generous and resonant tribute to Hutton, but on the whole he has scarcely had his due portion of national gratitude. We tend, as a people, to reserve our loudest cheers for the losers. On the balcony at Kennington Oval, when the multitude assembled after the finish of the fifth Test match, the applause increased in volume at the appearance of Hassett. Thus for Hassett the wheel had come an ironical full circle; for when he led Australia to a rubber's victory at Melbourne in 1951, the crowd shouted for F. R. Brown, and wouldn't go home but hailed him again and again. I happened to run into Hassett at the back of the pavilion; he was trying to find his car and get away before the crush. 'Listen to them,' he said, 'cheering Freddie Brown. They don't want the Australian captain. We have only won the rubber.' Then he paused, looked at me with comic wistfulness, and, apologetically taking from his pocket his fountain pen, said: 'Er—would you like my autograph?' This story, if not altogether true, is entirely characteristic of the most likeable and most friendly Australian captain of cricket ever to come to England. He has made his major errors—to the increase of his hold on our affections!— but in the main he has conducted his side at the right tempo, and done his best to encourage his young men.

The rise of Leicestershire to prominence in the county champion-ship delights me especially, for reasons of personal sentiment. When I was a very tiny Lancashire lad my first love in sport was not cricket but, as we called it then, 'assocy' football; and my hero was 'Billy' Meredith, who used to race down the wing for Manchester City, the ball flickering about his boots like some sort of shadow or lustre of them, leaving the track behind him strewn with frus-trated and rather dizzy opponents. One afternoon I found myself outside the county ground at Old Trafford; it was probably my second visit there. To this day I can't imagine how the admission fee of sixpence came into my possession. Lancashire were playing Leicestershire, and A. C. Maclaren made a century the majesty of which moves in my memory to this day. I decided on the spot that this was the game for me. And it so happened that one of the Leicestershire XI of that distant year was A. E. Knight, a profes-sional known not only for his clear-cut strokes and sound defence but also because of his interest in classic literature and his devotion to religion and good works. Under his name appeared the first book on cricket I ever read—*The Complete Cricketer*; and in it was a glowing romantic word-picture of Victor Trumper that awakened in me an ambition one day to become a writer on cricket myself.

Leicestershire's progress towards the summits owes much to the example of C. H. Palmer, the captain—just as the amateur captaincy of a young player has achieved in Sussex virtually a resurrection. David Sheppard, at the beginning of the season, was obliged to set to work on much the same material which had seemed to be heavy and unproductive and not at all related to Sussex cricket as we all knew and loved it in the years of 'George Brann, 'Ranji', Fry, Arthur Gilligan, Tate and Duleepsinhji and by example of skill, fortified and inspired by love and faith in the game and the men about him, Sheppard has indeed produced for us a Sussex side handsome to watch and hard to play. In time, and before he is much older, Colin Cowdrey will do as much for Kent.

The game is already all the better in health for the new blood that has been pumped into it these recent summers by young amateurs. Some of them, unfortunately, will not be able much longer to afford to go on playing simply for pleasure. And here we touch the sore spot of contemporary cricket. In spite of the glamour cast over the scene in general by the Test matches, too much of the day-to-day county routine is without imagination, true craftsmanship or individual relish. It is possible any day to spend hours on a county cricket ground and not see a square cut, a left-hand spinner, a straight drive, a leg-break, a truly fast ball, or a vivid hook. Now these are things which are part and parcel of the technique and art of the game; and if they are not constantly on view we are watching cricket in impoverished attenuation. The average professional player, worked hard without much rest from May to September, seems more and more to look for the sort of technical trick which is easiest and safest to exploit. The new ball! So he polishes it on his body, a sight which somehow always irritates me, especially when I see boys apeing the custom during an Eton and Harrow match. The M.C.C. might do cricket some service by returning to the ancient rule or procedure by which one ball, and one ball only, was used in the longest innings. Bowlers then were compelled to learn the lovely arts and devices of spin, changes of pace and of flight. Fast bowlers had to bowl at the wicket; even Lindwall is less dangerous by half when the ball has lost polish and prominence of seam. To bowl inswingers persistently to three short-leg fieldsmen is monstrous, witless, against the spirit; it is a bowler's confession of fear to face the challenge of a batsman's best strokes.

But week in and week out the cricket season of 1953 has honoured

111

Coronation year, and left us many scenes and excitements to cherish, best of all the power and strength of Lindwall's attack; and the agonized obduracy of Trevor Bailey, who twice stood in Australia's way when the path of victory looked clear enough for them, and batted in a manner that told them they would advance only over his dead body. And even Keith Miller wasn't prepared to go as far as all that.

THE CARIBBEAN FLAVOUR

THE first vision, or notion, that comes to the mind as we think of West Indies cricket is of joyful noise, a bat flailing the air, the ball whizzing here, there, everywhere, stumps flying, shining black faces and mouths laughing white-toothed, like melons. Such a mental picture of a West Indian cricketer is projected many times by Rohan Babulal Kanhai, who often seems to have only one object in life—to hit a cricket ball for six into the crowd at square-leg, falling on his back after performing the great swinging hit. The impetus of the hit, its sheer animal gusto, brings him down to earth, but it is a triumphant fall.

Cricket is an organism much conditioned by environment. West Indies cricket many times tells that its exponents have learned the game, played it as boys, in hot sun; and played it, moreover, intuitively, in uninhibited company, the sun going into the brain and blood. In the beginning the West Indian temperament ran riot. The pioneer discipline of George Challenor rationalized original impulse and sin, and tabulated a few necessary first principles and commandments concerning the virtues of reasonably straight bats and of patience. Today the conception of happy-go-lucky West Indian cricketers, bashing the ball all over the field, right and left, over after over, is entirely mistaken and illusory. Any visitor to Lord's the other Saturday morning, not knowing that West Indians were anywhere near the premises, could have watched the batting of Hunte and Carew and Butcher for hours, mistaking any one of these for any average English hard-working professional: colour of face excepted. West Indies have more than once in a Test match, fallen behind England's rate of scoring; nonetheless, they have sent forth some personal glow and vitality causing the impression of livelier, more mobile combatants. The difference between the West Indies' approach to cricket, and the English on the whole is, as far as batting goes, this: when a West Indian batsman is confined to scoreless defence both he, and the rest of us watching him, are surprised at this unfruitful behaviour. We wonder what has gone wrong. Whenever the everyday English batsman plays in this negative barren way, we are not surprised, we don't need to seek reasons for his inactivity and wariness; it is his natural way of play-ing the game. In his case, if he should hit a six, falling on his back, we should certainly wonder what was going wrong, technically and mentally.

The first creative raptures of West Indies cricket came to personal apotheosis in the flesh and spirit of Learie Constantine, now a man of title. He was coached by his father and by his mother. He soon developed into a cricketer in whose innermost being cricket and instinct to live became one and indivisible. He was the first and fullest representative West Indian cricketer. In all his movements, swift and apparently unpremeditated, he expressed the West Indian temperament. His bowling was very fast—Jack Hobbs vowed that Constantine's freshest overs were as fast as, if not faster than, any of his experience. He used a bat as an exultant announcement of his own and his countrymen's physical abandon and disregard of all *bourgeois* decorum. Constantine's fielding also had the racial agility; he was three men in the slips, omnipresent, long armed and, surely, boneless. One day at Lord's, in the mid 1920s when West Indies cricket was still struggling to receive serious international attention, Constantine performed miracles, leading his colleagues out of a very bare wilderness. Against Middlesex, the West Indies were going down to defeat; Middlesex had amassed 352 for 6 (declared), and 5 West Indies wickets had fallen for 79. In came Constantine, and in one glorious ferocious hour he scored 86, then wrecked the Middlesex second innings by taking 7 wickets for 57, in a whirlwind of lightning bowling and flying splintered stumps. He then actually won the match by a blinding quick motion 103 in an hour. During all this West Indian explosion of creative cricket energy and genius, a visitor from Barbados arrived at Lord's. Clearly it was his first entrance to Lord's, in those days a place of some elegance. So this visitor from Barbados had come to Lord's dressed for the occasion. He wore a light-grey frockcoat, striped trousers, white spats and a grey topper. Also he carried a tightly rolled umbrella. He watched the game from the covered stand, then a place of social exclusiveness near the pavilion. He watched the West Indies' tribulations in un-disguised dolour. But at the height of Constantine's brilliant resurgence, he rose from his seat in the enclosure of the select. Far away in the free seats at the Nursery-end a group of West Indians were cheering Constantine on. The immaculately adorned West Indian rushed from the select enclosure to the field and, waving his grey topper, he ran round the boundary towards the Nursery shouting to his compatriots there: 'I'se comin' to join you, I'se coming.' He had seen, that afternoon, the prophecy of Constantine's cricket. He could hardly have foreseen, no matter how beatific his vision, that one day, which probably he would live to see, would hail a West Indies XI as World Champions.

Such eminence and renown have not come to West Indian cricket by happy-go-lucky *calypso* cricket. The general public in England has rather got a wrong impression of Sobers, Kanhai, Butcher, Hunte and company. Several West Indian cricketers in recent years have earned good money playing professionally in the leagues of Lancashire and other unromantic places, where no vain swash-bucklings are encouraged. Consequently the first sunshine raptures of Caribbean cricket have been—dare I say?—sobered. Hunte, Carew, Butcher, even Sobers himself, could easily graduate to any Lancashire XI of the Harry Makepeace epoch, when the order of the day was 'No fours afore lunch; and not too many afore tea.' West Indian cricket, in short, has evolved from a game to an *art*, observing, mainly, the discipline that is the basis of any art. A scherzo doesn't unbalance the most classical symphony and Kanhai's gyrations don't disturb the ensemble of West Indies cricket as it is today, assembled for Test match purposes.

Naturally enough, fast bowling is the main weapon of the West Indies attack in the field. Every West Indian fresh from the cradle tries to bowl fast. Long before the coming of Hall and Griffith there were not Constantine but Francis and another Griffith, each of them so fast that a batsman needed to pick up his bat smartly. I remember the earlier Griffith mainly because one golden evening at Lord's he was fielding near the wicket and received a terrific crack on the skull, from some batsman's hook-stroke. The impact of ball on skull echoed around Lord's. But Griffith merely shook his head twice before picking up the ball and returning it to the bowler. And all our sympathies went out to the ball.

The present-day West Indies fast bowlers are a formidable pair to look at. Hall, I am told, sometimes goes into action wearing a crucifix on his chest, slung there from a ribbon round his neck. For my own part, I should think that it's the batsman who needs the crucifix. I am reminded here of A. E. Knight, the old-time Leicestershire professional. He was religious-minded. Whenever he arrived at the wicket to bat, he would take guard then bend his head in silent prayer. One day Leicestershire were playing Lancashire, with Walter Brearley on the war-path, avid for wickets while the ball retained the shine. In came Knight, took guard then bent his head. Walter Brearley whispered to the adjacent Lancashire fieldsman: 'What's the matter with him—is he ill?' 'No,' was the *sotto voce* answer, 'no, he always does it—he's praying.' 'Praying for what!' asked Brearley. 'Why, for divine guidance to a century.' Brearley, red in the face as a lobster, exploded: 'I'll ruddy well write to the MCC about this!'

Hall and his crucifix, Griffith with his 'suspect' action—here is attraction enough to draw to all cricket grounds all sorts and conditions of men and women, many of whom, judging by what I heard at Lord's the other day, wouldn't easily distinguish a no-ball from the pavilion cat. It is to be hoped, in all good humour, that there will be no organized hunt, off the field of play, after the 'chucker'. Let's leave it to the umpires. In any case, I can't believe that any fast bowler's arm can continue throwing and not soon go muscularly out of action. The law is quite clear on this 'chucking' matter. The umpire is not obliged to announce positively that a bowler throws or jerks; he can 'call' a suspect action if he is not entirely satisfied of the 'absolute' fairness of the delivery. Decades ago the famous Ernest Jones of Australia— the man who sent a cricket ball whizzing through W. G. Grace's whiskers—was thought by certain purists to throw. In a match between New South Wales and South Australia (Ernest Jones's State), a young batsman was sent in first to join in opening the NSW innings. After two NSW wickets had fallen, M. A. Noble (one of Australia's greatest cricketers) arrived at the crease. The second or third ball he received from Jones 'came back' a foot from the off at lightning speed, just missing the leg stump. At the end of the over, Noble walked down the pitch to talk to the young novice at the other end. 'Don't you think, son,' he asked, 'don't you think Jones is throwing one or two?' 'Yes, sir,' whispered the colt, 'yes, sir, he is—but don't say anything about it; they might take him off.' The young colt's name was Victor Trumper.

The present West Indies team is a mingling of all the cricketing talents. Every department of cricket's many skills is here on view; brilliant batsmen, dour batsmen, right-handed or left; fast bowlers, slow off spinners, again right-handed or left; slow left-handed spinners and the 'googly'. From watching these West Indians play cricket you could reconstruct the necessary elements and styles and techniques of the game if everyone of these requisites had somehow disappeared or got mislaid—as, in fact, many of them have got lost during the last years—first-class 'googly' bowling for example.

It is a remarkable fact that since West Indies cricket was baptized in Test company at Lord's in 1928, it has produced players fit to form a World XI, to play in some overworld a representative company of cricket immortals headed by 'W.G.' For example, Stollmeyer (the R. H. Spooner of West Indies), Butcher, Headley, Worrell, Weekes, Walcott, Sobers, Constantine, Gibbs, Hall and Griffith.

George Headley was one of the greatest batsmen of my acquaintance. On a bowler's wicket at Lord's he scored a century of such sure judgment and aim that if ever he edged a viciously spinning ball he did so with the edge's middle.

When West Indies won a rubber against England for the first time in this country sixteen years ago, Worrell, Weekes and Walcott made history at the crease as they scored multitudinous runs. And Valentine and Ramadhin put a spell of spin on all of England's batsmen, one of the greatest of whom confessed to me that, facing Ramadhin, he hadn't a notion which direction the ball would take after pitching.

West Indies cricket has renewed the first-class game, notably in Test matches, at a time when some rejuvenating injection was urgently wanted. Cricket, in first-class circles, was getting old, satiated with performance and records. All the known or discoverable strokes had been seen; every trick of bowling had been exploited. The West Indies brought back the first raptures, mingling the flush of adventure with the finest and most mature techniques. In captain Sobers alone, the West Indies can boast three brilliant exponents in one single ebullient personality: an accomplished batsman, a seam-bowler with the new ball, and a 'googly' spinner. He is already acclaimed as the greatest all-round cricketer of our own post-Grace period. Personally I would name Wally Hammond for this title: still, Sobers is gifted and versatile enough. But of all the delights West Indies cricket has showered on us, the galvanism of Constantine, the quiet mastery of Headley, the tripartite genius and stroke-play of Worrell, Weekes and Walcott, the enchanted improvisations of Ramadhin and Valentine, none has excited and delighted me, sent me so eagerly on the tip-toe of expectation, as

116

Kanhai, upright or flat on his back. We can only hope that prowess in Test cricket doesn't over-rationalize natural instinct in these West Indies cricketers. For all their acquired technical sophistications let there be some echo of the calypso to the end.

GREEN CAPS AND DEMONS

ACCORDING to the forecasts, or let us say prognostications, of the experts, the Australian cricket team of 1964 is the weakest in bowling of any witnessed within living memory and, at the moment these lines are being read, should be toiling sweatily on the turf of Trent Bridge, innocuous in the face of strong, confident English batsmen.

Somehow I can't believe it. I admit that on the strength of what I have seen of the Australian attack so far, I have discerned nothing in it that can't be found in the attack of any everyday first-class English county side. Indeed, were I an England opening batsman. I'd much prefer to tackle a new ball propelled at me by McKenzie and Hawke or Corling than by Shackleton of Hampshire and Statham of Lancashire. At Lord's the other Saturday, in a sort of Test rehearsal against the MCC, the Australian bowling looked to be so penny-plain in the eyes of an old-time Australian Test cricketer that he couldn't endure it all. He left the ground, rather feverishly babbling the names of Lindwall, Miller, O'Reilly and Grimmett. He could scarcely have got home before the MCC innings collapsed pitifully beyond repair. A few flickers and flexions from Simpson, suggestive of leg-spin, were enough to bring a sort of paralysis over the England batsmen's feet.

In this same rehearsal at Lord's the Australians also suffered an incipient collapse of their first innings. Three wickets fell to the energetic young Middlesex bowler, Price, and fell in two overs. Then Simpson came in to join O'Neill. And here's the point I wish to emphasize—in two or three subsequent overs the Australian innings emerged from crisis as though none had ever threatened. O'Neill didn't change his confident aggressive movements towards the supposedly advancing MCC attack. Simpson defended with time to spare. How often of recent summers have England batsmen coped with imminent trouble with this reliant equanimity?

The present Australian team obviously contains no bowler of genius of the giant stature. It hasn't—at least it hasn't so far—fielded with the traditional Australian swift and sure hostility, part of the actual attack. Nonetheless, it *is* a team of Australians wearing the green cap, so that in the sight of many England players these green caps are soon transformed to eleven terrible warriors in green buckram.

I think it is easier for a mediocre Australian bowler to get an average England batsman out than it is for the mediocre England bowler to account for Simpson, O'Neill, Booth and Co. Too many England batsmen appear ready or predestined to get themselves out. Dexter, the most original and fascinating appearance—I had nearly said apparition—in an England innings since the incomparable Denis Compton, is for ever bringing the hearts of his admirers to their mouths. He is subject to the aberrations of genius. Three times he will sweep his bat across the line of a leg-break—nearly a case of self-extermination lbw. Then he will sweep again, straight into the hands of square-leg. He is the most commanding of batsmen, the most regal, of any since A. C. MacLaren, sometimes disdainful of all bowlers. His trouble is that he seems too ready to abdicate. While he is at the wicket he ennobles the game, gives to it pride of carriage and the thrill of power. Then, apparently, he suffers some kingly mood of boredom. All very well; magnificent, but it isn't the sort of warfare needed to beat the Australians.

Yet on occasions this summer I have seen the Australian attack reduced to hardworking and not very resourceful endeavour by county performers of ours, two or three of whom have actually compiled the highest scores of their fairly anonymous careers against bowling which has exposed grave vulnerabilities of temperament in one or two of England's top batsmen, and, consequently, of technique. So commonplace and amiable has this Australian attack seemed to me that I had actually begun to feel sorry for it, until I remembered an old Johnsonian saying which experience of Australian cricket caused me to amend—'Don't feel compassionate about any Australian team in advance. Knock them down first, and feel sorry for them afterwards.' In 1909, an Australian team came to England, lost to the MCC, to two counties, then to England in the first Test match of the rubber. A London critic, out of kindness of heart, wrote that it would be a mercy for all concerned in this particular Australian tour if it could at once be disbanded and the

118

players sent home without delay. This same ill-starred Australian team won the rubber two-one.

Aubrey Faulkner, the great South African batsman and bowler, told me years ago that the main difference between Australian and England cricketers was this—in a Test match Australians play above normal form, England players below it. There is no technical reason whatever to prevent heavy scoring against McKenzie, Hawke, Corling, Veivers and the rest by Dexter, Cowdrey, Barrington and their colleagues. How much easier, surely, to cope with their more or less precise Bisley marksmanship than with the horrific nuclear assaults last summer of the West Indians, Hall and Griffiths!

Why, then, will many of us at Trent Bridge this weekend hesitate to risk a substantial wager on England's ability to score comfortably and prosperously? The Australians won't win, I fancy, because of any technical advantage. Should England lose, on a good stretch of turf, it will happen for a simple reason—our batsmen will get out quicker than Australia's, will be the readier to act as accessories to their own undoing. The Australian, whether he be cricketer, opera singer, soldier in action or aspirant to Wimbledon glories, usually has a good opinion of his power to cope. Many years ago, in a Test match at Lord's, Fred Root, bowling inswingers for England against Australia, knocked over the leg-stump of Herbert Collins, the Australian captain, in the game's first minutes. C. G. Macartney was the next batsman in, and as he walked through the Long Room on the way to the wicket, he flashed a glance at me, made an ominous gesture with his bat, and said: 'I'll attend to this cove.' He did, peremptorily and with gusto. He would have looked silly, on his return to the pavilion, had he been bowled for a poor score, I made this point to him. 'On a good wicket I always think the odds are in my favour. And I feel sorry for the cove that has to bowl at me.' Boastful? Not at all. Merely a master-technician's faith in his equipment.

Still, we needn't make a cant of Australian self-assurance and self-assertion. Sometimes these characteristics go with the so-called inferiority complex. We have had Australian cricket teams 'on the run' in our time—at least, Jim Laker has. England's technical assets are much more substantial and experienced than any now at the disposal of the Australian captain. We have at hand the large store of county cricketers to draw on. Let me put it this way—how happy Simpson would be if he could go into action at Trent Bridge this weekend with two bowlers at his service as good as Shackleton and Statham, both 'discards' for England. Given the mental concentration of the Australian, the quickness to see a loose ball and to punish it, who wouldn't expect Dexter, Edrich, Barrington, Cowdrey, Boycott, Parks and Sharpe to *annihilate* the bowling of McKenzie, Corling, Hawke, Veivers and the rest. But that 'loose ball', here's the rub! Australian batsmen seldom let it go by stroke-free. England batsmen too frequently wait to look suspiciously at it twice. Moreover, most of them are immobile at the crease, because of static footwork. At Lord's the other day, O'Neill moved yards forward to the off-spin of Allen, who for years has pitched the same near-half-volley length to English batsmen, who have pushed tentatively at it, and unproductively, most days. Poor Allen didn't know where to drop the ball at all as he saw the ominous forward movement of O'Neill's feet, bat rising behind superbly controlled, the wrists steering to an inch.

The England eleven now on view at Nottingham is probably the best available at the moment. Boycott, Edrich, Dexter, Cowdrey, Barrington, Sharpe, Parks—here are names which should certainly give the Australian attack cause to think hard, before the event. But England won't beat Australia if Edrich, Boycott, Barrington and Cowdrey each bat defensively, no matter how long any of them remain at the wicket. Trent Bridge on a sunny day, with the turf well rolled and cut, has always been a foretaste of the batsman's heaven, a 'Lotus land', it has been said, 'where it is always afternoon and 350 for 3'. On such a day at Trent Bridge, George Gunn, wearing a white panama, would walk out to the fastest bowling and have fun and games with it. On such a day, at Trent Bridge, George Gunn, when he was about sixty not out, turned to the slips of the fielding side and said: 'Gentlemen, time's hangin' a bit heavy on my hands just now. Is there any particular stroke you'd like me to perform for you?' Yet George Gunn was picked once only for England in this country.

If the present-day England eleven were all Australians I'd cheerfully back them to win the first Test match of this summer's rubber —in fact, the rubber outright. Things being what they are, I am inclined to hedge, and support England to the extent of five bob each way, win or draw, with a 'saver' on Australia.

THE TEST THAT NEVER WAS

A FEW summers ago, Groucho Marx was taken to Lord's,
during the course of a dull immobile county match. Through
the windows of the Long Room he looked on, while a friend
instructed him about the game's rules and know-how. 'Six balls
bowled from this end, then six from the other.' 'If the batsman hits
the ball where a fieldsman can't stop it, they run.' And so on.
Groucho listened attentively, 'I think I've got it. The field changes
over. They run. Yeah—I think I've got it.' He watched the game in
silence for five minutes, then said, 'Say—when does it begin?'

Groucho's remark returned to my memory many times at Lord's
this week, and when for the first two days of the Second Test no
progress or beginning occurred at all on the rain-soaked field of
play. Even after the action really and visibly had started, hours
passed by and no authentic England and Australian Test match was
to be seen—only a simulacrum of one.

Redpath, opening two Australian innings at Lord's for the first
time in his period of the green and yellow leaf, was able to stay in for
hours, even if during one period of fifty minutes he couldn't score a
run. Edrich, who as technician is nothing compared to Cowdrey,
actually scored a century, 120, his share of England's all-out total of
246, in his first Test match against Australia, a piece of resistance,
sensible, courageous and almost without the ease and relish of fine
art. On the other hand, Cowdrey again played an innings hedged
round by fallibility, uncertain of purpose, and anonymous in performance. Dexter presumed to go in first for England once more.
He 'got away' with it at Nottingham flamboyantly and prosperously,
thanks to a dropped catch giving him a second innings when his
score was next to nothing. One of the few great stroke-players in
cricket today, he lacks the solid defence required of a batsman to
cope with the new ball. This time he was immediately overwhelmed
—and, yet again, an England innings began discouragingly. To
emphasize further the *unintelligence* which marked the most inglorious and inept Test match I can remember, Simpson, one of the
most experienced opening batsmen in Test cricket today, chose to
go in to bat as late as number six in the order.

Again, to show folly heaping itself on folly, at a moment of
incipient crisis in England's first innings, four wickets down for
ninety-two, Simpson licensed himself to wheel up back-of-the-
hand spin (actual and probably possible) for two hours at a stretch,

121

for no wicket or sign of one. Next day, the closing day, Dexter persisted in keeping Coldwell bowling away over after over, for nearly two and a half hours. As Coldwell inevitably tired, Burge scored fifty in seventy minutes, the game's quickest run tempo at any part. When at last Dexter called on his spin bowlers, Titmus and Gifford, the Australian innings suffered promptly from self-doubts. Two wickets, Burge's and Redpath's, fell in quick sequence. When rain put an end to the proceedings, both Simpson and Booth were groping at the spin with a myopia which, surely, would soon have undone each of them.

Throughout the match recurrent examples of lack of class and poor breeding offended the eye of the connoisseur. In Australia's first innings of 176, one or two strokes as stylish and easeful in poise as any witnessed in the match were actually performed by Veivers, an honest Queenslander, the last man in the world to suggest that, as a maker of runs, he has a pedigree.

Neither team deserved to win at Lord's, or anywhere else for that matter. John Edrich's batting, like nearly all the other batting of both sides, would have had little appeal to me if the scoreboard had not been there. I can take no interest in any cricketer if I have to look to the scoreboard for a clue to the meaning of his existence at the wicket, or at the bowling crease. Hammond, Compton, Harvey, Worrell, Sobers—and sometimes O'Neill—can fascinate us scoring or not scoring. I could sit engrossed for hours by the bowling of Lindwall, Douglas Wright, Keith Miller, Bedser, to name a few artists of recent times, though not a wicket might fall their way for hours. The present rubber between England and Australia is certain to provide keen competitive interest, for the simple reason that it is being played by England against Australia. But, unless magical transformation and transfiguration occur soon, individually and collectively, the series seems doomed to bouts of mediocrity, relieved by flashes of quality.

The Test match that never began, never became a Test match, and was never finished! For my own part, the first blank two days of the engagement were the best, the days without cricket, because the playing area was waterlogged. And I am not sure that thousands of other visitors to Lord's on these two cricket-less days didn't share my happy experiences. On Thursday and Friday, ticket-holders were populous in the ground, the scene animated and loquacious. Outside the ground (the gates not opened), a huge queue was equally cheerful and garrulous. There was actually singing under the gloomy sky, despite the latest announcement: 'Wicket to be inspected at 3.45.' It is discomfort of this kind that brings out the British character full strength. Inside and outside of Lord's, in the Long Room, near the Art Gallery, in the gardens and near the Tavern, congestion, noise, discomfort, hilarity and conversation reigned supreme. Perfect strangers talked together. Not since the war have I seen part of the British public as cheerful as this.

On Saturday, after play had at last started. I went into the Long Room. Depression was already returning to the place. 'Terrible cricket,' somebody growled. 'Why can't they use their feet?' moaned somebody else. I now suggest that in every summer at Lord's two matches at least are arranged, under the following conditions and advantages:

Guaranteed No Play.
(Band, and rain, if possible).

SURREY HEROES

BY force of enthusiastic character and a skill of the sort which everybody can understand at sight, W. S. Surridge has inspired an excellent Surrey cricket team to win the county championship of 1952. The honour returns after thirty-eight years to a great cricket-ground. Surrey's conquests in 1914 were clouded at the end by the outbreak of war, and fifteen years had then gone by since the county had ruled supreme as, once in the mid-nineties, they apparently did by divine right. In 1914 Tom Hayward opened every Surrey innings with Hobbs, the greatest batsman of them all, not excelled in mastery of technique and achievement yet. And Hayward, for ever one of a half-dozen greatest professional batsmen, belonged to the champions of 1895, when K. J. Key was captain, and the names of Abel, Lockwood, Lohmann and Richardson were pronounced with breathless admiration by people not staled by 'records'—names that seemed to glow with a lustre not to be diminished by time. There is scarcely a doubt that in three or so decades to come middle-aged folk at the Oval will be glancing back in memory, while some contemporary 'master' compiles a hundred runs in four and a half hours, and saying, 'Ah—where's your Alec Bedser nowadays, and your May and Jim Laker, not to mention Fishlock?'

Surrey's success this year has proved once again that first-class bowling of variety, backed-up by quick opportunist fielding, will win matches that can only be left unfinished by superb batsmanship in an eleven with a mediocre attack. During the heyday of Hobbs, a Surrey innings would move processionally along the warm day, Ducat succeeding unto Sandham, Jardine unto Ducat, Fender arriving at the crease sixth or seventh wicket down with Alan Peach to follow, boundaries and brilliance to the end. But the county championship was not won this way. Collective effort, all-round efficiency, rather than anything so capricious as individual genius, are the signs of progress in our present age. We must consider, too, in all fairness, the possibility that the Surrey side led by Fender was unfortunate enough to play its best in summers in which Lancashire or Yorkshire cricket was at full bloom.

No lover of the game, none with a sense of history, won't be glad that Surrey cricket has, so to say, returned to the throneroom. Kennington Oval knows how to house greatness. The place does not vie with Lord's in aesthetics or deportment, but it has its own essential London character. At the Oval cricket is played in 'Cockayne'. South-east is South-east and North-west is North-west. Even to a Lancashire boy, who had not yet seen any other county field except Old Trafford, the famous chocolate-coloured cap could suggest a kind of dusty reflected glory of achievement; and I shall never forget my awe when I saw Hayward the first time, and how, when batting and between overs, he pushed his cap a little to the back of his head to cool his brow. Hayward for years was regarded as the embodiment of dignified poise and proportion in batsmanship. Some of us, barbarian Lancashire boys brought up on the cross-bat brilliance of J. T. Tyldesley, actually amused ourselves on drowsy afternoons at Old Trafford, when Surrey were playing Lancashire and not getting out quickly enough, by calling out to Hayward, 'Ole Surrey veteran; ole tap-ball!'

Hayward was then in his thirty-fifth year. And a newspaper article of the period discussed him rather in this way: 'Few people realize the value of self-restraint. Experience, a hard task-master, has taught Hayward this lesson. One of the secrets of his success is self-restraint.' Next day, or the day after, Hayward in a bad light at the Oval against Leicestershire scored 125 before lunch. The same season—1906—at Bristol, so the newspapers report, 'Surrey had an hour and three-quarters to bat and, but for a brilliant effort by Hayward, would have fared badly. As it was they lost three wickets for 127, of which the famous batsman made no less than 100.' A week or two later the same newspaper describes an innings of 208 by Hayward, made in three hours fifty-five minutes: 'In an hour after tea he scored 88 out of 146. As a fitting climax to some grand hitting he brought off five great drives in one over off Quaife. In each case Hayward jumped yards to make a half-volley. The first hit put the ball into the ladies' stand, the next cleared that building, the next Devey tried to catch, but his hands were over the wires in front of the pavilion, the fourth went into the ladies' stand, and the last, the biggest of all, cleared the wing of the pavilion.' These allusions and references, it may be well to observe, are not to G. L. Jessop but to Tom Hayward, historically known as a sound responsible and classic 'No. 1' batsman for Surrey and England.

I doubt if, when we come to think of it, any other county cricket-team has anything more to show of renown and glamour than Surrey. Hobbs, the greatest of all batsmen—as we have agreed. He played with and emerged from the classic form of attack: speed and length to the offside. He saw the advent of the 'googly' and 'swinger'. He showed the way to counter them. In his long career he had to cope with all the kinds of bowling which are now known and documented. In Australia, in South Africa (on matting wickets), in all conditions good and evil to batsmen, he was master all the time. He was recently asked, 'What did you think of yourself as a bat, Jack?' 'Well,' came the quiet modest answer, 'I think I was pretty good before the war of 1914.' 'But why, Jack? You scored thousands of runs after 1914.' 'Ah yes,' replied Hobbs, 'but I was obliged to play a lot off the back foot then.' Before 1914 Hobbs was as brilliant as Trumper himself.

Bobby Abel, a little man with a big average; Lohmann I never saw, but all who played with him agree that he was the ideal cricketer; Richardson and Lockwood, who, I am certain, were in conjunction the most wonderful fast attack of all time—the honest cleaving axe and the incalculable flash of lightning! The genius of J. N. Crawford, who one day crashed J. M. Gregory's furious speed into the pavilion at the Oval, on to the awning; D. R. Jardine, strongest of all captains of cricket; 'Razor' Smith, not excelled on a 'sticky' wicket; Hitch, Sandham, the Reads, Brockwell, Strudwick, E. M. Dowson, 'Ernie' Hayes, the terrific N. A. Knox and 'Shrimp' Leveson-Gower—there is no end to the roll, right down to the present moment and to those who work hard behind the scenes and in the nets: Brian Castor and 'Johnny' McMahon. It's a pity the poet Craig isn't at hand to write his noble numbers about them: 'And all the players are Gentlemen, and all the gentlemen are Players. . . .'

GOOD LANCASHIRE MEN WHO JUST MISSED GREATNESS

THE other day a fine cricketer died, and outside his own county few tributes were paid to his character and quality. 'Lol' Cook was one of the honourable company of those players who just missed greatness. Cricket history is still written too much in terms of the kings and dynasties; after all, the geniuses are only the sum-total of the vast anonymous activity that, so to say, tills the field. There is fascination in any study of frustrated talent, of skill and effort which missed the summits.

On his day Cook was one of the finest medium-paced bowlers who ever lived; why did his day not come to him nearly every day? What is the quality which marks the difference between a Cook and a Macaulay; a Cuttell and a J. T. Hearne; a Sandham and a Hayward; a Charles Hallows and a Warren Bardsley?

CUTTELL AND WEBB

Willis Cuttell is practically forgotten now; yet his bowling was amongst the best of its kind during the years 1898–1904; and that was the golden age of cricket. Cuttell could cause the ball to break back, and, better still, he could cause the next ball to break away; his length was accurate, and he knew how to disguise his pace and flight. Year after year he worried the greatest batsmen of the country; he was also a good batsman himself. But he never played for England, never even played for the Players. His trouble was lack of imaginative energy, the indefinable force which enables a man to see an opportunity and grasp it the moment it half-shows itself. It is a sort of faith.

Cuttell usually hoped for the best, but feared the worst; he was in temperament like another superb bowler who played for Lancashire in the same notable period: I mean Sydney Webb. On a sticky wicket Webb could exploit one of the deadliest off-breaks ever seen. But Webb seldom trusted his rare art. He was a Gummidge of cricket, a lorn creature, who obviously felt things more than most people. You could see Webb's very soul wilting whenever a batsman jumped out of the crease and thumped a good ball from him for four. 'Ah yes,' he seemed to say; 'I thought so. I'm not really in form today—didn't think I was when I got up this morning. And if he can hit my best ball, what will he do with my worst? And the pitch is not really "sticky". It's getting better every minute. And the glass is going up. The chances are that there'll be no more rain for months. And, of course, I can't possibly bowl on a hard wicket. Ah me, never mind; I suppose it'll be all the same in a hundred years. I hope so. There he goes again—another four off my off-break.'

D. J. KNIGHT

Some of us will die in the belief that D. J. Knight missed his footing on the upper slopes of greatness, slipped by accident into the void. He was a beautiful batsman, one of the few stylists of the post-war period. He played for England at Trent Bridge against Australia in 1921. In the second innings of England he faced Gregory and McDonald with composure; he flicked delicious strokes here and there by wristwork as lissom as Spooner's. His score reached the thirties; he seemed set for a century of grace and felicity. Then suddenly he was run out through no fault of his own. A hundred runs that day would have given Knight the confidence he needed. (But there's the point!—does anybody but the second-rater need such a gift?)

Knight failed ingloriously in the subsequent Test match at Lord's; the butterfly was smashed on Armstrong's grim wheel. Nonetheless, the batsmanship of D. J. Knight in the seasons of 1919–21 will not pass out of memory; it had a bloom which perhaps was too gentle for the rough-and-tumble of modern Test cricket.

V. F. S. CRAWFORD

One of the greatest batsmen of all time was V. F. S. Crawford— when he found his form. His driving had a glory of movement and power all his own; he was a creative hitter who could make a sad mess even of the attack of Barnes. In 1902, at Old Trafford, Vivian Crawford came out to bat when Barnes had broken the spine of Surrey's strength on a perfect wicket. Abel Hayward, Brockwell— all the famous heroes of the Oval—had been laid low by Barnes. Vivian Crawford attacked the greatest bowler of the day from his first ball; he scored ninety in round about an hour. Four outfields were reduced to immobility. Crawford could bat that way, when-ever he felt in the mood, against all living bowlers, one down, t'other come on. His strokes were classical in poise—upright, free, brave, mighty.

But Crawford was likely enough next innings and the innings after that, and so on for a month, to get out to the feeblest hits conceivable. He lacked concentration; cricket for him was not a devouring passion, as it must be always if a man is to achieve the consistency of genius. (It is a myth that genius is inconsistent; accidents *will* happen even to a Hobbs; but Hobbs is Hobbs always —ceaselessly watchful, ceaselessly intent on his machine, ceaselessly looking for his opportunity.) It was left for Vivian Crawford's brother, 'J. N.' to bring to magnificent flower a rich hereditary growth.

HEAP

If beauty of style and a cunning finger-spin were all that a slow, left-handed bowler needed for a place amongst the great ones, then Heap of Lancashire lost his way remarkably. His pretty action, his rhythmical swing-back of the whole body, his curving, insidious arm were a joy to behold. And his break spat venom; it pitched on the leg stump and whipped across so abruptly that first slip (usually MacLaren) could scarcely contain his anticipatory ecstasies. Heap once ran amuck at Old Trafford against Yorkshire, and took six for 16 and five for 23 in the match. He was a dashing batsman, too, in spirit the brother of Johnny Briggs, with a reckless love of a flick at the off-side ball. But Heap suffered from rheumatism, which ironically afflicted him in wet weather, the weather that suited his bowling like a confederate. He was constantly obliged to drop out of the Lancashire side because of his ailment. Once on a time a spell of warm weather restored him to health; he was again chosen to play for his county at the Oval. Heap determined to demonstrate that he was as fit and young as any of his colleagues. Lancashire lost the toss, and Surrey began to pile up the runs. Heap fielded at mid-off. Suddenly Hayward drove a ball past Heap, and Heap ran after it for all he was worth. 'I'll show 'em!' he said to himself, as he made scalding pursuit. He picked up the ball an inch from the boundary, threw it in to Dean the bowler, and returned to his position at mid-off a little out of breath but triumphant. 'How many did they run, Harry?' he asked proudly. 'Only five!' answered Dean.

Heap was one of Old Trafford's 'characters' at a time when Lancashire cricket was so rich with human nature that I sometimes get it mixed up in memory with pages out of Dickens. I once asked Harry Dean what were his emotions when he was bowling on a perfect wicket against Ranjitsinhji. 'Didn't you feel the hopelessness of the job?' I asked. 'No,' replied Dean; 'no, not exactly, so to speak. I used to say to myself, "Well, it's him against me."'

HUDDLESTON

The best bowler for Lancashire who never quite reached the levels of distinction was Huddleston. On a 'turning' pitch he was unplayable. I remember the season of 1904, when Lancashire were racing for the county championship. In July they arrived at the Oval unbeaten. A defeat in those days, when '100 per cent' meant everything, would have been crucial. At lunch on the third day Surrey were winning easily; they needed some 300 runs for victory, and they were more than 200 for two wickets. I was a schoolboy then, and I dared not open the afternoon papers. I bought one in Albert Square and carried it unopened for half a mile. Then I approached the 'stop press' column from a distance, holding the paper a long way off and gradually drawing it closer to my vision. My heart leapt up when I saw a long column with a succession of 'c MacLarens b Huddlestons'. After lunch Huddleston swept the Surrey batsmen out of his way one after another; Lancashire won easily, and a small boy blessed Huddleston for ever.

From the host of the Might-have-beens a team could be named good enough for the best English eleven of the moment. Here, it is: F. L. Fane, D. J. Knight, Seymour of Kent, P. R. Johnson, A. J. Turner, V. F. S. Crawford, E. M. Dowson, Cuttell, Heap, Wilson (the Worcestershire fast bowler), and the immortal Gaukrodger (because of his name). As C. H. Spurgeon once said: 'If you can't be a lighthouse you can be a nightlight.'

CONVERSATION WITH RHODES, 1950

IN their old age the mild wide blue eyes of Wilfred Rhodes have lost the keenness that missed nothing on a thousand fields of play; they have become dim, after much peering down the wicket in search of lbw's. Though he visits Test matches still he sees only a 'shadowy coast', but he is not blind, as Philip Mead is; yet Mead also attends an occasional Hampshire match. Not long ago, after some young man had played an innings for his county, and as soon as he got out, Mead requested that he should be brought before him. Mead then asked for the young man's bat, and he held it for a while, running the fingers of his right hand over the blade. 'You're not "middling" 'em yet,' was his only comment. Cricket by Braille.

Rhodes can distinguish white flannels from green grass and find his way about happily enough. He came into the pavilion at Trent Bridge on that awful Thursday morning in June 1948 when England collapsed against Australia. At the moment I met him Toshack and W. Johnston were bowling.

'Ah can't see properly now, yo' know,' he said, 'but they keep on tellin' me that there's two left-handers on, both bowlin' over t' wicket.' I assured him that it was indeed the truth.

'So they keep tellin' me,' said Wilfred, 'but Ah can't see for meself properly, but they keep *on* tellin' me that there's two left-handed bowlers "on", both bowlin' over t' wicket, but Ah can't see properly, but they keep on tellin' me. . . .'

To those of my readers who cannot get the humour of these remarks without a technical clue, I can only say that for me to provide it would spoil the richness of one of the most amusing and most lovably characteristic remarks I have heard in a lifetime spent in cricket pavilions. Now that Rhodes cannot see much of what is going on he compensates himself by talk—he, once the taciturn Wilfred, cannot be stopped in his flow of chatter, and what is more, nobody would wish to stop him, for history comes from his mouth in rivers. He stopped me at Trent Bridge behind the pavilion while Worrell in front of it was playing a dazzling innings against England in 1950; he button-holed me, and much as I longed to look upon Worrell, I was held as by the eye of the Ancient Mariner; and contemporary greatness happening round the corner was dissolved for me and fused into the immortal past, with Rhodes speaking of it to me in the flesh.

Half a century ago, almost, I had seen him when I was a schoolboy of ten, seen him at Old Trafford standing at the wicket's other end while poor Fred Tate was bowled and England lost a rubber by three runs. Many times had I watched him, with George Hirst, in action against my county of Lancashire; and I had hated the sight of both of them, and had feared them.

And here he was, and here was I, behind the Trent Bridge pavilion in July 1950, the roars of the crowd in the air around us; and Wilfred's talk turned the clock back, yet at the same time somehow merged departed glory with all that was alive and happening here and now, on a lovely summer morning.

I deliberately 'drew' him. 'What was "Ranji" like?'

'Aye, "Ranji",' said Wilfred, 'aye, he were a good bat. But Ah used to like bowlin' at him. . . .' (Imagine the high throaty voice of Rhodes, the staccato dialect.) '. . . Aye, Ah, liked bowlin' at "Ranji". That leg-glance of his. Ah could get 'im out, y'know. Ah used to send him a top-spinner and he'd miss it . . . But he were a good bat; aye, he were a good bat.'

'And Victor Trumper?'

'Aye, Victor Trumper. Aye. He were a good bat were Victor. Ah liked bowlin' at him, though. He was always givin' you a chance. But aye; he were a good bat.'

'And Maclaren?'

'Aye, Mr Maclaren; aye, he were a good bat. But that Harrow drive of his; yo' know if he'd waited a bit he could have hit ball squarer and safer. Aye, Mr Maclaren, he were a good bat.'

He lavished on no man higher praise than that he was a 'good bat'; none of your extravagances of 'great' or 'marvellous'. 'Aye,' he nattered on, 'M. A. Noble. But Ah never liked bowlin' at him. He never let you see his wicket all day . . . but he were a good bat. Aye, M. A. Noble.'

'Aye, Johnny Tyldesley, now he were a good bat—on a "sticky" wicket best I ever bowled agenst. But Ah could get him out, yo' know; he used to drive my spinnin' half-volley and get caught off-side. Aye—sometimes a spinnin' half-volley's best ball of any on "sticky" pitch, if batter's quick and a bit rash on his feet, like Johnny. But he were a good bat.'

His eyes twinkled; if they couldn't see clearly across the street today, they could see far back and for ever. His cheeks were as fresh-coloured as in his youth when he rose quickly to fame as a slow left-arm bowler worthy to put on the mantle of Peel.

He first played for England at Nottingham in 1899, against Australia: this was 'W.G.'s' last match for England and C. B. Fry's and Johnny Tyldesley's first. In 1902 Rhodes was in at the death, as a batsman, in two of the most excruciating Test match 'finishes' on record; at Manchester when England lost the rubber by three runs, and in the subsequent match at the Oval when England won by one wicket, thanks to an incredible innings of 104 by Jessop, cut and driven in one hour and a quarter to the accompaniment of falling slates from the roofs in the Kennington Road and environs.

'Aye,' said Wilfred, his eyes seeing his visions still more clearly, 'Ah remember—it were a Saturday afternoon at Old Trafford—we used to finish third day then on Saturdays—sometimes Wednesdays —and Dick Lilley were in wi' me, only Fred Tate to come, and we had to get about twelve to win; and Hughie Trumble bowls me a half-volley. Ah can see it now—he bowled from far end—Ah think they call it Stretford end—and as soon as Ah sees ball comin' Ah says to miself, "Ah can 'it this," and so Ah let go. And Ah drives it clear over yon rails. . . .' Then he paused and another glow of revelation came to his eyes. 'Aye, and what's more,' he added, staccato as a woodpecker, 'what's more, it only counted four for a hit over rails into crowd in those days. Yo' had to hit out of ground for a six. So reightly speakin' we only lost match by one run, and Ah should have been not out 6 instead of 4.'

'Aye,' he meditated, 'it were a good match. When Dick Lilley and me were in, there were eight on us out and only Fred Tate left. And when we only wanted eight, Dick Lilley hits Trumble, deep square-leg, as good a hit as ever you see, and Clem Hill ran length of a cricket pitch and caught it. Aye, it were a good match. England only wanted 124 to win, and we were 36 for none at lunch. But pitch was doin' a lot and Hughie Trumble bowled off-spinners. He were a good bowler were Hughie. . . .'

On this afternoon of 26th July 1902—at which I was present, a small agonized boy—Maclaren was caught, the first of England's wickets to fall, in the deep field by Duff, off Trumble. Sullen clouds were looming up the sky, and Maclaren feared rain would steal victory from England, and all our chances in the rubber. So he risked it and drove hard, high, majestically, fatally. When he came back to the amateurs' dressing-room he flung his bat on a locker and said to old William Howard, the dressing-room attendant, 'William —I've lost the match and the—rubber.' But F. S. Jackson died in the belief that it was a mistake on his part that threw the match away. In the first innings he had made 128; in his second innings Saunders sent him a full-toss. Jackson vowed to his life's end that he could safely have pushed it to the on or off or anywhere, for a two; but the goal was so near, so alluring, that he hit too hard and made a present of a catch to Sydney Gregory at cover. In this same intolerable innings Jackson, Abel, Braund, K. S. Ranjitsinhji, Lilley and Lockwood, all perished, after Maclaren's downfall, for less than 90. 'Ranji' was lbw Trumble for 2. He was dropped from the England XI forthwith and never played in a Test match again.

Less than three weeks after this Test match at Old Trafford, Rhodes not out 4 ('should 'a counted 6') in at the death—he went in last for England at Kennington Oval, where Trumble, Saunders, Noble and Armstrong awaited him, with seven other Australians. George Hirst waited for him too; fifteen runs were needed for a victory to wash down the dish of irony thrust under our noses at Manchester. It is generally understood that Hirst greeted Rhodes with these words: 'Wilfred, we'll get them in singles.' It is not more fanciful to say that he added to his instruction: 'Aye, and if tha gets out, Wilfred, Ah'll warm thee.' The runs were obtained, in singles.

But Hugh Trumble, one of the finest men I have known, one of nature's gentlest, swore to me when he was a septuagenarian in Melbourne, that Hirst was 'dead' leg before wicket to him when England's score was 259 for nine. If the decision had been answered in Trumble's favour two consecutive Test matches between England and Australia would have been won and lost by three runs.

Last man in for England, sharing the honours in the most stupendous of all victories by England against Australia; then, a few months more than ten years afterwards, Rhodes went in for England at Melbourne with Jack Hobbs, and played his part in the most prosperous partnership of all for a first-wicket in a Test match— 'c. Carter, b. Minett, 179'. 'Aye,' he told me, 'Ah remember. Just before we won toss Ah split me fav'rite bat at nets and George Gunn asked me to borrow his, but Ah said, "It's too heavy for me, George" —two pound ten it were. George always played with a two-pound-tenner—but he said, "That's what you want, Wilfred, on these fast wickets—it's on "sticky" wickets you want light bat so's it'll coom up quickly.'

'Well,' continued Rhodes, eyes again lost to the dark present in the full glowing sight of the past, 'Ah borrowed George's bat and, d'yo' know, when Ah starts playin' forward, just defensive, ball goes for four, ay, just defensive push and it goes for four, aye, it goes for four, just a defensive push. . . .' His countenance became suffused with joy—nearly half a century after the event. Something for nothing. Yorkshire. 'Aye,' he went on, 'there was no need to lift George's bat oop; ball went like a gun off middle of wood, defensive pushes, aye, and they went for fours. . . .'

The Hobbs–Rhodes achievement happened in 1912, eight years after Rhodes, on the same ground, had taken fifteen wickets for 124. He had given up bowling in 1912; during the Test matches of this, his great season as Hobbs' colleague at the outset of an England innings, he bowled only eighteen overs for 57 runs and no wickets. After the war of 1914–1918, Yorkshire direly wanted slow bowling, so Rhodes picked up a discarded art exactly where, decades since, he laid it down; and, recalled to the England XI in a lean period, he bowled against Australia yet again and was not the least important factor in a victory which brought the 'Ashes' to us after we had spent fourteen years in the wilderness. He foxed out for 79, Woodfull, A. J. Richardson (twice), Bardsley, Ponsford and Collins. When, to 'draw' him, I suggested he wasn't spinning them at that time of his life, he laughed his bland soundless laugh and replied: 'If batter thinks Ah'm spinnin' 'em, well, Ah'm spinnin' 'em.' At the end of

his career it was his modest boast that 'Ah were never hooked an'
Ah were never cut.' It was his sly humour that prompted him to his
famous remark about Verity. He travelled from Harrow, where he
was coaching, to 'look at' his successor at Lord's. After a close
inspection, from near the Green Bank, he said: 'Aye, he'll do; he's a
good bowler. Aye. He can bounce 'em.' Then, following a pause:
'Aye, an' he can bowl a ball as I never *could* have.' We all sat up in
astonished curiosity. A tribute from the Master! 'What is it,
Wilfred?' 'Why, the ball they can tickle down leg-side for a single.'
But there was none prouder than Rhodes at Verity's prowess,
though Verity was not really in the Peel–Rhodes tradition; he was
too quick through the air and not seductively curved enough in
flight for that. 'Best ball a slow left-hander can bowl,' he often told
me, 'is spinnin' half-volley—on a "sticky" pitch.' His second
thoughts or reservations are delicious. Of Bradman he said: 'Best bat
I've ever seen, aye, best bat I've ever seen—off ba-ack foot.' Of
square-cuts, when I deplored to him that nowadays we seldom see
cutting the like of J. T. Tyldesley's: 'Aye, a good bat, Johnny. But
cut never were a business stroke.' He played 'hard'. It is alleged that
one day he walked down the wicket while batting to admonish a
newcomer to the team, a greenhorn who began his innings by hitting
two fours, one a cover-drive, in the first over bowled to him. 'Hey,'
is the remark attributed to Wilfred on this occasion, 'hey, young
feller, what y' doin'—we doan't play cricket in Yorkshire for foon.'
But he took his portion of fun all the same. It lent salt to the joke
that he was a man of some caution. When the M.C.C. elected as
life-members a number of distinguished old professional players
(regrettably omitting one of the most venerable and, in his day,
celebrated—W. G. Quaife), the Yorkshire newspapers next morning
rang up those cricketers of the county included among the chosen
few. Each said the right and expected thing. 'I'm proud not only for
myself but for Pudsey and Yorkshire.' 'It's a great pleasure in my
old age and I hope I deserves it.' But Wilfred, when asked for *his*
opinion on the honour received, said: 'Well—Ah don't rightly
know what it means yet—but Ah'm very pleased all same.'

In an attempt some years ago to write a sketch of Rhodes I called
him 'legendary', but that was in my green and salad and rather
yellow days. He is and will remain a Yorkshireman of any period,
typical and indigenous. His spirit lives on, his technique persists.
'The third line of defence for any batsman of sense, lad; bat, left pad
close to it, then—quick wi' thi'—right pad over, too—never mind
what fancy writin' fellows say about "two-eyed stance" and swash-

buckle through covers. We doan't play cricket for foon in York-shire.' ('Hear, hear,' from Emmott Robinson.)

The career of Rhodes spanned two epochs different in concep-tion of the game or the way the minds of players approach it. He began under the amateur influence, when cricket was regarded as one form of outdoor sport amongst others in which an opponent's challenge should be accepted and answered in reason; when indeed cricket was actually played for fun. He lived to see a change of heart; he himself became one of the first and most influential of the realists who reacted against the romantics, one of the hard dour school. 'Mak' 'em fetch 'em,' was his first principle or attitude. 'Give nothing away.' The defensive field on batsmen's wickets; the length that made a long-armed drive difficult even to attempt. Yet if we look up scores in *Wisden* of the great period in Yorkshire cricket dominated by Lord Hawke in the early nineteen hundreds, we will find, match after match, a recurring phrase, 'c. Denton, b. Rhodes', as familiar during a season of fine weather as the other recurrent phrase of the same illustrious period in wet seasons, 'c. Tunnicliffe, b. Rhodes'. Denton usually fielded at deep long-off where I have, with my own eyes, seen him hold not a few catches from big drives off Rhodes; somebody swallowed the bait and we thought nonethe-less of him for it.

David Denton was one of the best outfields in the land; and as a batsman he himself rendered the lives of all outfielders busy and apprehensive. The Lancashire and Yorkshire match, once on a time, was one of the most brilliant and chivalrous that was played, as indeed it could scarcely help being, with Lord Hawke and Maclaren or Hornby captains, the other combatants including such as F. S. Jackson, Spooner, Frank Mitchell, T. L. Taylor; for the profes-sionals were encouraged, not to say commanded, to trust to their strokes, with the exception of the one or two batsmen whose job it was to hold one end of the wicket steadily. Every team possessed one stout 'stonewaller'; Albert Ward went in first with Maclaren for Lancashire in the years of which I am now writing; Tunnicliffe went in first for Yorkshire with J. T. Brown. (But Ward and Tunnicliffe were usually making the recognizable motions of batsmanship, observing the rhythm of it even while they left the boundaries to the activity of others.) It was in a Lancashire and Yorkshire match that George Ulyett tried to drive Johnny Briggs over the boundary for the winning hit, with only one wicket to fall. Ward caught him on the rails and Yorkshire lost by five runs.

About a quarter of a century afterwards two runs were needed for a victory in a Lancashire and Yorkshire match, one wicket to fall, in the last over of the day. Parkin the bowler pitched rather wide to the off, so Rhodes, the batsman, cannily 'let them alone' and the match was drawn.

I am pointing no moral story; I merely emphasize again a difference in tactics and mental approach. Both schools of thought have produced cricketers equally great, Rhodes adorned each school. And if the Lancashire and Yorkshire match of Lord Hawke's day was brilliant, the Lancashire and Yorkshire match of the Rhodes–Robinson governance was not less great; for humour and North-Country shrewdness took the place of the cosmopolitan gesture and accent of the amateur presence. During the 1920's, matches at Old Trafford between Lancashire and Yorkshire were seldom finished. On flawless wickets the watchword was: 'No fours before lunch on principle, and gradely few afterwards.' Visitors from the South of England, not knowing the clue, complained wearily: 'What sort of a cricket match is this? Look at the score. Fifty in two hours.' But if they had known the secret they would have understood that in a Lancashire and Yorkshire match of those years the score-board meant little or nothing, that the players had other things to do besides worrying about runs. There were all sorts of private and personal grievances to attend to. To enjoy the 'foon' you needed to know your Makepeace, your Macaulay, your Emmott Robinson, your Kilner, your Waddington, your Wilfred Rhodes.

No cricketer has more than Rhodes shaped a county's policy, instructed the technical expression of it, linked past skill with present, informed everything with a native wit and wisdom which expressed the man himself and the soil and air which bred him and still breeds all the sons of Yorkshire. If he says he can't see much nowadays, what of it? He always 'smelled-out' as much as he saw. That was the 'foon' of it.

SOME THOUGHTS

ENGLAND *v* AUSTRALIA

1956

INFLUENCE OF AGE AND INJURIES

THE absence of Tyson from the England team at Nottingham
will spoil the drama of the occasion. With their minds still
vivid with impressions made on them in Australia by Tyson's
pace, the Australian batsmen must surely have been rendered taut
of nerve and determined not to retreat an inch this time, at least not
perceptibly, from his line of fire. But the absence of Archer would
be as damaging to Australia's attack as Tyson's is to England's. I am
not certain that Archer, fit and in form, would not sustain a searching quick attack longer than is nowadays within Lindwall's power.

Lindwall, in fact, and Miller too, are likely to be deployed in short
thrusts with the new ball. Archer, a younger man, can bowl at a
sharp penetrating speed over a long period; and he is not entirely
dependent on the new ball's seam. Lindwall, of course, has resources
of experience and can bring into play other factors than pace. For
half an hour or so at the beginning of an England innings we can be
fairly sure that Lindwall and Miller will launch an attack of red-
hot, red-balled violence. After the burden of increasing years has
made itself felt on either of them, the Australian reserves of bowling
on a good wicket should soon be exhausted by batsmen fit to play for
England. Ian Johnson seems unable to spin the ball with the snap
that compels a hurried stroke, and so far Benaud has not convinced
us that he is a more dangerous leg-break bowler than he was in 1953.
Davidson is a tolerably good left-handed bowler if he is allowed to
obey nature and aim at pace and good length. But unless there is a
metamorphosis at Trent Bridge, sudden and magical, the Australian
attack promises, for the most part, after the new ball has waned, to
have an amiability which might have bored Hobbs or Sutcliffe or
Washbrook or Compton, and amused Eddie Paynter.

We must bear in mind, I suppose, that Australian cricketers often
grow in stature in a challenging scene; at least, tradition tells us they

do. But there was no noticeable structural elongation amongst any of them when challenged not long ago by Tyson and Statham. And nobody yet has found evidence that the batsmen in Johnson's command are firmer and straighter in defence against a fast ball, or more mobile of feet coping with spin, than the major Australian batsmen were who, in two consecutive rubbers, faltered repeatedly and lamentably not only against Tyson and Statham but in turn against Bedser, Wardle, Lock and Laker—against, in short, all sorts of bowling, fast or slow. If England are unable to win this summer's rubber, the reason will be, I fancy, not that Australia are the better team but that England are worse—if my meaning is clear.

In 1909 an Australian team came to England and lost two matches, one to Surrey and one to the M.C.C., out of their first five engagements. A critic of eminence, who was also a good cricketer, expressed the view that it might be to the advantage of Australian prestige in cricket if the team could somehow cancel the tour and return home. But this 1909 Australian team won the rubber, winning two of the three Test matches that were played out, and having the best of the drawn ones. The joke is that the Australians also lost the first Test match. The moral for us is not far to seek; though, lest it depress weak hearts unduly, the fact should be mentioned that the Australian eleven of 1909 included Victor Trumper, C. G. Macartney, Warren Bardsley, W. W. Armstrong, M. A. Noble, Albert Cotter, Vernon Ransford, and S. E. Gregory.

It seems hard nowadays for a cricket selection committee to pick a representative team, but it is harder still to get it to the ground physically safe and sound, and strong enough of limb and muscle to support the heat and burden of a Test match. If, as appears likely, Test match cricketers are bound to suffer strain and contusion as the sparks fly upward, wisdom would recall Denis Compton at once. Some players thrive on injuries; Trevor Bailey practically insists on them. Once, long ago, J. T. Tyldesley was struck on the head at Old Trafford by Kortright, perhaps the most dangerously fast of all bowlers. Tyldesley was helped from the field, but returned to the wicket later in the day, and proceeded to treat Kortright's bowling with a savage brutality. Kortright himself put it all down to bad temper on Tyldesley's part.

Why cricketers have become susceptible as never before to physical strain is hard to say. Never before have they been so carefully looked after, body, soul, and pocket, as now; never before so much massaged and taken up and down the country for their engagements in comfort and at times convenient to them, even if stumps have to be drawn at half-past four on a sunny afternoon. No fast bowler these days bowls a thousand overs a year. Trueman, last summer, bowled nearly a thousand overs, but mainly our Stathams, Tysons, Lindwalls, Millers, seldom in a season bowl more than half the overs sent down most years by Tom Richardson, E. A. Macdonald, A. Gover, Nichols of Essex, W. E. Bowes. In 1926, Macdonald bowled 1,249 overs and took 205 wickets. Tom Richardson, with an action more strenuous than Macdonald's lovely one, bowled 1,690 overs in 1895, taking 290 wickets.

It is not necessarily bad luck that brings to a cricketer a slipped disc or a 'pulled' sinew. Part of a cricketer's equipment and qualifications to do his job at all is physical fitness and endurance. If a fast bowler's action, his run or his swingover, are ungainly and not easy of rhythm and in accordance with laws of muscular adjustment and movement, he is sooner or later likely to strain something; the cause is bad style or bad technique, not 'bad luck'. Sir Pelham Warner, when he was captain of Middlesex, was one morning before a match approached by one of his fast bowlers, who showed him a finger bruised in the nets, saying 'Don't think I'll be able to play today, sir.' And 'Plum', having looked at a faint discolouration on the finger, said 'Do you mean to tell me, Tompkins, that because of a little bruise you think you can't play? Why, a cricketer should be prepared to bleed for Middlesex.'

MILLER AND HARVEY THE EXCEPTIONS AT TRENT BRIDGE IN A MEDIOCRE ELEVEN

Australia will surely go into the Test match next week at Lord's a resurrected team. The stand by Burke and Burge brought about a reprieve and nothing less. At no time during the match at Trent Bridge was the wicket really vicious; but on Monday afternoon, and for a brief period after lunch on Tuesday, it enabled Lock and Laker to suggest to the Australians that they were spinning the ball, or about to spin it spitefully any minute; and most Australian batsmen of present-day schooling are apt to imagine that a cricket ball spins almost by its own volition as soon as the barometer falls. In days before wickets were covered in first-class matches in Australia players such as Trumper, Duff, Bardsley, Macartney, and Collins were masters at coping with spin on English turf.

When Miller was out on Tuesday afternoon, the Australian cause seemed to be in grave danger. More than two hours was left for play, and England needed to take six wickets, none of them likely to be defended, as we all imagined, by batsmen resourceful of technique against a triumphant Lock and taken on a damp if improving pitch.

The match was saved by two young Australians, one of whom had yet to show that he knew the first thing about defensive batsmanship on a turf affected, even slightly, by rain. Moreover, these young men surely must have seen in the overthrow of Harvey and Miller signs that the odds against them were gathering in force. By splendid resolution, they held on, over after over and at last England were frustrated. It was good to see Australia rescued by youth, just as it had been splendid to see England led far on the way to victory by youth.

Nonetheless, though the result was fair enough, considering the ill-luck that befell Australia, England had cause for acute disappointment. Circumstances had put Australia in a slough of moral or psychological bankruptcy. They were allowed to emerge from it by bowlers of experience who were very much 'on top'. It is assumed nowadays that a bowler must have help from the pitch to get him wickets. The recovery by Burke and Burge was made in the best Australian traditions—traditions very much in need of some new polish.

The batting of Richardson in his first Test match against Australia was truly heartening. His first innings had a veteran coolness and sagacity. His second innings, to begin with, was not certain of touch, but at the cue for attack he was quick of movement and strong if not always accurate of aim. Already he has been hailed as the successor of Hutton as an opening batsman for England: but he still has much to learn, and much to go through, before he is the successor of Washbrook, let alone Hutton. But his promise is immense and he is bound to develop, for he is sensible and quick to learn.

Such is cricket, that his first appearance in the England eleven against Australia might easily have been his last—at least for a long time to come. Accurate fielding would have run him out for next to nothing in his first innings: and in his second, he was missed at leg-slip before he had scored. He and Cowdrey held England's first wicket strongly and quite serenely on Thursday; and at the right moment they attacked gallantly and well.

I did not like to see Cowdrey depending wholly on his pads against balls that were by no means pitched out of the danger zone. Nonetheless, he often performed the strokes which in power and style are proper to a Test match.

P. B. H. May also batted as an England cricketer and an England captain should—with ease and calm and handsome poise. Also he seemed well in control over his men in the field, and obviously every one of them was a willing collaborator. We were all the time watching a team, not an assembling of separate parts. Some of the English fieldsmen may have at times looked slow at bending, but they were in touch with one another. The Australians, on the other hand, fielded more or less as detached individuals; and frankly not always with the historical Australian certainty and confidence.

It was an unkindness to Australia that they were caught in the first game of the rubber in moist conditions not to their liking—and caught after a month of poor or variable form against the counties. There is no doubt talent enough in the team to support Harvey and Miller, the only two great players confidently at Johnson's service. All cricketers should hope that Lindwall may yet again be seen gloriously in action: the chances at the moment are that he won't.

Archer, Benaud, and Davidson are natural cricketers, Davidson perhaps the nearest to qualify of the three. His accident at Nottingham was a cruel blow. Benaud is inexplicable: he has extraordinary gifts as a forcing batsman, and as a leg-spin bowler. His fielding is electrical. He bowled admirably at Trent Bridge in circumstances entirely against any confident exploitation of leg-spin. He has done things with bat and ball which nobody merely talented is able to do. Yet in the highest class he persistently commits gross and elementary errors. I believe that under an M. A. Noble, an Armstrong, or a Bradman, Benaud would soon discipline and organize the skill and instincts given to him in his cradle.

Harvey's innings of 64 was unmistakably that of a great player. He used unaccustomed restraint: he watched the ball, saw it quickly, kept to the line of it. The familiar Harvey chanciness, intermittent but fatal, was checked by judgment and self-denial for four hours. But whether scoring or defending, he was a lovely sight, swift of foot, no energy wasted, and all his movements graceful, his power so concealed that his severest stroke could not offend a bowler's dignity. This innings might have been played with Victor Trumper at the other end of the wicket and would have kept inside the picture's frame.

Harvey was challenged by Lock at Lock's most vehement and

141

fiercely accurate. Lock deservedly got him in the end. Lock's bowling was as menacingly beastly to see as to bat against; and that is saying much. On his day and on his wicket, he is the most eruptively destructive left-arm bowler known in living memory. And a hostile opportunist fieldsman as well!

Much cricket in this game was below Test match standard. On the second afternoon, following May's dismissal, England's batting on an easing wicket lacked strokes and purpose. Time was now Australia's ally. They were psychologically in the depths. Caught on the kind of moist turf they distrust, two of their finest players had been put out of action by misfortune. Yet at this moment, when England should have pressed home advantage triumphantly and in quick time, a mere 37 runs were added in 85 minutes, for the loss of five wickets. At ten minutes to three England's score was 180 for three: when May declared the innings closed, at a quarter past four, it was 217 for eight.

There was no need on Saturday for Bailey's passive resistance. He was chiefly responsible for wasted previous moments. Bailey is a grand saver of England from defeat in Test matches: but this year this occupation seems gone. I doubt if England will need Bailey's passionate obstinacy, his self-inflicted martyrdom, against the present Australian team, not very strong to begin with, and now weakened by physical infirmity.

Is it generally understood that five or six of this year's Australians would have little chance of finding places in the England eleven? Would we exchange Cowdrey or Richardson for McDonald or Burke: Graveney for Burge? Ian Johnson as an off-spinner would not replace Laker; and with all Bailey's stern, tight-lipped inactivity, I fancy he is a better all-round cricketer in a Test match than the perpetually potential and frustrated Benaud. Lindwall today is not, over a longish stretch of bowling, more dangerous than Tyson or Statham, assuming athletic soundness of wind and limb in all three.

There are only two Australians in Johnson's command who, without argument, would go into the England eleven with no protest even from the displaced men. There are, in fact, in this Australian contingent, several cricketers who might find themselves worked very hard during an English summer to hold their places in any of our stronger counties: would either Burge, or McDonald, or MacKay, or Wilson, or Ian Johnson strengthen Surrey or Yorkshire just now?

On Monday, the absence of purpose in Australian methods, at the wicket and in the field, was remarkable and deplorable. While Harvey batted beautifully and masterfully on a pitch now slow and fairly trustworthy, Benaud, having hit a superb six in the last over before lunch, was clean bowled shortly after the interval, out to a hideous, fast-footed, cross-bat heave of the bat into thin air. Obviously Australia's game hereabouts was to prolong the innings, absorbing time, especially as Harvey was protecting one end of the wicket with increasing ease and felicity of style. Ian Johnson defended stoutly for a while: but after Harvey's sudden, unexpected downfall—he missed a quick ball from Lock which kept low—Ian Johnson threw his wicket away, caught in the deep at long-on, cleverly caught, by Bailey. Lindwall was a victim to the same unreason: and I should have thought that in his unsound muscular condition, a passive, straight bat would have better served his side and his own physical wellbeing.

When England batted again, there was a continuance of Australia's aimlessness. I could not gather from evidence visible to the naked eye whether Johnson was intent on saving or losing the match. There was at times no hurry in the field, and while only one slip was placed to a fast bowler, and he in no useful or truly definable place, with two third men; and while many balls were pitched defensively wide, Benaud was given leave to send along eighteen overs of legspin on a wicket on which no leg-spinner would wish to expose the inevitable defects of his qualities. Archer, able always to keep runs down, bowled only three overs (maybe Johnson still had doubts of his fitness); Johnson, who should at least possess run-saving ability as a bowler, sent down twelve overs.

Miller bowled as though in another dimension, or in another match—as though weary of the present engagement, so fallen away in greatness of atmosphere. He improvised ball by ball, tossing back his mane, fast balls, slow off-spinners, near-wides, a 'bumper' as a final commentary, all done as if he were making experiments in a net vacant of a batsman. He plays with his animal spirits in charge, impulsive and spontaneous. If his mind and knowledge of the game occasionally step in, it would seem as though to comment satirically on the contemporary state and situation of Australian cricket. He is an artist, and an individual, and he remains with us as a reminder of the greatness of the Australian XI of 1948. On Monday, surrounded mainly by mediocrity amongst his colleagues, he put me in mind of some forest-tangled lion, rendered captive and caged, in a zoo of animals and pets very much domestic. From this indictment Harvey is, of course, always excepted.

And if the indictment appears hard and forthright, it is based on observations which later were confirmed by at least one England cricketer of only yesteryear. It is necessary to insist on the highest standards, especially on Australian standards for so much comment and criticism nowadays comes over the air and in print from old players turned writers and broadcasters who, in the kindness and fullness of their hearts and pockets, cannot bring themselves to utter hard words about their friends and fraternity, still actively in the game.

ENGLAND'S OPPORTUNITY FOR REVENGE AT LORD'S

Since the beginning of the present century Australia have won four Test matches at Lord's and England one only. Verity vanquished Woodfull, Bradman, and the rest there in 1934, and Australia's victories were achieved in 1909, 1921, 1930, and 1948. This year England should take the chance of a lifetime to wreak revenge—on the most renowned and imposing of cricket fields.

And England should see to it that there is no doubt or half-measures about the victory; for in fairly recent times Australia have administered some severe thrashings and punishments to our cricketers in this country. They won by 562 runs at the Oval in 1934, by 409 runs at Lord's in 1948, and by an innings and 149 runs in the same at the Oval. In 1938, also at the Oval, England rubbed Australia in the dust to the tune of an innings and 579 runs, but on that occasion casualties deprived Australia at the pinch of an innings by Bradman and an innings by Fingleton.

On current form, only by some aberation of purpose or sudden paralysis of skill should England find themselves at all hard pressed this time at Lord's by the unfortunate and not exactly felicitous Australian team led by Ian Johnson. For one thing, the match is not likely to be played on the kind of fast wicket which Australian batsmen and bowlers seem nowadays to depend upon for a confident exploitation of their powers. Also, wretched luck has taken away much of their attacking resources by injuries to Davidson and Lindwall. But, as he contemplates Australia's unhappy experiences since the season's opening, the hardened English sportsman may pause in his optimistic prognostications, remembering that when fortune changes at cricket there is often a drastic, not to say dramatic, swing-round.

The form of the Australians has been too bad wholly to be true; for if Johnson cannot boast an eleven palpably of Test match pedigree, he can put faith in one or two players of ominous potentiality. A great cricketer, once he has known greatness, if only momentarily, can again be visited by greatness as long as he remains capable of reasonably healthy physical motions and responses. No team can be taken for granted as beaten before the match begins if it contains Harvey, Miller, Archer, Burke, and Benaud. A slight raising of the eyebrow may well be caused by the mention of Benaud's name in this context; for this young cricketer's performances in Test matches against England have not been, in Mr Attlee's term, outstanding. He has batted fifteen times and only once has he scored as many as 34 in an innings; and only once has he taken as many as four wickets in an innings, for which he had to allow 120 runs. I doubt if any English player would be trusted by our selection committee so far and for so long, with no more practical or visible contribution to the cause than Benaud's. Yet he is plainly gifted.

When he first came to England in 1953, Benaud in the third match of the tour against Yorkshire at Bradford scored 97 in two hours, then took seven wickets for 46. Now it is not possible for mediocrity even to rise to the level of this kind of mastery. And what a man has done once he can do again. On several occasions, outside England and Australia Test matches, Benaud has seemed a vessel of plenary inspiration, and, with the bat especially has played with the imprint of rare skill and individuality. I saw him at the nets at Lord's on Tuesday, defending seriously, scrupulously behind the ball; and his strokes, when he liberated them, were clean, true, strong. His reactions were swift and natural. Benaud is certainly a born cricketer and I think born to levels not scaled by ordinary talent.

What does he lack? Why does he get out to reckless, injudicious, cross-bat heaves at the pitch of the ball, feet rooted to the earth, as at Trent Bridge last week? I am a confirmed believer in natural instincts and propensities in cricket and in all other activities. Benaud is 25 and looks every inch a cricketer. It will be no matter for wonder if at any moment he confounds those of his critics who have more or less 'written him off'.

At the moment of writing the wicket at Lord's seems unlikely to have the hard surface and speed which are amenable to the

Australian bowlers. They will probably consist of Miller, Archer, Johnson, Crawford, and Burke, with reserves improvised from Mackay or Wilson. I hope we shall not see Miller again reduced to the undignified chores of a utility or run-saving attack. Australia must be commiserated on over the loss of Davidson at this critical stage of the rubber, for he is a fine all-rounder and a bowler of penetration. On a moist or 'lifting' Lord's wicket Archer might help Miller in a breakthrough of the England innings while the ball is new. But, on the whole, the Australian bowling has a nondescript look, which should strengthen confidence among England's batsmen.

Charles Macartney once came down to breakfast on the morning of a Test match at Lord's and, looking through the window, said: 'Lovely day. By cripes, I feel sorry for any poor cove who has to bowl at me today!' For years and years the note of Australian assurance has apparently depressed English cricketers; and now is the occasion for a change of tune and heart. No Australian team has looked as vulnerable as this one, though, as I have tried to argue, it possesses certain possibilities of quality. But as advocate in the Australian cause, I confess to a brief that is soon exhausted.

As stated at the head of this article, the chance has come not only to beat Australia but to thrash them soundly for all the world to see. I could in fact almost feel sorry for the Australians in their present period of leanness and misfortune; then I remember the advice of Doctor Johnson about compassion on behalf of all opponents, invaders, marauders or burglars whatsoever; knock the man down first and feel sorry for him afterwards.

There is of course room for improvement in England's batting towards the lower regions of the order of going in. In unsettled weather neither side should need two fast bowlers; and indeed the modern notion that fast bowlers must of necessity work in pairs can be overdone. Trueman has scarcely bowled himself free of stiffness after absence from day-to-day labours; England's team, for all its 'psychological' advantages, dare not risk its batting to accommodate a bowler not in his top form. A quick removal of Cowdrey or Richardson might compel Godfrey Evans to put on his pads and get himself ready to stem a collapse of the 'tail'. Given unsettled weather, four bowlers should be enough for England's purpose at Lord's. A. C. MacLaren maintained that four were always enough, but they had to be the best of their kind.

It was refreshing at Nottingham to see an England innings opening in a mood of enterprise and hopefulness, with the batsmen both as quick to punish the loose ball as they were to defend stoutly against the good one. But I could not share the general view that Cowdrey and Richardson inspired complete peace of mind; from time to time each made a mistake which against the Miller and Lindwall of 1948 would surely have been fatal. I do not like the way Cowdrey allows a ball to collide with his pads, his bat held in abeyance, hoping for the best, and Richardson, who will quickly learn by trial and error, has an edge to his bat, there for all eyes to see. The England innings may well be given solidity by the inclusion of Insole. His consistent scoring season by season is sometimes belittled by a remark to the effect that he is not 'a Test match' batsman. If it comes to that, is Macdonald, Burke, Benaud, Archer, Mackay, Rutherford, Craig or Johnson, a Test match batsman?

England's only need is fine weather—and good resolution. Here we are, the season at the half-way stage, with the Australians still looking for victory in a match against a county. Their record up to date—one defeat and seven draws—would qualify for a position in the lowest deeps of the county championship table. Let the sun shine generously at Lord's. Everything is ready there for a great game and a grand spectacle—the players, the crowd, the scorers, the press and the radio men, the umpires, and, of course, the ambulance men.

NO CALL FOR SWEEPING CHANGES

The Lord's Test match of 1956 will be remembered as Keith Miller's. His bowling, electric with improvisations which probably surprised himself now and again, wrecked England's first innings, undermined the second; and blew it sky high when with a ball of sudden and vicious velocity, aimed as though from an ambush, he got May caught at the wicket.

He is not only dangerous with a new ball at an innings' outset: he is able to transform himself into a change bowler never to be trusted in that usually secondary occupation. The ball that defeated May and clinched the issue of the match was not by any means an old one; but Miller's action, less than intense and not highly strung at this point of affairs, had scarcely hinted of the demonic. But May, a little earlier in the day, had been brilliantly missed at the wicket by Langley who, with Evans, gave as splendid an exhibition behind the stumps as any seen at Lord's in a lifetime.

Nothing is calculable about Miller. Sometimes he bowls as though with his mind elsewhere, or the direct attack having failed, he is apparently trying experiments for his own amusement's sake. Occasionally, he looks to be merely marking time, 'keeping one end going', his thoughts dwelling on distant things, romantic or other. It is at such moments that the inexperienced batsman is prone to lapse into a mood of false security. It is a fact that people, after an eruption of a volcano, will begin to build homes again on the slopes, hoping for the best. Many batsmen have imagined themselves comfortably housed, for a while at least, as the Miller fires have seemed to smoulder.

On Saturday, in Australia's second innings, when the game was being won by Trueman, who bowled as if ready and willing to break his back and burst his heart, Miller played an innings made out of the tempered steel of batsmanship; then, when he was caught at the wicket off a ball which he might have claimed as one from his own fiery armoury, he raised his bat on high as a salute to Trueman, who had overthrown him, seven minutes from close of play. Most batsmen, in the circumstances and at that time of day, might justifiably have beaten the earth with their bats. No: Miller let us see the finest gesture ever known on a cricket field in a Test match. Here is a player who would grace any eleven, any great company, of any period.

In an article preliminary to the match, I wrote in these columns to the effect that though England should win, as the stronger side on paper, the form so far of the Australians 'has been too bad to be true, for if Johnson cannot boast an eleven of palpably Test match pedigree, he can put faith in one or two players of ominous potentiality.' One of these players, I ventured to assert, was Benaud. His innings on Monday was superb. The situation of his team, as he began this innings, was precarious. His own position in the Australian eleven was in the balance. He was nearly caught from Trueman with his score not many more than three; but he did not withdraw to a protective shell. At once he pulled Trueman for six. Here was an example for all English batsmen to follow. And did they follow it? On the contrary.

The long innings of Mackay was not wearisome to the observer of character. Mackay clearly enjoyed every slow-moving minute of it. His innings was a triumph of mind, or something approximating to mind, over matter. His purpose was modest—just to stop the ball when he thought it was straight. He was so accurate in his aim when he missed the balls which missed the wicket, or the edge of his bat, that there appeared to be no legal way of removing him from the crease.

For years cricket has been evolving a Mackay, for the purposes of five-day Test matches. All other batsmen, supposedly wholly defensive and strokeless, have been only the imitations of durability compared to Mackay, merely embryonic. It is true that on Thursday he drove for four past cover and was caught on the off-side trying to repeat the hit. These were plainly throwbacks to some crude ancestry of cricket, throw-backs to a Macartney or a McCabe. On the whole, I fancy Mackay will remain 'true to type'.

Mackay's innings, of course, was the main obstacle to England's advance on Saturday; and without it Benaud could not have achieved his dauntless thrust for victory. I cannot understand why Laker was not in quick time given a chance to try, by off-spin turning away from Mackay's left-handed bat, to find the edge of it, or the middle, or wherever the seat of fallibility reposes in it.

Australia wriggled from a parlous position at Trent Bridge with only nine players: and they have won at Lord's with ten. A week ago they must surely have been psychologically in the depths. Now they are again infused with the traditional Australian confidence. England have missed a golden chance, while the stock was low and Lindwall, Davidson, and Craig were out of action.

If a team which is only mediocre possesses a genius, it must be regarded as dangerous, and capable of anything. The Lord's match was Keith Miller's match let us say it again, let us sing it in choric numbers. The injuries to Lindwall and Davidson put a heavy responsibility on him as a bowler. They were increased at Lord's by the quick physical breakdown of Crawford. The Australian attack, their fate in the match and indeed in the rubber itself, depended on him.

The proof of greatness is in the answer to the challenge and in the performance of duties which test a man beyond the scope and powers of ordinary mortals. Miller responded to every demand: he bowled 70 overs in the match and took ten wickets for 152: and only a few weeks ago his bowling days were thought to be finished, because of some weakness of muscle in his thirty-seventh year. He announced, in his last Test match at Lord's, the power of will: also he showed us how a fight can be keenly fought, no quarter shown, yet with chivalry and gusto. Here is the representative Australian. They should put up a statue to him in Canberra, to encourage the politicians there to see visions and dream dreams.

TIME FOR CHANGE IN ENGLAND'S LUCK AT LEEDS

The England team picked to play against Australia at Leeds seems stronger than the poor-hearted one beaten deservedly at Lord's. Clearly the selectors' aim is improvement in the batting, even if not more than four bowlers should be at May's command.

A. C. Maclaren always maintained that four bowlers were enough on any kind of wicket, but he played at a time precedent to the discovery of the slipped disc, when many bowlers, even fast, were strong enough of muscle to go through a full season and not suffer premature infirmities. It was Maclaren, by the way, who, when he heard of the team chosen to serve under him at Old Trafford in 1902, groaned out of his heart: 'My God, look what they have sent me!' The players 'sent him' were F. S. Jackson, K. S. Ranjitsinhij, J. T. Tyldesley, Abel, Braund, L. C. H. Palairet, Lilley, Rhodes, Lockwood, and 'Fred' Tate.

The Leeds wicket has not often been friendly to fast bowlers in Test matches, though in two games on this ground Lindwall and Miller have taken some twenty wickets between them at 26 runs each. But A. V. Bedser found it an easy task at Leeds in 1948 to bat three hours after facing Lindwall at the beginning of the morning. In a typical Leeds air or atmosphere Bailey might use the new ball skilfully enough to act as excellent foil to the accredited fast bowler, Trueman or Statham: for the chairman of the selection committee has stated that the player likely to be left out of the England eleven will be one of the fast bowlers.

The recall of Washbrook should certainly bring back to the eleven a necessary experience, dash of panache, and the presence expected from an England cricketer. The mystery is why for five years, while we have been looking in vain for a reliable opening batsman, discarding many in turn, Washbrook has been neglected altogether.

But he has not been called back now to go in first again for England. The chairman of the selection committee, unusually communicative, has said that Cowdrey and Richardson would open the innings at Leeds—an unusual forecast or 'anticipation'. Most of us would wish that P. B. H. May wrote out the order, with Cowdrey number four. The inclusion of Insole and Oakman must surely stiffen the batting, making some reinsurance against a rearguard consisting of Lock, Statham (or Trueman), Laker and Evans, which does not look as insecure as at Lord's. The first seven of England's batsmen will probably be Cowdrey, Richardson, May, Insole, Washbrook, Oakman and Bailey: and I doubt if better men for the job are available. Obviously the strategy behind the choice of seven batsmen of proven technique is first of all to avoid defeat. Another defeat would mean goodbye to the Ashes, for we could scarcely hope to win two out of two matches remaining.

The great thing needed is a change of heart in the approach of the England batsmen, and, indeed, sometimes in the England generalship. At Lord's, Benaud upset the England bowling plan by his resolute hitting. May apparently was afraid of using his slow spinners against him. And—here is the irony!—when Benaud himself bowled leg-spin, our batsmen were afraid of hitting him. I am still of the opinion that the present Australian team is one of the most fallible ever assembled. In the county championship they would today be placed near the bottom, and rightly so, for not only has this team played uncertain cricket technically, it has bored the public as no previous Australian cricketers have ever done.

Leeds has not been a happy ground for England, who have never won there against Australia since Test matches were first played at Headingley in 1899. But Australia have won four times, in 1909, 1921, 1938, and 1948.

Jack Hobbs was afflicted with appendicitis at Leeds in the Test match of 1921; Johnny Briggs had a seizure at Leeds in the Test match of 1899. At the beginning of the Test match of 1909, at Leeds, G. L. Jessop so severely strained the muscles of his back that he was unable to play cricket again during the season. In 1951, at Leeds, Bailey strained his back in the Test match against South Africa; but, as usual, he thrived on pain and scored 95. At Leeds Macartney scored a century before lunch against England, and 304 in a day. In 1934, also at Leeds, Bradman scored another triple century. In 1951, at Leeds, South Africa scored 538 against England, E. A. Rowan 236. Last year, at Leeds, South Africa won the toss against England, lost five wickets for 38, then won by 224, after scoring 500 in their second innings.

It is time for luck to blow England's way at Leeds. It is certainly time that an England batsman scored a century before lunch at Leeds against Australia—or anywhere else.

ENGLAND MUST EXAMINE TOP OF BATTING LIST

The Australians were no doubt unlucky to get caught at Leeds on a dubious wicket on the closing day. But they lost the match, more or less, when they lost six wickets for 69 on Friday in circumstances not at all insurmountable for batsmen having an ordinarily professional technique to cope with occasional spin. Obviously the better team won. With Keith Miller unfortunately unable to bowl, Australia's attack was generally not dangerous after Archer had used the new ball, which he did most cleverly at the beginning of the match.

On any pitch likely to take spin, or even appearing to be ready to take spin, no Australian bowler could claim half the skill and experience of Laker and Lock. And apart from Harvey and Miller, and Benaud in a lesser way, none of Australia's batsmen possesses at present more than a rudimentary knowledge of the art of the passive bat and the front foot play needed to stay at the wicket any length of time against bowling which does not follow the line of flight after pitching, or rises at an angle not advertised by the line of flight. We must charitably and chivalrously remember that Australia's all-round resources have been curtailed by the accident to Davidson; moreover, their supply of organized batting was decreased at Leeds by the peculiar omission from the team of Craig. It is to be hoped that Davidson will be fit for the match at Old Trafford: I saw him batting in the nets at Lord's the other afternoon, and he looked good and in a class definitely first-class.

Though England have beaten Australia decisively, with some aid from fortune to support technical superiority, the selection committee will need to think once more about the batting at the innings' outset. On Thursday, Richardson, Cowdrey, and Oakman had no patriot's vote of confidence. Something should be done, even desperately, to return Cowdrey to the position in the order in which, not so long ago, he was one of the best number four batsmen in the world and, surely, the successor of Hammond, whom he sometimes resembles in style.

Wharton continues to score consistently. If it is argued that he is not entirely sound in method, the answer is that Richardson certainly is not either. Richardson batted an hour for four when he opened England's innings on Thursday with Cowdrey; if Wharton were to stay in an hour he would score not much less than 40 against any bowling extant.

The bowling of Laker and Lock has rightly been warmly praised; Laker certainly rises beyond his average Test match ability if Lock is co-operating with him. Australia, of course, missed a golden chance to save themselves at Leeds when, needing only 34 to save the follow-on, they lost their last four wickets for one run. Miller and Benaud, after resolute cricket, got out at the crisis, Miller rather thoughtlessly. Talent does what it can, genius what it must.

If Washbrook had failed on Thursday, England's situation would have been dire. As soon as he reached the wicket, in fact, on his way to it, the atmosphere of the England innings became easier to breathe in; he administered refreshing air to May. He played with time to spare and, even in defence, there was panache about his carriage, an independence of manner, yet with it all we could feel the certain touch that can be quiet and wait. We could realise, too, that here was a batsman of a period stronger and more self-reliant than ours; May was excellent, but the difference between Washbrook and May was that of a vintage and a good non-vintage wine. But May proved his calibre by conquering the challenging hour, in spite of momentary uncertainty. Only the great player is able to score a century in spite of the fact that he is, to begin with, not altogether 'in touch'.

Before Australia's first innings opened no less an authority on the Headingley turf than Emmott Robinson told me that it would not take spin sharply until Monday, failing rain. The Australian first innings' collapse on Friday—six for 69—has been generally put down to great bowling on a pitch definitely helpful to spin. My own view is that the cause was deplorably inadequate technique and a general want of experience in the face of Laker and Lock on a turf which allowed spin to occur occasionally, but seldom with the nip or lift which is really dangerous. Burke, Harvey, and Archer were victims not of spin but of bad judgment.

Then the behaviour of Mackay at the wicket probably spellbound his younger colleagues into the delusion that the pitch was a pitfall, a subsiding oleaginous earth and entire universe in perpetual and obtusely angular movement. He defended with his pads as though not to one spinning ball only but to several, aimed at him simultaneously from all parts of the field. No umpire could have given him out leg before, for the simple reason that he was never in one position for more than a split second of time. Though he hopped and floundered like the boneless wonder, to the amusement of thousands, I could not quite understand how he could legally be removed from the wicket; in other words, how he could be got out.

But then he made the fatal mistake—he used his bat. On turning wickets Mackay does himself injustice by thinking he needs a bat; what is more, he handicaps himself by using a bat at all. He is not expected to score, at any rate not quicker than he could, with practice, score leg-byes. In future, let him give his bat to the umpire— there is no rule, as far as I know, which insists that a batsman should use a bat persistently and habitually.

The general failure of Australia's batting at Headingley can be accounted for in the drastic but honest phrase of Dr Johnson— 'Pure ignorance'. Since wickets in Australia have been covered in most first-class matches few Australian batsmen have done well in an English summer of unsettled weather. On Tuesday when Australia gave up the ghost in an encircling gloom the wicket was not definitely 'sticky'. No batsman of sense, possessing Miller's hitting power, would stay in two hours for 26 on a truly 'sticky' pitch—not if he had any cricket sense at all.

The defeat of Australia in the present rubber has been confidently anticipated by the present writer since the season's beginning. But England's batting skill conceals the heel of Achilles; considering the suspect spot, Keith Miller may well say: 'Give me the right mood at Old Trafford and I'll show you—again—where it is.'

NOW TO OLD TRAFFORD

Whichever player is left out of the dozen chosen to confront the Australians in the Test match beginning at Old Trafford today, England should win without need of undue effort on any wicket at all amenable to fast or spin bowling. The Old Trafford turf nowadays is usually of good pace in dry weather, so I am told: it is to be hoped then that Statham and Trueman are included even if a batsman must go by the board. I am assuming, of course, that no act of midsummer lunacy omits either Laker or Lock.

If I were P. B. H. May, I would feel very much inclined to open the innings with Richardson (now that Graveney cannot play) and Sheppard: I would gladly risk losing my first wicket cheaply to be able to send Cowdrey in number four rather than expose him to a new ball bowled by Lindwall and Miller. True that Sheppard has not recently been going in number one or two: but a great batsman is adaptable and Sheppard opening an innings for England this week would be a reversion to original type. The fact that he does not play cricket habitually nowadays need not worry us more than apparently it worries Sheppard himself, the thoroughbred player is not obliged to keep his nose to the grindstone of routine practice. Besides, Sheppard at the opening of an England innings is bound to look its part; he will launch the England ship with champagne, not small beer, even if the bottle breaks in his hands—and I hope that this idea or figure does not provoke protest from the temperance reformers by its suggestion that champagne and the cloth can come together without profanity.

The England XI I would like to see taking the field is this: Sheppard, Richardson, May, Cowdrey, Washbrook, Bailey, Evans, Laker, Lock, Statham, and Trueman. Since 1953 the Australian batsmen have collapsed against the swing of Bedser, against fast bowling in their own country, and against Laker or Lock on English wickets not openly 'sticky'. (Had the wicket at Leeds been truly sticky on the closing day Lock would surely have made Laker hurry to take his share of victims going to the slaughter like newly born lambs.)

No great act of prevision is wanted to prophesy that on a really difficult turf Lock would send most of the present Australians to the right about for a total score of round about sixty or seventy, including byes, leg-byes, no-balls, wides, overthrows, etc. On a firm fast pitch, Australia's powers should naturally wax strong as possible. For all our confidence we must bear in mind that though as a team Ian Johnson's contingent is about the least accomplished technically and in experience the rawest ever gathered together, it contains in its ranks at least four cricketers extremely dangerous given the mood and the hour. And the day may well be about to dawn on which Miller, Harvey, Lindwall, and Benaud, are visited by inspiration simultaneously.

At Lord's the other day Lindwall began to bowl at the morning's outset with an aspect of middle-aged amiability at a pace which for him was nearly apologetic. Then artfully he released a perfect outswinger full of length and not beyond medium speed; such a ball is capable of defeating the greatest of batsmen. So with Benaud; from time to time he spins a quite insidious leg-break. Archer, of course, is a seam bowler of rare accuracy and resilience. As for Miller—well we all know his power to take a whole match and situation by the scruff of the neck and bend it to his will and way.

Sympathy has recently been expressed on behalf of the Australians: for it is maintained in certain soft-hearted places that Ian Johnson and his colleagues have experienced very bad luck on this tour, poor fellows. I can only quote again the words of Dr Johnson to point the inadvisability of showing fellow-feeling for those who assault us, oppose us, or have nefarious designs on our property or person: 'Knock them down first, sir, then show compassion afterwards.' Or words to the same effect.

There is a school of thought which favours the dropping of Bailey rather than an accredited stroke-player, to allow England freedom to use four bowlers. The argument here is that as the balance of the rubber is now even with England in possession of the Ashes, England should go all out and make sure of victory at Old Trafford. Bailey, of course, is in Test cricket, essentially a match-saver, not a match-winner. The fact is surely that the more need there is for the stroke-players of England to take an intelligent offensive the more Bailey will be needed in case things go awry. Besides, Bailey in the field is always in the game, often offensively omnipresent. He is the best change bowler since the Hon F. S. Jackson.

Old Trafford will inevitably hear this week the old jokes about the weather, rain or shine. No irony from the South can dim the great ground's history—Ranjitsinhji's marvellous 154 not out when he glanced Ernest Jones off his left ear, and Tom Richardson's 110 overs in the same match (13 wickets for 244); Trumper's century before lunch and Australia's victory by three runs in 1902, with Barnes, Hirst, C. B. Fry, G. L. Jessop, and Haigh left out of the England team: England's grand total of 627 for 9 scored during a heat wave of 1934 in which three Australians at least became afflicted with sun stroke: Compton's courageous and confident and vivacious 145 not out in 1948 after he had been knocked half senseless by a bumper from Lindwall (only the greatest batsman of his time could have played this innings).

All these immortal deeds have been done at Old Trafford against Australians. So even if the rain should interfere yet again with a Test match at Old Trafford there should be plenty to see with imagination's eye and to talk about. Not all the ghosts will inhabit the press box.

WHAT KIND OF BOWLING DOES AUSTRALIA WANT?

Providence saw to it that justice was done at Old Trafford on Tuesday to the fine arts of Laker, whose skill and judgment on Friday were belittled by many critics, not all Australian, who apparently were ready to account for his success almost entirely in terms of a dusty pitch. On Tuesday, recurrent sunshine collaborated gently but not drastically with Laker, who performed something of a miracle of combined cleverness and endurance.

The Australians may justifiably claim that they were unfortunate to be trapped on a drying turf, but at the same time they might pause to bear in mind that it was a turf on which all the other English bowlers, Lock included, were shorn of their usual powers. As a fact, too much has been made of Laker's spin and not enough of his superbly controlled flight, subtly changed, which defeated the wicket when it was unhelpful to spin, and, what is more, often defeated the Australian batsmen before the ball pitched.

The Australians should be grateful to Laker, though overwhelmed by him, for re-educating them in a science they have recently neglected. The superb innings of McDonald was proof of quickness to learn and of flexible and adaptable talents. Here was an innings organized technically, the best played this year by any Australian for the purposes of lengthy tenure on an English wicket in a Test match. Craig, too, proved himself an educated, resourceful player, though he was not able to cope with Laker the moment the wicket on Tuesday began to stir a little in its sleep.

The wicket in the Old Trafford Test match may possibly have helped the spin of Laker at times: but to account for an Australian batting collapse nowadays we are not obliged to suppose unreliable English turf or overzealous English groundsmen. Since 1953 Australian batsmen in Tests against England have collapsed wholesale at least nine times in fourteen matches—here are some facts and figures:

1953 at Trent Bridge: Australia in the first innings lost six wickets for 6 to Bedser. In the second innings eight wickets crashed for 79. At Manchester: Australia lost eight wickets for 35, mainly to Wardle. At the Oval: Australia succumbed to Lock and Laker.

1954–5 at Sydney: Australia collapsed second innings to Tyson and Statham; eight wickets fell for 112. At Melbourne: eight

Australian wickets fell in the second innings for 36—all out 111. Tyson and Statham again. At Adelaide: in Australia's second innings, six wickets fell for 34—111 all out—to Tyson and Statham. At Sydney: Australia 111 for six, mainly to Wardle.

So it will be seen that in three consecutive rubbers the Australian batsmen have collapsed wholesale to all sorts of bowling, on all sorts of wickets, here and in their own country, where, of course, wickets are prepared without fear or favour. In the present rubber they seem incapable of coping with flight and spin. What kind of bowling would they like us to serve to them? We have in succession treated them to fast bowling, medium-paced bowling, seam-bowling and spin bowling. We have bowled at them in every style on our own and on their own wickets. They are hard to please.

It is a curious fact that four dreadful Australian batting break-downs since 1953 against England have occurred in a second innings. And not one or two batsmen have collapsed, but the entire team, excepting Harvey now and again. Evidence is here of poor resolution, lack of strong nerve—far more evidence of want of will-power than the amount of evidence discoverable at Leeds or Manchester this year of badly prepared turf.

Suppose for the sake of argument that the Old Trafford wicket on the second day for half an hour enabled Laker to spin his off-break dangerously. Is it a new thing in Test cricket to see spin on the second day of a Test match? Have Australian critics forgotten the period in which an Australian Test eleven had little use at all for fast bowling or the new ball, but brought into attack O'Reilly and Grimmett to spin at the beginning of a first or second day? In three-day Test matches spin was in action the first over. Laker is chosen to play for England because he bowls spin. The Australians of today's vintage apparently think that he should bowl straight, at least until they have completed one innings.

The sure sign of a difficult dry wicket is not spurts of dust but the ball that lifts or rises abruptly. Spin itself is not evidence of a bad wicket. Few balls at Old Trafford lifted acutely on Friday. A Test match bowler who is not fast, or an exploiter of the seam, is expected to exploit spin. Do the present-day writers and commentators imagine that Hobbs, Sutcliffe, Woodfull, Macartney, Bradman, Ponsford, Hammond, Leyland, Kippax, and others scored all their runs in Test matches against bowling that was straight until the beginning of a third day's play?

On the abused Old Trafford pitch during the second day, Evans scored 47 with impunity, and Lock was unbeaten for an effortless 25.

Burke stayed in three hours on this Old Trafford wicket when it was thought to be at its worst. The Australian collapse at Old Trafford happened in the space of half an hour. Before this collapse, Burke and McDonald had played with tranquillity for 48 to open the innings. After the collapse, not one Australian wicket fell in 65 minutes, except Harvey's, who was caught hitting dementedly at a full-toss. Indeed, much evidence can be found to the effect that this Old Trafford wicket was reasonably co-operative to batsmen, taking it as a whole.

The accusations levelled at Old Trafford's groundsman were so unjust that at one time I expected Jim Laker, good-natured man that he is, to give himself up, and make a confession. 'I done it, with a blunt instrument. A cricket ball. But I had no malicious intent. I forgot that in Tests against Australia today spin is illegal. It all comes, your Worship, of bad habits picked up at Kennington Oval.' And I imagine that his Worship's sentence would have been just: 'In view of the fact that you are appearing in this court under the First Offenders Act. I am inclined to take a lenient view of your offence. Still, the law must be upheld. My sentence is that you be taken from this place, to another—Taunton or Bath—and be detained there with six months' hard labour, bowling at Somerset batsmen.'

In our praise for Laker we must not forget the foundations well and solidly laid for victory by England's young amateur batsmen: Cowdrey, Richardson, Sheppard, and May. Years have passed since an England innings gave as much pleasure to well-bred watchers of cricket as the large amount given in this match on Thursday and Friday. To the Rev David Sheppard a special tribute is due. Only a batsman of pedigree can hope to score a century in a Test match after a considerable period of absence from first-class cricket. But class will tell in a flash of a moment.

England's two victories, each by an innings, have been administered with a properly retaliative ruthlessness; and the victory at Manchester also had greatness of style in it. Let the good work be continued three weeks hence at Kennington Oval, with the conquerors of Old Trafford left intact to convince the Australians—and an English critic or two—which really and obviously is the better team.

IMPROVED FORM DUE FROM AUSTRALIA AT THE OVAL

Though the 'Ashes' remain in England's keeping, the Fifth Test match which begins at the Oval today will certainly be fought severely, without quarter. Australia are eager to prove that, for all their limitations, there has been little, except English weather and wickets, between the two teams in skill. England, of course, hope to prove in no uncertain voice—as Lock, G. A. R., would agree—that there has been, and undoubtedly is, a vast difference.

The selection committee, by inviting twelve experienced players to the Oval, demonstrated a serious view of the occasion. It is rather melancholy, by the way, that against an Australian team of unusually indifferent quality, England, with the 'Ashes' safe, can find scarcely any recently discovered talent fit to be trusted, but must needs call again on the gallant and not long ago half-crippled Compton, and the noble war-horse Washbrook. These two stalwarts can be both included in the England team only by dropping Bailey, or by leaving out a bowler. An England eleven nowadays without Bailey is bound to resemble 'Hamlet' without, say, the first gravedigger.

Most of us are eager to see Tyson, Statham, Lock, and Laker as a bowling ensemble; and as a victory for England in this match is almost a necessity of prestige, maybe for once in a while Bailey may, with sense and without discourtesy, be relegated to the pavilion, though for my part I would always wish him by me were I England's captain.

The irony of Compton's career is that in his prime he should have suffered an injury which must inevitably, even in times of some-times marvellous surgical dexterity, cramp the movements of his feet. Compton is one of the few batsmen of the present time who really and truly uses his feet. Most of his contemporaries would do as well on wooden legs. Genius can rise high over impediments, but it is a question whether Compton now is able to rise high enough and quickly enough to take a sharp chance of catching anywhere near the wicket, especially if he is obliged to leap suddenly sideways.

The Australians have recently shown immense improvement in form against one or two of our less formidable counties. The return to soundness of limb of Davidson should bring a much wanted reinforcement, though Ian Johnson might occasionally feel himself embarrassed by excess of quick seam-bowlers and of batsmen-bowlers not quite good enough as specialists in either department. We must all wish the Australians dry, warm weather and a fast true wicket. Then, they will meet Tyson and Statham again, refreshed by pleasant memories from their own country.

As a wit at Lord's remarked the other day, it is to be hoped that the groundsman won't be suspected of putting uranium in the wicket. Though the Oval wicket is a fast drier, it is hardly likely to be fast in time for this morning or even tomorrow, unless a sun burns down furiously on Kennington. Maybe the Australians will draw comfort from the knowledge that an opportunity was taken by Surrey to give Laker a 'rest' during the last few days, even though a crucial engagement with Middlesex had to be played at Lord's, in conditions made for off-spin, and in which Titmus took fourteen wickets in the match.

Granted fine weather, we must expect the Australians to make an improvement on their form at Manchester. They could scarcely do worse. A typical innings by Harvey is overdue in a Test match, and the same may be said of Miller. There is more ability at Johnson's command than we have consistently been allowed to see in this season of distressful weather.

Many cricketers will join Johnson in his prayers for sun and a hard ground. Patriotic Englishmen will be content to hope that Tyson and Statham remain strong of heart, limb and muscle. The Australians need a change of bowling. They have supped full of spin and Laker.

AUSTRALIA'S WEAKNESSES AND ENGLAND'S SHORTCOMINGS

The issue of the rubber was seldom uncertain to anybody with a close knowledge of the main traits of Australian cricket during recent years. Since 1953 Australia has persistently produced batsmen fallible against (1) pace, (2) swerve, and (3) spin, in conditions where these time-honoured bowling factors could find full scope. Also, Australia has for long lacked accurate spin bowling on any wicket.

Given level turf, with the ball behaving with well-bred geometry—the turf of the West Indies—all Australian batsmen are dangerous, with averages ranging from Harvey's 100 to Lindwall's 37—in Test matches at that. Only a twelvemonth or so after the Australian holiday in the West Indies, on turf reflecting the Elysian fields of batsmen, the same players have been reduced to fearful empiricism on wickets no better than those which English county cricketers are obliged to tackle every day.

Yet it is the fact that in a season conspiratory to spin, several Australian batsmen have done as well as more than ordinarily good English batsmen. According to statistics, as I write these astonishing words, the best batsman of the season is none other than K. Mackay, with 972 runs, average 51·15, the same Mackay who put bowling and cricket into another dimension at Leeds. Even these remarkable statistics do less than justice to his genius; but they rather, I think, obscure the point under discussion, which is known or charted batsmanship.

Burke is a batsman recognizable at first sight; so are Harvey, McDonald, Burge, Miller, Benaud, and Craig. All of these have maintained averages, day by day, of 35 and over, in spite of spin, in spite of soft wickets. Seven Australian batsmen in Johnson's hapless team are qualified to go statistically alongside our best dozen.

If Lock and Laker were Australians, would any, excepting one or two, among English batsmen produce methods much more dependable than those of the Australians on pitches sensitive to spin. Day by day in county cricket it needs much less than a Laker to spin out English batsmen neck and crop.

Shepherd, of Glamorganshire, has taken 160 wickets at 14·76 runs each, with off-breaks he cultivated only yesteryear. Illingworth, another apprentice off-spinner, has taken nearly 100 wickets at 13 runs each. Amiable Wells, of Gloucestershire, not a Laker nor yet a Tattersall, has taken 100 wickets at 18 runs each. Tattersall, in a season in which his county decides he is not bowling well enough, has so far taken over 100 at 16 runs each.

The Test matches are widely supposed to have witnessed a resurgence of English batsmanship. Why then was it necessary to recall Washbrook, to lean heavily on Compton, brave and skilful as ever but physically not above suspicion? It was a joy to see the Rev. David Sheppard in the England eleven once more; but here was another case of an oblique S.O.S. At the Oval the other day Compton lifted English batsmanship, indeed all contemporary batsmanship, to a loftier plane than it has habited for years, a plane of felicitous mastery, of versatile stroke-play.

It is easy to name three really versatile stroke-players today in English cricket who are not or nearly 40 years old. Peter May is a wonderful dependable batsman who, in a season during which he has not been really in form for his county, has finely responded to the challenge of Test cricket. But he has needed to withhold many of his strokes.

The beautiful batting of Sheppard at the Oval reflected the glow of the amateur tradition, and there is promise in the busy stroke-play of Richardson, but, taking cricket by and large, there are still many technical shortcomings against spin in the performances of the bulk of English batsmen. Five noughts made holes in England's first innings in the Oval Test; and all of Washbrook's nerve, skill, and insousiance was needed to prevent a collapse at Leeds.

A trustworthy batsman is lacking yet to open an England innings. The ideal man for the job is, of course, Sheppard; but he has better work to do elsewhere. At all reasonable risks, Cowdrey should be restored to the place in the order of batting where he proved himself the finest young player of the day.

One of the most satisfying features of the Tests was the dominance of the amateur in the England batting. At Old Trafford, where England stayed at the wicket all day and scored 300 runs, none but an amateur batsman was on view—Cowdrey, Richardson, May, Sheppard, and Bailey. I can recall no other instance of a like independence of professional assistance for a whole day in a Test match between England and Australia.

Not one century was scored in the rubber by an Australian batsman. I can find no precedent for individual abstinence of this kind among Australians against England since the rubber of 1890.

It is lucky for a bowler if he can pick and choose his period. I remember Larwood in Australia, after he had retired from the game; he was watching the wickets falling in an England v. Australia Test match, wickets of the new generation, wickets of Brown, Close, Parkhouse, Dewes, and other scarcely fledged aspirants. He contemplated the comings and goings from and back to the pavilion, then said out of his heart: 'When I think of my Test-match career, I seem to have spent all my time bowling at Bradman.'

Laker's wonderful performance of 46 wickets in a rubber at 9·60 runs each is not likely soon to be equalled, unless Australian batsmen continue to play back to almost half-volleys, with and without spin, on soft wickets transformed by lurid imagination into morasses of infernal mischief.

But with all my appreciation of Laker, I would not envy his

'record' if I were J. N. Crawford and I had taken 30 wickets, when not much more than a boy, on Australian wickets of perfect ease, taken these 30 wickets in a rubber, having dismissed the following-named batsmen: Trumper (three times), Clem Hill (twice), M. A. Noble (three times), Armstrong (five times), S. E. Gregory (twice), Macartney (three times). This is a 'record' which will not be equalled until Australia, or any other country, is able in one and the same rubber, to put into the field batsmen of the calibre of young Crawford's vanquished.

It is a pity that the Oval Test was not favoured with sunshine throughout and a good hard wicket. In dry weather, I am confident that Tyson and Statham would yet again have overwhelmed Australian batsmen. The Australians are free now to point out that in only one of the five Tests were they granted a firm pitch to play on and were not unfairly handicapped by rain. This was the Lord's match—and they won it. That, as Captain James Hook might say, is where the canker gnaws.

OLD TRAFFORD'S CENTURY

O F Old Trafford's hundred years of history and great cricket played by men of character I have had the good luck to enjoy at least half a century's portion. I first entered the ground in July, 1899, on Monday the 24th. Lancashire were playing Gloucestershire, and as I pushed my way through the heavy stiff turnstile (where did I get my sixpence from?) I heard a terrific yell coming from the field. I thought somebody had been killed. It was Charlie Smith, Lancashire's stumper, appealing for a catch at the wicket. I was then a small boy, and in the manner of all small boys I was always hungry, so in order to avoid the crowd at lunch I at once went to the refreshment bar to buy a ha'penny bun. As I stretched up to the counter to pay an explosion happened; glass splinters flew about. I was terrified, until a kindly Lancashire voice from a man in a cloth cap said, 'It's all right, sonny, it's only Jessop just coom in.' A prophetic introduction of Old Trafford to me, and to the 'Cricketer' to come, and to my Makepeace and my Hallows long ago.

Tom Lancaster played for Lancashire that day; and I reflected on the romance of things that with such a name he should indeed be playing for Lancashire. Who today remembers the Lancashire Eleven which contained my first heroes?—Ward, A. H. Hornby, Tyldesley, C. R. Hartley, Cuttell, A. Eccles, Sharp, Lancaster, Webb, Smith, Mold. Old Trafford was situated half a century ago in the country, surrounded by meadows. Stretford was a village. At the top of Warwick Road the Botanical Gardens was situated. I saw Johnny Briggs there one evening, but he was not studying botany.

It was difficult to become a member of the Lancashire County Cricket Club 50 years ago. I have seen (from a distance) tall hats on the pavilion at Old Trafford. The Ladies' Pavilion was a joy to sit in on sunny days. The black-and-white wooden house made a pretty picture, and afternoon tea was served by girls in frills and lace. One very hot day, with the sun bringing up blobs of paint on the wooden seats, Jimmy Heap, the Lancashire cricketer, joined me and sat down. He was wearing his flannels. He jumped up immediately, so hot was the seat. 'Jupiter Pluvius,' he said. The Lancashire players during this period occasionally dragged into their conversation, rightly or wrongly, a classical allusion, remembered probably from cricket reports of the period. Cecil Parkin, happiest of all bowlers (when he was taking wickets), assured me that 'when the day comes when I can't play cricket. I'll do as them Roman emperors did—I'll get into a hot bath and cut mi ruddy throat.'

Scene and the atmosphere have much influence in making the style of a cricketer. It was against a green and pleasant background at Old Trafford that R. H. Spooner made the grass musical with his strokes. In a period of Manchester's cosmopolitan opulence, A. C. MacLaren dispersed all hints of provincialism from Lancashire cricket and Old Trafford as he lorded the earth, at the wicket or directing operations from his position of authority at first slip. The first three Lancashire batsmen in the order of going in of those days were MacLaren, Spooner, and J. T. Tyldesley. No county has had an innings opened with so much mingled grandeur, graciousness, and sword-like brilliance as these three cricketers spread over the field day by day. They were my heroes, my gods, when I was a boy of twelve, yet though I believed in the superiority of each over any other batsman alive or dead I was obliged to pray that they would not get out as I watched them facing the attack.

After I had grown to manhood, a miracle happened. I actually found myself engaged in a match at Old Trafford with A. C. MacLaren and R. H. Spooner opening the batting. I was captain of

165

the fielding side—a 'Manchester Guardian Eleven'. Imagine it; by the strange wheel of time the boy who had looked from a distance at these two cricketers playing for England and Lancashire on Old Trafford's historic sward was now clothed in flannels with them, drawn into the circle of history. Here was the chance of a lifetime. I decided to open the bowling. If I could get the wicket of MacLaren, life would be made worth while having been lived through. The whole meaning of life might at once become clear.

The last ball of my first over broke from the off, and just missed MacLaren's leg-stump. He played forward. The ball shaved the leg-stump. As the field changed over MacLaren said to me, 'Well bowled—but I didn't suspect that you could bring them back. So long as we know!' Then, every time I bowled an off-break, he moved back on his wicket and swept the ball effortlessly over the square-leg boundary. 'So long as we know!'

J. T. Tyldesley I came to know as a friend in a thousand. He asked me one day to play for a team he was taking to Romiley, at the end of a season, a village match. When Saturday came rain was drowning all Manchester. Also gross darkness covered the city. At midday the rain was still falling; the clouds were still heavy and Stygian. I confess that I decided that the journey to Romiley would be a waste of time. On the following Monday morning I went into a café where Tyldesley and I frequently met. He was sitting there reading a paper. 'Where were you on Saturday?' he at once asked. I explained —the weather. 'Why, Johnny, there was never the faintest chance.' He interrupted with these memorable words: 'You, of all people, should know that the first duty of a cricketer is to turn up.' I recommend the axiom as one of general and even universal moral application.

Long before my friendship with Tyldesley began I had spoken to him. One Saturday at Old Trafford rain fell in torrents at noon. I was still in my early teens. Urged by the hope of small boys I waited. I stood under the wall outside the ground. The rain persisted mercilessly. Everybody went home. But boys sometimes believe in magic and prayer. I willed the sun to shine. The rain fell faster. Then a man in a raincoat and blue serge came out of the ground, at the members' gate. I immediately penetrated his disguise. It was J. T. Tyldesley. And he spoke to me. 'What are you waiting for, sonny?' 'Won't they play again?' I supplicated. He told me the match had been abandoned hours ago. 'Get off home,' he said, and gave me a sixpenny piece. This was a boy's finest hour.

The same boy was present at Old Trafford when England lost the rubber to Australia by three runs, in July, 1902. Fred Tate's tragic match. He missed Darling, the Australian captain, ruinously, and was bowled by Saunders at the pinch. In this gigantic game Ranjitsinhji failed twice—lbw b. Trumble 2; lbw b. Trumble 0. He was in his prime and pomp, but he was promptly dropped from the England Eleven. That day, while England crashed to defeat, the end was watched by S. F. Barnes, George Hirst, C. B. Fry, and G. L. Jessop, each temporarily dropped by the selection committee. As Ranjitsinhji waited to go in to bat, he for once in his wonderful career suffered from nerves. And while he waited he carved his initials 'K.S.R.' on the ledge of the rails of the amateurs' balcony.

The Australians have always liked to play at Old Trafford. 'The light is so good there,' they maintain—an unexpected compliment. But Old Trafford is one of the few great cricket grounds where sightscreens are placed at each end of the wicket, with the pavilion broadside. The fact that the pavilion at Old Trafford is at a right-angle to the flight of the ball is, however, no deterrent to the pavilion's convictions upon matters of leg-before-wicket.

When did Old Trafford's golden age occur? I suppose the answer depends on one's date of birth. I was too late on the scene to watch Hornby and Barlow. In 1904, when Lancashire won the championship undefeated, the team contained at least five England players—MacLaren, Tyldesley, Spooner, Brearley, and Sharp. But my own view is that Lancashire cricket has never excelled the combined technical skill and personal genius of the summers of 1926, 1927, 1928, when the championship was enthroned at Old Trafford three years in succession, with Leonard Green a captain of understanding and control. And control was needed, for the team included Lancashire men of uninhibited character and vocabulary. Eight or nine of the players of this period were of England stature—Makepeace, Hallows, Ernest Tyldesley, Frank Watson, Duckworth, Richard Tyldesley, and Iddon. There was also the most beautiful and on his day the most satanically destructive of fast bowlers—E. A. Macdonald, who ran to the wicket so silently that Leonard Braund said that when he was umpiring he could hear the approach of Macdonald to bowl only by the rustling of his shirt.

On Whit Monday, 1926, Lancashire amassed the total of 509 for nine against Yorkshire. At lunch the score was 451 for four. As the 500 was neared, Leonard Green was batting. He decided that as Lancashire most likely would never again get as many as 500 against Yorkshire he would score the five hundredth run or perish in the attempt. So he blocked a ball from Rhodes and ran like a hare.

The ball was vehemently fielded by Emmott Robinson and hurled to the bowler. The ball struck Rhodes in the wrist and as he picked it up, hot and bothered, and as Green got safely home, he was heard to mutter: 'There's somebody runnin' up and down this wicket; Ah don't know who it is, but there's somebody runnin' up and down this wicket."

In these years the Old Trafford wicket was so prepared that even Macdonald at times was rendered harmless. The Lancashire and Yorkshire match was seldom finished. But the players had a richness that made even stalemate alive and humorous. 'Foony match, Lancashire and Yorkshire,' said dear old Roy Kilner; 'two teams meet at beginning and we say "Good morning"; then we never speak agin for three days, except to appeal.' But the Old Trafford wicket was not always a batsman's bed of roses. In 1901 the playing pitch was rough and fiery 'While it remained bad,' reports 'Wisden', 'the totals at Manchester recalled the cricket of 40 years ago. Sharp profited to a great extent by the bad wickets, making the ball fly in a manner that was, at his great pace, absolutely dangerous.' Yet, though playing half his innings at Old Trafford on a 'dangerous' turf, J. T. Tyldesley in the season scored 3,041 runs, average 55·22. I don't believe that any batsman, Bradman or Hobbs, has, considering the circumstances, equalled this performance.

In 1928 Hallows scored a thousand runs in the month of May; and in the season Ernest Tyldesley scored 3,024 runs, average 79·57. Ernest Tyldesley, one of the most accomplished batsmen Old Trafford ever nurtured, played only twice for England against Australia at Old Trafford, in 1921 and in 1926; in two innings he scored 78 not out and 81. Yet he could not stake a sure claim to England honours, so keen was competition, so high the standard of batsmanship.

Cecil Parkin's heyday ended before the achievements at Old Trafford of 1926–8. At his best he was the most hostile off-spinner I have ever seen, unplayable on a 'sticky' pitch. His pace through the air was quick, his break from the earth was knife-edged and murderous. Even on a flawless turf he could turn the ball back; but under the then existing lbw rule batsmen were free to save their wickets by putting their pads in front if the ball had pitched outside the off-stump. One day at Worcester on a lawn of green silk, Parkin time after time beat the bat by beautiful spin. And each master ball was frustrated by dull-thudding pads. At the end of the hot day Parkin showed me his bowling analysis—30 overs, 92 runs, one wicket. 'And,' he said, 'they send missionaries to China!' I believe

168

that his ashes were scattered over the playing pitch at Old Trafford, and that on each anniversary of his death his lovable Lancashire wife placed a red rose at each end of the pitch. He was original, vital, dark-skinned, and upright. He walked to his bowling mark tossing his black hair; then he swung round, ducked, and with a great cartwheel action let loose the spin. On a good day he accompanied his bowling by his own singing—popular melodies of the period, generally about the sky is 'blew and I love yew—how's zat?' His energy shot out in spring-heel darlings, in angular flashes, in sudden waves of curving physical grace. As the sun burnished his raven head, it was hard to believe that such gusto ever would be exhausted or become ineffectual or old.

Lancashire professionals of this period talked cricket at nights after a match; they would sit for hours matching plot with plot, craftsman's secret with craftsman's secret. At eleven o'clock the 'skipper' would order 'one more for the road.' 'Noa,' Richard Tyldesley would say. 'Noa, thanks, skipper . . . well, maybe . . . half a pint . . . just half a pint . . . well . . . oh, tha might as well mek it a pint.' The Lancashire soil was in these men and pervasive. It got into the skin of Macdonald, an Australian ('A Tasmanian,' Emmott Robinson called him, as though to worsen still Lancashire's practice of playing an Australian). The Lancashire stuff is not worked out, I hope, or diluted today. There is Washbrook still as dominating as MacLaren himself. There is Statham honouring the fast bowling tradition established by Mold, Brearley, Sharp, and Macdonald. There is Hilton, as Lancashire as Eddie Paynter himself, who was as great a Lancashire lad and player as any. And we have only to look at Tattersall to know that we are at, and of Old Trafford, bone of Lancashire's bone. The ground is full of ghosts. No cricket field has known greater players, greater games, rain or shine. Not the least of Old Trafford's distinctions is that W. G. Grace was unable to score a century there; he scored centuries everywhere else. The Lancashire (or the Australian) bowling was too good for him.

In my own active membership of Old Trafford, I was lucky to have on the committee hosts as generous as Sir Edwin Stockton, O. P. Lancashire, T. A. Higson, Myles Kenyon, and J. C. Fallows. They made Old Trafford a happy place to go to and live in, summer by summer. There was William Howard, too, the dressing-room attendant, and—by no means least—the old man at the gate of the members' entrance in Warwick Road. In the year of Old Trafford's centenary let all these servants of the club be remembered and appropriately saluted.

TEST MATCHES

ENGLAND *v* AUSTRALIA

1926

PICKING THE TEST TEAM

MOST of us have picked our 'England XI's' by now, and, like the novices we are at the job, we have done it all in 'high priori' fashion, backing our favourites—hero-worship making us sometimes forget that an England team must achieve a balance of parts, with each cricketer more or less a foil in character and technique to somebody else.

For example: enthusiastic and self-appointed 'selection committees' throughout the country are anxious that Tate, Macaulay, and Root should all bowl for England at Trent Bridge next Saturday but one. The case for each of these cricketers is, of course, excellent. But though the three of them seem to make an excellent attack in the abstract, actual practice might easily find Macaulay, Root, and Tate getting in one another's way. Here we have three bowlers who are at their most dangerous with a new ball; plainly, they cannot *all* be asked to attack at the game's beginning and when the 200 has been reached. And three seam-bowlers on the same side means (on a hard wicket) three bowlers who are not certain to bowl deadly stuff with the 'old' ball. Tate attacks keenly throughout the longest day, on the hardest ground; nonetheless, experience has not infrequently found him losing something of venom bit by bit as the seam of the ball gets flatter and flatter. Macaulay is not consistently dangerous on a batsman's pitch with the old ball; nor is Root. Our amateur selector does not keep these technical points in mind; the authentic Selection Committee, let us trust, is hardly likely to overlook them.

The England XI for the Trial match at Lord's on Saturday will depend for bowling mainly on Tate, Macaulay, G. O. Allen, and Kilner. Three of these cricketers 'prefer' the new ball. Kilner is the one bowler on the side that commands finger spin. This, of course, will not do. The Australian batsmen have been nurtured on fastish straight stuff; England must try and find bowlers capable of breaking the ball *away* from the bats of Messrs. Ponsford, Woodfull, Ryder, Andrews, and Richardson.

170

Tate and Macaulay to bowl while the ball's seam and 'shine' are there—no cricketer will challenge this choice. What of the bowlers for the 'old' ball, which, of course, must occasionally be turned? Ah, these fashions in bowling! A few years ago Wainwright, the old Yorkshire cricketer, used to say to me, 'Rub t' ball on t' ground and get t' slippiness off'n it—else you can't grip it and spin it.' Nowadays swerve is the rage; bowlers rub the ball on their arms and seek to keep 't' slippiness' on. Hence, by the way, the decline in spin-stuff on good wickets. Kilner 'picks himself' as a spin bowler—not to mention his courageous batting, quick fielding, and Yorkshire spirit. On a 'sticky' pitch Kilner and Macaulay would, I imagine, get Australia out as cheaply as any other admixture of bowling in presentday English cricket. We must not put too much faith, though, in a 'sticky' wicket as an ally of England; Australia might bat (such is the fortune of war) while the turf was easy, and England while it was difficult! Macartney and Arthur Richardson, so rumour has whispered, can both spin a cricket ball to some purpose.

England's best all-round attack for this country—in weather of all sorts—would probably be: Tate, Macaulay, Kilner, Fender or Stevens, with Woolley to lend a hand the very moment Australia's score got beyond 357 for two wickets. It is not a fearsome attack on paper, I admit. Where will you find a better—keeping in view the various technical ends that must be attended to in modern English cricket? Time was when we had bowlers like Arnold, Relf, and Barnes, who were able to make the best of the new ball by their 'swerves' and 'swingers', and then, with the polish gone and the seam flat as a fluke, change methods and bowl beautiful breakbacks or leg-spinners pitched on the middle stump. Today we cannot boast a single great medium-paced spin bowler—for a hard turf. Cricketers have allowed the old mysteries of break go hang—all for the trick of swerving. And, as we can find out any day by watching a game from a place behind the bowler's arm, there are not more than three bowlers in England who have the power to make a ball swerve once the seam has been worn down. That is to say, the traditional wheezes of break (I am still writing of hard-wicket bowling) which served the uses of, say, J. T. Hearne throughout the hottest day— these reliable wheezes have been neglected in order that medium-paced bowlers might give the ball a swerve for half an hour after a match has started and for half an hour after the 200 has gone up!

It is the English bowling problem which is the Selection Committee's chief anxiety. Hobbs, Sutcliffe, Hendren, Carr, Woolley, Chapman, and Fender or Stevens ought, against Collins's moderate attack, to get runs enough. It is Australia's batting we have to defeat within three days. If we were somehow able to unearth three or four bowlers clever enough to get Australia out for round about 250, it would not matter much if all of these bowlers were 'rabbits'. A total of 400 or 500 is not wanted in England, as usually it is in Australia. In England bowling and fielding win Test matches—in Australia batting and fielding. England's batsmen today could afford to 'carry a tail' if that 'tail' were Tom Richardson and J. T. Hearne.

No cricketer in the country really believes we shall prove equal to the task of bowling out Australia twice within three fine days for convenient scores. And hope deferred during these many years looks, naturally, to soft wickets for assistance. But even with rain about, are we likely to get 'sticky' pitches in the Tests? Are not the groundsmen at Lord's, the Oval, Old Trafford, Leeds, and Trent Bridge day by day tending their green plots with a care (and an amount of 'top dressing') calculated to defy the hottest sun after the heaviest rain? It is rumoured that these most ancient and quiet groundsmen are determined to 'larn' Mr Gregory whether he can 'bump 'em or not'. Well, Collins holds the rubber; he will not object to docile turf on which his batsmen might conceivably feel that Trent Bridge, after all, is not a long way distant from Sydney.

FIRST TEST 1926
Trent Bridge

ENGLAND

A. W. Carr (Notts), captain, A. P. F. Chapman (Kent), J. B. Hobbs (Surrey), H. Strudwick (Surrey), F. E. Woolley (Kent), E. Hendren (Middlesex), M. W. Tate (Sussex), F. Root (Worcestershire), H. Sutcliffe (Yorkshire), J. W. Hearne (Middlesex), R. Kilner (Yorkshire).

AUSTRALIA (selected from).

H. L. Collins (N.S.W), captain, W. Bardsley (N.S.W.), W. M. Woodfull (Victoria), J. M. Taylor (N.S.W.), A. A. Mailey (N.S.W.), C. G. Macartney (N.S.W.), T. J. E. Andrews (N.S.W.), J. Ryder (Victoria), J. M. Gregory (N.S.W.), W. H. Ponsford (Victoria), A. J. Richardson (South Australia), W. A. Oldfield (N.S.W.), G. V. Grimmett (South Australia), S. C. Everett (N.S.W.), J. L. Ellis (Victoria).

Sensible cricketers never prophesy; before the event they will tell you only what ought to happen. But poetic justice is not infrequently abused in this world. Besides, it would be hard to say which team deserves most to win the first Test match. There is little to choose between the two, either in skill or style. England, perhaps, can boast the finer individual talent; Australia, though, will show us what the musicians call ensemble.

At the moment of writing, rain is in the wind. Many folk of this country no doubt will expect as a matter of course an England victory on a bowler's pitch. Cricketers themselves do not hold this expectation unanimously. A wettish turf at Trent Bridge will take much of the sting out of Tate's attack. With rain about, Macartney and Richardson might easily prove deadlier bowlers than Kilner and Woolley. Why did our Selection Committee not choose another 'sticky' wicket bowler—Rhodes, for example—as twelfth man, and call upon him during rainy weather in place, say, of Hearne?

If Tate is England's main hope as far as match-winning goes, then we must pray for a fast Trent Bridge wicket. Tate likes to find 'bounce' in the earth. Root depends for his wickets on a cross-wind or on some heaviness of atmosphere, rather than on the state of the pitch. If he can bowl at Nottingham as he bowled last week at Birmingham—and if the Australians bat against him as absurdly as they did then—well, we shall beat Australia easily enough. But what mighty 'Ifs' these are! I am hopeful about Root, though. The Australians will need to be clever indeed if they are to learn in time the technique usually demanded from batsmen face to face with Root's extraordinary leg swerve. But if Root is unable to bowl his best this time, and if the Trent Bridge wicket is of easy pace, Tate and Kilner will likely enough pass through very hard labour! Against Australian batsmen that are in form, Hearne and Woolley, can scarcely be troublesome—unless both of them discover at the same moment a spin and length which neither has known in Test matches for years and years.

The English batting is strong 'on paper'—it has usually been strong 'on paper' since 1920. I look to Carr to put toughness into the side's 'psychology'; I look also to a violent assault on Australia's bowling by Hobbs, Woolley, Chapman, and Carr, our forcing batsmen. Little use will be done to English cricket just now by drawn Test matches; they will, indeed, play into Collins's hands. If we cannot beat the Australians this summer, our next opportunity will not come until the Australians are in this country again. English cricket is not at the moment breeding the class of cricketer capable of overthrowing the Australians in Australia.

Friday evening in Nottingham, so far, has been sunny and full of wind. The Trent Bridge wicket is in beautiful condition, and of course the groundsman has, since noon, had the option of covering his masterpiece in marl—a stretch of authentic Nottingham marl

173

which was first planted in November last. The game is likely to begin, therefore, with the conditions in favour of the batsman, and as the weather during the next few days is expected to prove unsettled, the act of tossing for innings tomorrow morning will be fateful indeed. It is surely rather scandalous that these great matches should in this country be frequently at the mercy of the weather. The chances are more often than not in any summer against three days of uninterrupted cricket. For this reason alone it is unfortunate that Mr Warner's plan of a four days' Test was not adopted for this year. Nobody wishes to see Test cricket in England drawn out to the unheavenly length known in Australia. In the driest season here four days would usually bring a decision. One wet day under the present time limit almost certainly means a barren engagement—especially as sticky wickets do not often occur in this period of over-dressed pitches. I am not arguing in favour of Australian cricket conditions with their disregard of the clock; a four-day Test in this country would still do justice to time as a protagonist. Yet with four days for action the chances would always tend to favour a decision. Our whole attitude to a Test match, our imaginative sense of the event, would be quickened if we could think as we looked at the play that one side or other was doomed to bite the dust. Drama with its relentless inevitability would be on the field always; no escape for one opponent!

FIRST TEST 1926
1st Day, Trent Bridge

ENGLAND
First Innings

Hobbs, not out	19
Sutcliffe, not out	13
	—
Total (for 0)	32

A. W. Carr, A. P. F. Chapman, Strudwick, Woolley (F. E.), Hendren, Hearne, Kilner, (R.), Tate, and Root to bat.

AUSTRALIA: H. L. Collins, W. Bardsley, C. G. Macartney, J. M. Taylor, T. J. B. Andrews, W. M. Woodfull, J. Ryder, J. M. Gregory, A. J. Richardson, W. A. Oldfield, and A. A. Mailey.

NOTTINGHAM, SATURDAY

Fifty minutes of cricket was our brief portion at Trent Bridge on Saturday; then thunder-rain flooded the field, at one o'clock. We waited miserably till a quarter to six, moist, unpleasant bodies the lot of us. The postponement would possibly have come sooner than this had the umpires been sole judges of the wicket's condition.

But upon the latter point, more anon, as the old-time writers pleasantly used to say.

Showers delayed the game's beginning till ten minutes past twelve. A vast service was performed to his side by Carr when he won the toss. Much absurd chatter has gone round this land about Gilligan's bad luck with 'the spin of the coin' in Australia. But, of course, tossing for innings is in this country a much more 'influential' business than ever it is in Australia. The loss of the toss at Sydney rarely, if ever, means a certain ruined wicket for the side that does not bat first; in England it frequently does—and Saturday at Trent Bridge might well prove a case in point in the long run. At any rate, England had choice of innings on as perfect a stretch of turf as a batsman could wish to discover even at Trent Bridge; today the Australians may find themselves compelled to bat on a wicket with its top knocked about considerably. In that event the Australians will have real cause for bewailing the luck of the toss. Yet I doubt if they will make as much hubbub about it all as most of us did over here during the last English tour in the land of perfect and almost imperishable turf.

Saturday's scant cricket was, frankly, far below Test match class. The Australians were handicapped by a greasy ball. Even Gregory could not make his bowling come to the bat with any killing energy; and Macartney's left-hand, over-the-wicket stuff was obviously gentle as a lamb. A sorry commentary on Australia's attack this year that Macartney—the period's rarest genius amongst batsmen—should at his time of life have been at the necessity of relearning his bowling. He went about his work in much seriousness on Saturday; his field included a mid-on, three men close in on the leg side, one slip, a backward point, a cover, a mid-off, and one man in the deep—almost 'straight'. As I say, Macartney bowled over the wicket to one slip only—sure sign, this, that his spin (if any) was not biting on the docile earth. There was something comical about this little man's way of attacking Hobbs and Sutcliffe; he bowled with a suggestion of cynicism in his easy action, as though he were saying 'Well, if I must bowl, I must. But remember, you've also got to bat, my son. Centuries are more in your line. Go easy then, Charles— they won't hit you yet; it isn't done at the beginning of a Test match.' And really 'it' isn't—at least it wasn't on Saturday. Many balls from Macartney lost pace after pitching; they seemed to humble themselves before the bats of Hobbs and Sutcliffe, as if to say: 'O mighty cricketers of England; glorify us by letting us serve your greatness. Here we bow before your will; we petition that in all

175

your wonderful sovereignty you do us the honour of hitting us to the boundary for the good of England.'

Unfortunately Hobbs was not wearing his imperial purple just now. He batted skilfully, of course, but he seemed more desirous of pushing and gliding the ball gently here and there and running short runs than of letting us see his bat turn into a royal rod of punishment. Sutcliffe, too, was circumspect and modest in his strokes. Still, I will not join in the criticism directed at him by many good judges of the game who held that he ought to have attacked Macartney's doubtful length violently. It must be remembered that Sutcliffe was not feeling too confident about his muscular fitness; he had to move cautiously for a while. I objected, for this reason, to Hobbs's quick dashes for stolen runs. On the rather slippery turf, with his partner a batsman who only the other day was suffering from physical hurt. Hobbs might for a while have denied himself what no doubt is a rare pleasure—for he runs his short ones with palpable enjoyment. In Saturday's fifty minutes of activity, only three boundaries were hit—two from no-balls. The length of these no-balls was not, as far as I could see, different from the length of many 'legal' balls which were treated respectfully. Today, let us hope, Hobbs will serve each ball he plays strictly according to its merits. I trust, too, that when the first English wicket has fallen Woolley or Carr will be sent forth to bat. England must get quick runs—especially if there should be the chance of a bowler's wicket towards the fall of the afternoon. Had MacLaren and Spooner batted on Saturday, England would have scored sixty runs at least. This is not a mere idealistic speculation; it is an inference drawn from countless demonstrations given us in the past by these two unforgettable batsmen (against far better bowling than that of the present Australian XI) of how to force the pace on an easy pitch at the outset of a match. I saw Spooner at Trent Bridge on Saturday, and as I did so I thought of an afternoon that happened on this old field many years ago, when Spooner drove past cover with a brilliance that seemed to send ripples of light over the grass. Also I saw MacLaren during the afternoon—poised in magnificence on the pavilion balcony, apparently illustrating a stroke, and telling somebody the way to do it in high Roman fashion.

Gregory bowled eight overs for eighteen runs; then Collins rested him for Richardson. The turf was against fast bowling, yet Gregory hurled all of his fine strength into his attack, ran his old run of menace to the wicket, leaped the old leap of energy. The action is rather laboured now and the pace definitely less formidable than it was in 1921, not only from the ground (which, of course, alters in speed from day to day according to the weather, but also through the air. Nonetheless, I shall look for wickets coming Gregory's way in summer weather. His field, as he began his action on Saturday, was: Ryder, Mailey, Woodfull, Collins, slips; Taylor, third man; Andrews, cover; Macartney, mid-off; Bardsley, fine leg; and Richardson, forward leg. He moved Collins from slip to short leg after bowling three overs—an indication that he was able to make the ball 'come back' at times. It was a break-back by Gregory indeed that once troubled Hobbs and caused the master, after countering the ball, to walk down the pitch and look very closely at it for a while. The best hit of the morning was an off-drive by Sutcliffe from Macartney—a stroke of beautiful poise and ease. Sutcliffe also got a boundary by a gentle forward push-stroke which travelled straight past the bowler through an outfield vacant of men.

The patience of the crowd throughout the long wait in the afternoon was admirable. A little banter hailed the two captains as they inspected the pitch at five o'clock, and again at a quarter to six. This time Carr and Collins presumably could not agree. Carr naturally must have wished to make all possible use of conditions favourable for quick runs; Collins just as naturally must have wished to spare his bowlers, as far as he legally could, from the hardships of a slippery ball. So the captains walked up and down the pitch, and, to all appearances, made the question one of fine argu-able shades. At last the umpires were consulted; they, without hesitation, abandoned play for the afternoon. All of which was significant of much concerning the rule which reads: 'The two captains shall decide as to the fitness of the wicket for play. If they disagree the decision of the two umpires shall be final'. This rule was drawn up by the Board of Control for Test matches. It goes counter to the forty-third of the Laws of Cricket, as controlled by the M.C.C. This law says: 'The umpires are the sole judges of the fitness of the ground'. Moreover, the M.C.C.'s instructions to umpires contain this passage: 'In case of interruption from rain . . . the umpires shall inspect the wicket, unaccompanied by any of the players. . . .' I think rule 43 of the Laws of Cricket, and this instruc-tion of the M.C.C. to umpires for ordinary first-class cricket ought to apply in Test matches. The Board of Control's rule which gives the captains a voice in the question of the condition of a pitch might frequently mean that Test captains, consciously or unconsciously, will tend to let the job of ground inspection become part of their general strategy. The most sportsmanlike cricket captain is, when all is said and done, bound to be a partisan; the umpires are not. Carr and Collins could not arrive at an agreement on Saturday upon a point which was settled by the umpires after a very summary glance at the turf. When Chester and Burrows called the afternoon 'off', all the logic-chopping of Carr and Collins was rather reduced to absurdity, and as I saw Chester wave his hand decisively, murmured, 'A Daniel come to judgment; yea, a Daniel!'

FIRST TEST
2nd Day, Trent Bridge

ENGLAND
First Innings

Hobbs, not out	19
Sutcliffe, not out	13
	—
Total (for 0)	32

A. W. Carr, A. P. F. Chapman, Strudwick, Woolley (F. E.), Hendren, Hearne, Kilner (R.), Tate, and Root to bat.

AUSTRALIA: H. L. Collins, W. Bardsley, C. G. Macartney, J. M. Taylor, T. J. E. Andrews, W. M. Woodfull, J. Ryder, J. M. Gregory, A. J. Richardson, W. A. Oldfield, and A. A. Mailey.

NOTTINGHAM, MONDAY

There was never the faintest chance for cricket today. Rain fell in torrents all morning and did not stop till after three o'clock. The ground is now in a pitiful state, and unless we have tomorrow miracles of bowling and fine weather the first Test will go to an unmourned end. One wet day out of three is, of course, enough to render any English Test match sterile.

In the olden times rainy weather often meant a sticky wicket: for that reason great games have been known to reach a thrilling decision after a blank day. But groundsmen of our period do their job so well that bowlers' pitches rarely happen even when the sun is shining on sodden turf. Cricketers must agitate for the four-day Test match, or for some limitation to the groundsman's art. As things stand at present fine weather means a wicket so perfect that high-class batting teams cannot be got out twice within three days. And in a rainy season one blank day means an almost certain draw.

Whatever the weather, dry or wet, the chances in this country now are definitely against a finished Test match of only three days' length. I am not arguing for Test cricket without a time limit; the clock must, for the good of the English game, continue as the enemy of slow batting. The four days' Test match would provide scope for a result in fine weather, and would also provide some sort of insurance against the one wet day in every three which has come to be the common lot amongst cricketers of our green and pleasant land.

FIRST TEST
3rd Day, Trent Bridge

ENGLAND
First Innings

Hobbs, not out		19
Sutcliffe, not out		13
Total (for 0)		32

BOWLING ANALYSIS
ENGLAND—First Innings

	O.	M.	R.	W.		O.	M.	R.	W.
Gregory	8	1	18	0	Richardson	1	1	0	0
Macartney	8·2	2	14	0					

A. W. Carr, A. P. F. Chapman, Strudwick, Woolley (F. E.), Hendren, Hearne, Kilner (R.), Tate, and Root to bat.

AUSTRALIA: H. L. Collins, W. Bardsley, C. G. Macartney, J. M. Taylor, T. J. E. Andrews, W. M. Woodfull, J. Ryder, J. M. Gregory, A. J. Richardson, W. A. Oldfield, and A. A. Mailey.

There was so much rain at Nottingham on Monday and during the night that there was no possible chance of play in the Test match being resumed. The captains were the only members of the teams who took the trouble to go to Trent Bridge, and they at once agreed to abandon the game in which there had been only 50 minutes' play.

SECOND TEST 1926
1st Day, Lord's

AUSTRALIA
First Innings

H. L. Collins, b Root	1
W. Bardsley, not out	173
C. G. Macartney, c Sutcliffe, b Larwood	39
W. M. Woodfull, c Strudwick, b Root	13
T. J. E. Andrews, c and b Kilner	10
J. M. Gregory, b Larwood	7
J. M. Taylor, c Carr, b Tate	9
A. J. Richardson, b Kilner	35
J. Ryder, c Strudwick, b Tate	28
Extras (b 11, lb 12)	23
Total (for 8 wickets)	338

W. A. Oldfield and A. A. Mailey to bat.

Fall of the wickets:

1	2	8	4	5	6	7	8
11	84	127	158	187	208	282	338

ENGLAND: A. W. Carr, A. P. F. Chapman, Hobbs, Sutcliffe, Woolley, Hendren, Kilner, Larwood, Tate, Root, and Strudwick.

LONDON, SATURDAY

Today at Lord's was full of summer sunshine, and the waters of Trent Bridge were forgotten. We have seen England and Australia in action again with Lord's in a June light.

Collins won the toss—a misfortune for this country, not only because Australia batted first on a perfect wicket, but also because Collins's accurate guess at the coin's spin will perpetuate that horrible term 'Horseshoe Collins'—language more in keeping with Newmarket than Lord's. At half-past eleven the conflict began. Our eyes were all for Root. Strong, silent men on the pavilion cast out of their minds for a while their indignation against Mr Cook and asked themselves: 'Will Root do it again?' For a brief space it seemed that he would. His seventh ball did not swerve to leg, as Collins imagined it would, but travelled straight through and uprooted the leg stump. Collins did not attempt an authentic stroke at this deceitful ball. He stood with his bat on high and was wholly 'circumwented', to use Sam Weller's graphic term. Collins is at most times a man of a grave, not to say mournful, aspect. On Saturday he actually smiled after his wicket fell, and as he walked back to the pavilion he was, no doubt, the most merciless satirist on the ground of his gullibility. This ball of Root's which 'straightens' itself is almost a leg-break, though its angle is not acute.

As Macartney went out to join Bardsley. I had a feeling that the next few overs by Root would be crucial—perhaps even decisive. If he could exploit still further the mood of indecision which he must by now have provoked in the Australian psychology—well, the match would be ours. On the pavilion balcony the Australians watched Macartney and Bardsley with eyes which were very pin-points of attention and concern. Possibly apprehensions came in crowds to their breasts. Root strove manfully to jump to his opportunity. Even Macartney watched his swerve like a man in the presence of a perilous ambush. Round his leg side crouched Sutcliffe, Hendren, Chapman, and Carr, holding out hands as though in supplication. Bardsley, being a left-handed batsman, did not, of course, find in Root's attack a problem as difficult as that which Macartney had to tackle. Root's swerve 'goes away' from

180

Bardsley and not at all dangerously, it even favours a late cut. Macartney was clever at forcing Root through the leg trap by means of a wrist stroke. Yet he was clearly unwilling to risk an offensive hit against Root—and it is not every bowler who is able to turn Macartney's bat into a door bolted against unknown peril.

Bardsley and Macartney both played excellent cricket, circumspect but cool. The score reached the thirties, and then, I thought, Carr made a mistake. He took Root off after Root had bowled seven overs for six singles, two twos, and a wicket. As Root went out of action so early in the day, I fancied a sigh of relief was to be heard in the ranks of Australia. Surely it would have been good 'psychology' to keep Root bowling a little longer than this. His asset now was the Australians' uncertainty about the correct way to counter him—an uncertainty that had been intensified by the quick overthrow of Collins. Carr 'rested' Root before Macartney and Bardsley had played themselves in; when he was asked to bowl again fifty minutes afterwards the Australians had contrived to pull the game round, and could face Root with some runs behind them to 'work upon'. Macartney and Bardsley found nothing strange in the attack of Larwood, Tate, and Kilner. Here was good but conventional bowling. Root was picked to play for England less for any self-sufficient technical points in his bowling than for the potentialities in his peculiar strategy. This strategy thrives on indecision in the minds of batsmen who are not acquainted over much with the leg-swerve.

Even Macartney, the world's most resourceful batsman, had not quite played himself out of indecision against Root when Carr asked Larwood to bowl instead of Root. Not once again, all Saturday, did Root attack with quite the air of confidence he let us see in his first few overs. The spell was broken after that.

From Larwood's first four overs 24 runs were hit, including a brilliant cut and an on-side push by Macartney, both strokes glowing with the polish of wrist action. Root could not get the quick pace or the sharp rise from the turf that he got at Birmingham, consequently the batsmen were at liberty to strike late at his leg-swinger, get over the ball, and play it to the ground. At Birmingham Root's sharp and forceful angle from the pitch made a purely defensive stroke 'carry' the ball to the leg-trap. That 'extra' nip gave at Birmingham to the most passive stroke energy enough to send a catch to the encircling fieldsmen. Granted the right wicket, I am confident Root would yet again upset the Australians considerably.

Macartney and Bardsley scored 73 for the Australian second wicket in 75 minutes. Then Macartney flashed a daring bat at an off-side ball and got himself out, caught in the slips. This little innings of Macartney's was delightful to watch. The game's critical condition caused Macartney to curb his customary tantrums, yet now and again the inveterate and lovable imp of mischief in the man would peep out, and then a swift, lawless hit would astonish decorum. Macartney was not Figaro this time, but, rather, Till Eulenspiegel under the eye of old, dignified law. In the solemn occasion the excellent rogue tried hard to be on his best behaviour, but the abandoned nature of him came out from here and there in some almost furtive piece of impropriety with a gay cross-bat. Bardsley and Macartney are a picture of dignity and impudence at the wicket. Bardsley's batsmanship has that serene contentment with formal beauty which marks the classic style. Macartney enchants us with the 'wild civility' which is more bewitching than art that is too precise in every part. Not that Bardsley's innings was flawless on Saturday; it had its loosenesses of execution and touch, but in mood it was the work of a ripe master who is satisfied with the craftsmanship taught by the ancient schools.

At lunch Australia were 112 for two, Bardsley not out 52. Henceforward to the long day's fall. Bardsley alone batted in the Test match manner. Woodfull fell to a fine catch at the wicket low down on the earth from a glance to leg. The leg-glance is a useless stroke against Root; you must either leave his leg-swinger alone or force it through the field with the bat's full face. Andrews never settled down, and got out ignominiously. He hit at the pitch of a ball from Kilner and gave a return catch that was dropped. From the very next ball, which had a slightly shorter length, he attempted exactly the same rash stroke and sent another catch to Kilner, who did not fumble again. As Kilner gripped his catch and so retrieved a blunder his Yorkshire smile said plainly enough, 'Who'd 'a thought it?' Gregory, fifth out at 187, tried to smite a half-volley into the pavilion, and somehow hit over and across the ball. Whenever Gregory makes a big score in high-class company it is less a success of technique than a vindication of his native and almost untutored genius for hard hitting. Taylor also failed; he is completely out of luck's way. He showed his quality in a dramatic hook to square leg from a no-ball—easily the greatest stroke of the afternoon. Then he ran into the one and only deadly ball which Tate bowled all day. It pitched on the leg stump, whipped across, and rose sharply at the last second. Only a good batsman could have 'found contact' at all with this ball. Taylor returned sorrowfully to the pavilion—no doubt with visions of his achievements in Australia mocking him. He cannot do the right thing here this season.

With six Australians out for 208, England were making a handsome advance. And with the new ball in action and Tate using it we had momentary hopes of an Australian collapse. Unhappily, Tate was out of form; his bowling rarely 'fizzed' from the turf as usually it does. Richardson and Bardsley played a canny game for eighty minutes and added 74 for the seventh wicket. There was merit in the way Richardson changed from his customary boisterous game and acted the part of cool, correct defence. Kilner bowled him with a delicious break which pitched on his leg stump and hit the middle of the off wicket. Ryder scarcely exploited the tactics needed to put Australia in a winning position. Bardsley now was too tired to hit hard, and the English bowling had a weary air. Ryder batted half an hour for his first nine runs, and when he did at length bestir himself Australia's pace of scoring had fallen a little behind the clock. In the afternoon's last hundred minutes not more than 89 runs came to Australia. This, of course, was not match-winning batsmanship.

Bardsley's innings persisted to the finish. He gave chances to my knowledge at 112 and 139, both to Strudwick. The beginning of his cricket was indeterminate; many of his earlier strokes through the slips were dubious. He started his day's work like a cricketer who was uncertain whether or not he was in form. Clever slip fielding or clever wicketkeeping might well have caught him out before he reached twenty. His innings for a while reminded me of the artist in 'Don Quixote', who, when asked what animal he was painting, replied diffidently, 'That is as it may turn out.' Not until after lunch did Bardsley seem certain of his touch. But between lunch and tea his cricket was stately and assured; his caseful mastery caused the failures of his companions to seem a little incredible, for Bardsley never let the English attack trouble him in the slightest. The one or two chances he gave were like faint scratches or flaws on the cool marble of a great innings. He was always responsible for a half at least of his side's total. He made his first 50 out of 108, his century out of 189, his 150 out of 287. So far his innings has lasted four hours and 50 minutes. A third of his runs have come from delicate leg glances, another third from effortless push drives between cover and mid-off.

On paper it might seem that the English bowlers maintained a high-class attack. The truth is they were flattered by batting which was scarcely worthy of Australia's reputation—excepting the innings of Macartney and Bardsley. Tate, Larwood, and Root all depend too much on the new ball; once the seam and gloss had been knocked away their work was without resourceful variations either of break, pace, or flight. Kilner was our only imaginative bowler; he was the solitary man who seemed to work on a plan and give to the 'old' ball an amount of artifice in the shape of spin. England's fielding had its brilliant periods, but Root, Larwood, and Woolley are not exactly fieldsmen of Test match ability. Strudwick had a bad day.

SECOND TEST 1926
2nd Day, Lord's

AUSTRALIA
First Innings

H. L. Collins, b Root	1
W. Bardsley, not out	193
C. G. Macartney, c Sutcliffe, b Larwood	39
W. M. Woodfull, c Strudwick, b Root	13
T. J. E. Andrews, c and b Kilner	10
J. M. Gregory, b Larwood	7
J. M. Taylor, c Carr, b Tate	9
A. J. Richardson, b Kilner	35
J. Ryder, c Strudwick, b Tate	28
W. A. Oldfield, c Sutcliffe, b Kilner	19
A. A. Mailey, lbw b Kilner	1
Extras (b 12, lb 16)	28
Total	383

ENGLAND
First Innings

Hobbs, c Richardson, b Macartney	119
Sutcliffe, b Richardson	82
Woolley, not out	50
Hendren, not out	42
Extras (b 3, nb 1)	4
Total (for 2 wickets)	297

Fall of the wickets:
Australia.—First Innings

1	2	3	4	5	6	7	8	9	10
11	84	127	158	187	208	282	338	379	383

England.—First Innings

1	2
182	219

There was a slight mishap at the beginning of this lovely June morning. From some cause or other a hose-pipe was left running its water. An amount of moisture went into the very middle of the Test Match wicket, but the faint damage was done well outside the place where a good ball ought to drop. Near the actual pitch the water needed to be dried by a big stretch of sawdust, and this sprawled unbeautifully over the grass, making the place round about cover-point look like the floor of a butcher's shop. One trembles to think of the consequences had this hose soaked the pitch in the bowler's danger-zone. There would have been work for a Star Chamber, surely.

When the match went on at eleven o'clock it quickly suffered two interruptions. First we had some bother about the ball, and another was used (though not a new one) after a solemn consultation between Carr and the umpires during which the damaged ball was closely looked at and held up in the air for scrutiny as though it were an egg of doubtful quality. Then the game came to a short interval while Bardsley went into the pavilion to get attention to his right hand after it had received a painful though not lasting hurt. The rhythm of the cricket was thus broken until the time of day came to fifteen minutes past eleven. Meanwhile the crowd grew bigger and bigger and the sun shone a more and more ample warmth. This was a morning on which it was excellent to be alive and a cricketer. Mid-summer fires were now burning at Lord's; the very air of the place was sweet with the game's seasonal flavour. As the match fell from time to time into those delicious silences which come over a cricket field on a summer day you might well have heard history beating her wings—for at Lord's tradition is a living presence; the great old days of cricket mingle here with the new days; time is at a rest in this cricketers' heaven, the past and the present come to a meeting-place at historic, nay, legendary Lord's.

Bardsley and Oldfield lifted the Australian score to 370, and then Oldfield struck at a ludicrously high full-toss which plainly slipped out of Kilner's hand. It was caught on the leg-side—an inglorious end to as stylish an innings as one could wish to see. Oldfield is a batsman of true culture; his strokes are refined, handsome, and strong. With Mailey in, last man, Bardsley's total stood at 190. Mailey was quickly out leg before wicket, and Bardsley came back to the pavilion undefeated to the finish. His innings had passed along the processional length of six hours and three-quarters; all the time he had given us play which in every action told us of

Bardsley's accumulated experience, told us of his numberless days in the sun on this and on the other side of the earth.

The English attack was keen but not deadly. Again Kilner seemed to be the only bowler able to spin the ball and order his flight through the air changefully and thoughtfully. And again Tate's nip from the pitch was missing—without that he is an unresourceful bowler. Carr did not call on Root's swerve at all. Another spin bowler will be needed the next time England plays Australia on a hard ground. Throughout the English fielding was eager and hard-working, with Carr perhaps the most tireless and the most accurate of the lot. To see him chasing a ball to the edge of the field, his head down, his face flushed with determination's heat, his teeth clenched, the whole man flung into the pursuit—here was a sight for the immortals of cricket to see as they sat watching somewhere on high, as sit they must whenever a Test Match goes on at Lord's, which is the Valhalla of cricketers.

The English innings began at twenty minutes past twelve in a brilliant way. Hobbs drove Gregory's first ball—a full toss—to the off for three, the stroke making a violent noise, while Hobbs's action had an almost contemptuous ease, as though to say, 'What rubbish to bowl at me in a Test Match.' Sutcliffe hit the last ball of Gregory's first over also to the off for three, and then cut Macartney sweetly past the left side of point to the boundary. Another boundary was got by a straight drive from Gregory in Hobbs's most majestic manner, and Sutcliffe, with another neat offside stroke, sent a ball of Macartney's to the crowd sitting on the grass near the Mound Stand. Here was the cricket we have all been waiting to see Englishmen show to Australians these many years; the gay light of this batsmanship shot over the field and challenged the radiance of the sun itself. The noise of the busy bats came up to the high press-box like the crackling of a fire ready to burn a gaudy bonfire of runs for England. Gregory quickly passed out of action after bowling five overs for 21 runs. Then, with Mailey and Arthur Richardson in control of the attack, the scoring diminished suddenly in speed and lustre. It was as though some damp fuel had been thrown on our batsmen's fine fires. In 35 minutes we had seen 50 runs hit to all parts of the field; in another 35 minutes only 27 were scored. Sutcliffe batted for half an hour and made four; Richardson bowled ten overs for ten runs. The Australians, so it seemed now, were out to keep the cricket quiet, and so work for a quite sterile draw. With Gregory revealed to them as a spent force the Australians had every reason to feel that at last their Test Match vein of victory had been, as the man in Dickens put it, 'considerably used up'. Mailey's spin had clever moments, and Richardson pitched his old-fashioned offbreaks accurately. But this was a common, every-day county bowling side, and could hope for little more than to 'keep the runs down'. Remembering Armstrong's Attila ride over English batsmanship in 1921, it was almost sad to look upon this helplessness of Collins's bowlers. But the tears live in a crocodile's eyes that should water my sorrow at Australia's puny attack today. I suffered much in 1921 as I saw Gregory and Macdonald rub English batsmanship in the dust; our revenge was won by the Hobbs and Sutcliffe stand this afternoon—at least it was for a while.

After lunch further assault and battery was dealt against the attack of Gregory—though he bowled hard, even passionately. If will-power alone had counted for everything Gregory would have shattered wickets with each ball he hurled down. The day would have been a batsmen's nightmare of spinning wickets. But Gregory's efforts vaulted far beyond his powers of accomplishment; his action was heavy with toil, there was no suppleness in his arm, no killing pace in his attack. He bowled like a man in the face of an impeding wind; five years ago he bowled as though a fierce wind were behind him like a willing ally. As I watched Gregory strive in vain to re-capture his old thunder, as I watched this shadow of Gregory, I thought of the irony that comes to poor mortal man as time passes by him and steals his possessions from him stealthily and lets him discover his loss whenever he may.

I have one serious complaint to make, though, against this heartening first-wicket stand of our own admirable Hobbs and Sutcliffe. They did not increase the rate of scoring in proportion to the steady failing in power of the Australian bowlers. England's first 50 runs came in 35 minutes, the second 50 came in 50 minutes, the third 50 also needed 50 minutes for its making. England's best plan for a snatch at victory depended on runs coming to them at this point of the game with more and more speed as the minutes went by and the Australians became wearier and wearier. I confess that I harboured the wish as the heat burned on the grass at half-past three that Sutcliffe and Hobbs would get out now and make way for Woolley, Chapman, and Carr. Hobbs dawdled needlessly in the nineties; perhaps he was requiring some rest, and Sutcliffe is not a quick scorer either by style or nature. Both men had done superb work for English cricket. Their splendid foundation to the innings was ready for the entrance of really primitive batsmen; they had sown the soil, and surely Woolley or Carr or Chapman, perhaps all three, would reap a quick harvest of boundaries—given a chance before the tea interval brought a breathing space to Collins's faltering bowlers. Hobbs loitered for 45 minutes while his score went from 88 to 97—and all the time runs were at his bat's end if only he would pick them up. This slow movement of Hobbs to his century rather spoiled a worthy innings; England will never beat Australia within three days if her batsmen are going to travel covetously and imperceptibly along the narrow tract that separates a score of ninety from a century. Hobbs got his first 50 runs in 65 minutes; in another three-quarters of an hour he entered his seventies; after that, between three o'clock and twenty past four, he made merely 25—and, as I say, the Australian attack was hereabout in a condition most favourable for a bid for victory by fierce hitting from our batsmen.

Sutcliffe was bowled with England's total 182; the stand lasted three hours and a quarter. Sutcliffe's bat was always making pretty curves, but he does not seem able to take full advantage of the loose ball. Mailey's spin troubled him because he is not mobile of foot. He is rather a statuesque batsman and likes a ball that comes 'straight through'. Hobbs arrived at his century in due course after batting three hours and twenty minutes; his second 50 took him two hours and ten minutes to get—which was not match-winning cricket in the presence of weak bowling. Hobbs, as he played before lunch, would have sent, between lunch and tea, England's score dancing along well towards Australia's total, and then the others could have gone for the Australian attack bald-headed, as they say. In no circumstances ought a great batsman to spend an hour moving from 90 to 100. I cannot imagine that Hobbs idled the opportune period away on the assumption that with more than half of the second day gone a victory by England was not possible. The Test match batsman of the proper faith believes that victory is always possible. It might be argued in extenuation of Hobbs's impolitic inactivity between his 90 and his 100 that Ryder was bowling a little wide to the off-side. This is an extenuation which might save the face of a less accomplished cricketer than Hobbs. We expect our greatest batsman to rise superior to such an old wheeze as off-theory bowling as a device in a team playing for 'keeps'. There is also another reason why Hobbs today should have gone on with his militant cricket before lunch. Whether England can beat Australia within three days is not the only issue to be settled this summer: it is for our batsmen, finished or unfinished matches, to destroy once and for all the notion of Australia's supremacy in cricket of the present time. For too long has Australian bowling had English batsmanship in thrall: the hour is ripe for a complete breaking of the spell cast upon us by Warwick Armstrong. We must not go about the job of breaking this spell tentatively, as though we were apprehensive that it might explode and consume us. It was clear enough this afternoon that the Australians, once they realized their attack was not going to be deadly, worked to the ancient plan of keeping the batsmen quiet. Armstrong, years ago bowled outside the leg stump in a Test match with his field crowded on the leg side. His strategy was that if Australia was unable to win, then England must be prevented from winning. J. T. Tyldesley almost frustrated this cunning by jumping well towards leg and driving Armstrong's attack powerfully through the covers. Hobbs is not a J. T. Tyldesley —and this afternoon England might have passed Australia's 383 had he been a J. T. Tyldesley.

From the purely technical point of view, Hobbs's innings was beyond criticism; he batted just as any man of us breathes and walks —that is, without taking thought of how difficult and intricate a work it was that he was doing all the time. His innings came to an end at half-past five; Richardson caught a low cut, and, having gripped the ball, Richardson ran to Andrews at cover-point and hugged him in his delight at the overthrow of England's master. Hobbs's innings of 119 lasted four hours and five minutes, and he was caught with England's total 219, the second wicket to fall. With Hobbs out of the way Australia lifted up her heart, and at 223 a dazzling throw-in from deep third man almost ran Woolley out. I left the match with a feeling that England had missed an opportunity. Our cricketers put the Australian attack down on the mat at three o'clock, and afterwards did not trample it underfoot for sheer want of imagination. The familiar lesson has been read to us again: our batsmen are not equal to the task of getting quick runs from decent-length bowling. Too readily this day was Collins permitted to instruct his bowlers to pitch the length that connives at the negative policy of 'Never mind the wickets, save the runs'. The humour of this remark resides in the fact that this Australian team is about the weakest in bowling on hard wickets we have ever seen in this country during living memory. The Australian fielding was good on the whole, and Oldfield kept a pretty wicket. The grit and determination of Richardson's bowling in a hot sun was the finest point of all the Australians' heavy labours in the field.

SECOND TEST
3rd Day, Lord's

AUSTRALIA

First Innings	
H. L. Collins, b Root	1
W. Bardsley, not out	193
C. G. Macartney, c Sutcliffe, b Larwood	39
W. M. Woodfull, c Strudwick, b Root	13
T. J. E. Andrews, c and b Kilner	10
J. M. Gregory, b Larwood	7
J. M. Taylor, c Carr, b Tate	9
A. J. Richardson, b Kilner	35
J. Ryder, c Strudwick, b Tate	28
W. A. Oldfield, c Sutcliffe, b Kilner	19
A. A. Mailey, lbw b Kilner	1
Extras (b 12, lb 16)	28
Total	**383**

Second Innings	
H. L. Collins, c Sutcliffe, b Larwood	24
J. M. Gregory, c Sutcliffe, b Root	0
C. G. Macartney, not out	133
T. J. E. Andrews, b Root	9
W. A. Oldfield, c Sutcliffe, b Tate	11
W. M. Woodfull, c Root, b Woolley	0
J. Ryder, not out	0
Extras (b 5, lb 12)	17
Total (for 5 wickets)	**194**

ENGLAND
First Innings

Hobbs, c Richardson, b Macartney	119
Sutcliffe, b Richardson	82
Woolley, lbw b Ryder	87
Hendren, not out	127
Chapman, not out	50
Extras (b 4, lb 4, w 1, nb 1)	10
Total (for 3 wickets)	**475**

Innings declared.

BOWLING ANALYSIS

AUSTRALIA—First Innings

	O.	M.	R.	W.		O.	M.	R.	W.
Tate	50	12	111	2	Larwood	32	2	99	2
Root	36	11	70	2	Woolley	2	0	5	0
Kilner	35·4	11	70	4					

Second Innings

	O.	M.	R.	W.		O.	M.	R.	W.
Tate	25	11	38	1	Larwood	15	3	37	1
Root	19	9	40	2	Woolley	7	1	13	1
Kilner	22	2	49	0					

ENGLAND—First Innings

	O.	M.	R.	W.		O.	M.	R.	W.
Gregory	30	3	125	0	Richardson	48	18	73	1
Macartney	33	8	90	1	Ryder	25	3	70	1
Mailey	30	6	96	0	Collins	2	0	11	0

Fall of the wickets:
Australia.—First Innings

1	2	3	4	5	6	7	8	9
11	84	127	158	187	208	282	338	379

Second Innings

1	2	3	4	5
2	125	163	187	194

England.—First Innings

1	2	3
182	219	359

LORD'S, TUESDAY

In my message yesterday a mistake in telegraphing made me refer to Woolley, Chapman, and Carr as 'primitive' batsmen; the word I used was 'punitive'.

This morning Woolley set about Gregory's bowling in rare match-winning style. Four times in five overs he drove the fast bowler through the covers to the boundary and also cut brilliantly through the slips. The mingled grace and ferocity of Woolley's cricket made me think of the panther on the kill. In quick sequence Woolley hit seven boundaries, two of them crashing drives from Ryder. This was, indeed, batsmanship with the trumpet note of victory in it. Would that Woolley could have 'got at' the Australian bowlers yesterday afternoon after Hobbs and Sutcliffe had laid a splendid base from which to race to a win. Hendren this morning let 25 minutes pass before making a run. Then he played admirably, cutting and driving in his own jolly way, giving us skill and nature excellently blended.

Woolley's beautiful innings finished at ten minutes to twelve; he batted two and three-quarter hours in all and hit 13 fours, many of them bejewelled strokes. Hendren was 63 when Woolley got out at noon. The Australian total was passed amid mighty cheering at twenty minutes after twelve, a superb off-drive by Hendren giving England the lead. Now, I felt certain, we would see some swash-buckling batting from Chapman and Hendren. With only an afternoon left for play and England absolutely safe, with everything to gain and nothing to lose by violent hitting, I expected Chapman and Hendren would hurl their bats at every ball, good, bad, or indifferent. As a fact the cricket proceeded in the style and at the pace we normally get in any match. Hendren reached his first century against

191

Australia at a quarter to one; henceforward until lunch, three-quarters of an hour afterwards, he scored 27. When England over-hauled Australia's 383 for three wickets only, Chapman was eight. He arrived at his fifty some seventy minutes later, but at one period of the morning he played for an hour for 25.

It will be understood that England's rate of scoring was not calculated to thrill the imagination in the circumstances, though the cricket was technically always good. At 11.45 the English total was 350; at 12.30 it was 400; at ten past one it was 450, and at half-past one it was 475. In two hours and a half this morning England, with the game as safe as houses, scored 178—which was merely an excellent speed for any normal period in a game. Credit must, of course, be given to Australia's steady bowlers, especially to Richard-son, whose length was good, but I would have liked to see Hendren and Chapman throw correctitude to the winds altogether. If it were possible to play forward to Richardson and push his bowling away safely for singles almost on the half-volley, might not a resolute jumping drive to the pitch of the ball have brought many a glorious boundary! Still, we must not allow 'what might have beens' to spoil appreciation of what actually has happened in this Test. At long last we have witnessed English batsmen right on top of Australian bowling, playing it in easy spirit, toying with it in fact.

Hobbs by his superb cricket before lunch on Monday raised hopes that a gorgeous hurricane ride of English batsmanship was about to take place. It was his clarion call to vigorous action that caused our sense of anticlimax, as we realized later on that we were looking at high-class batting, but scarcely a 'stampeding' of Collins's respect-able bowling. Up to a point, our cricket, in fact, did put the Aus-tralian attack to rout, and Richardson's length was responsible for the recovery of an Australian steadiness whereby our batsmen were compelled to slacken an advance which for a while gave England some outside prospect of victory. But Richardson's match-saving length was hardly challenged combatively enough by our cricketers once they had made the game safe, and they flattered Ryder's hard-working but commonplace bowling for much too long on Monday.

England reached 383 in a quarter of an hour less than the time spent on this total by Australia, but we must bear in mind that Australia were losing wickets most of the while. Hendren's innings lasted three hours and a half. It was good to see him come at last into his own against Australia. We may look forward now towards seeing the real Hendren in Test cricket—the Hendren who smashed the Yorkshire attack to smithereens a few days ago. Carr declared at lunch 92 to the good, with England's score 54 better than the previous highest in a Test at Lord's.

The Australians had nothing to play for but a draw when they went in again, and Collins was two hours making fourteen. Nonetheless the Australians between lunch and tea scored six runs more than England did in the same period on Monday. Today Australia, a team fighting for a draw, made 113 for one wicket between 2.15 and 4.30—this after losing Gregory's wicket with only one run on the board. On Monday, England between 2.15 and 4.30 made 107 after getting 77 for none before lunch. These figures would be spoiled by comment. Macartney played deliciously, despite Australia's forlorn position. This was proper cricket, true to the spirit of the game. He indulged in no silly risks, he merely did a great batsman's duty by playing every ball strictly on its merits. He made his first 50 in 70 minutes and his century in two hours and three-quarters.

The three-day Tests this year seem doomed to stalemate. Neither side is likely to be good enough in bowling to force a decision on hard wickets. Tate's attack lacked sting this afternoon even as it did on Saturday. The match, indeed, has exposed the limitation of the modern seam-swerver who has cultivated his 'new ball' tricks at the cost of the traditional qualities of spin and flight-variation—qualities which will serve the bowler's purpose throughout the longest day and on any wicket. The match has had few points better worth watching for long than Oldfield's stumping and the fielding of Carr and Taylor. A stroke by Woolley damaged Taylor's hand on the edge of the field. I have rarely seen a ball come with this terrific pace to the boundary. Yet Woolley seemed merely to wave his bat in a nonchalant way.

TEST MATCH AFTERTHOUGHTS

IT was Hobbs's own fault that some of us were rather unkind about his century against Australia at Lord's. He lifted us to the heights of expectancy by a glorious onslaught on Gregory; it looked indeed that he had smitten Collins and his supermen to rout and ruin. Then our greatest batsman, so it seemed to us watching from the edge of the field, let Collins put his valiant batsmanship into chains and, what was more bitter for us to believe, submitted

G 193

without a struggle to the captivity. In an hour he dragged his manacled way from 90 to 100. True is it that Ryder and Richardson bowled a good length. But has it come to this in English Test cricket—that our best batsmen are able to score only from loose bowling! We do not expect to see much loose bowling in a match between England and Australia. The next decent club cricketer is capable of hitting the bad ball. A great batsman has, we expect, the power to score from an attack of some accuracy. Did any bowler ever keep Victor Trumper 'quiet' when he was set on a good wicket —merely by pitching the ball a foot outside his off stump? Or J. T. Tyldesley or George Hirst? Ten runs in an hour, on a hot day, with your side's total 150 for no wicket—here is batsmanship of a sort that it would be impossible to 'explain away' in *any* circumstances of cricket, save those which imperatively call for a deliberate manoeuvre after a draw. England, I trust, was not playing for a draw last Monday afternoon but one, when her innings was regally poised at 150 for none.

Those of us who grumbled at Hobbs were, as Smee would observe, really paying him a handsome compliment. We declined to believe that he was unable to score at a reasonable pace from this Australian bowling. We looked at the easy mastery of his cricket; we felt the enormous reserve power of it all. And we asked 'Why does he play like this in this hour?' Hobbs has told us that he got runs last Monday but one as quickly as he was able. I think he takes too modest a view of his genius. And I am certain he will, in the next Test match, himself provide the strongest criticism of any upon his tactical error at Lord's. Homer nodded, and Hobbs nodded—not to say slumbered deeply—last week at the turning point of the game. There is little cause for lamentation over this lapse from the proper sovereignty of Hobbs. Criticism can do him no important hurt now; we have only to reflect upon his services to English cricket, upon the way this Atlas has supported our world of hopes in cricket these many years—we have but to dwell on these things and we could weep for joy about our Hobbs. Because we hold him fast in our admiration we have a right to be incredulous whenever he falters—as, being human, he must falter at times. At Leeds, let us forget Lord's —'Soonest ended, soonest mended'.

Hobbs perhaps has had to stomach much criticism which some of his colleagues ought to have taken. On Monday, when Hobbs dawdled, England had not exactly got Australia on the mat, though she was half-way there. But on Tuesday morning the occasion called for fierce cricket; England now were 297 for two against Australia's

383 all out. Woolley began the day with cricket that was a challenge to bold action; in spite of his example, only 178 runs were scored in 150 minutes before lunch. And all the time, I take it, Carr was wanting to make a sensible 'declaration'. It may be argued that the match was an almost certain draw on the closing morning, and that some of our batsmen therefore were free not to take the risks the situation gave them leave to take. My answer to this argument would be that, win or draw, it is for English batsmen this year to smite Australian bowling hip and thigh while they have the opportunity. If we cannot defeat Australia within three days let us at least make a valiant gesture. If our batsmen are not going to attack Australian bowling for all they are worth when England's score is 200 for two (or 150 for none) then whenever are they going to attack it? Perhaps one may as well state here that Ryder did not keep the runs down by the device of bowling wide on the off side of the wicket. His length pitched reasonably close to the batsman; a bold thrust of the left foot would have got to the line of the ball. Watching Ryder's attack closely, I came to the conclusion that this was the kind of bowling that I myself used to try to send down at the nets at Shrewsbury School to boys who were anxious to learn how to cut.

Collins's funereal innings at the end of the Lord's Test was only cricket in a rather inglorious conception of the game. A batsman has a right to risk nothing in a 'match-saving' situation. But never, as a cricketer, ought he deliberately to push a ball away unfruitfully which it is in his power safely to hit. Collins once did actually make a boundary during the aeon of his unbeautiful innings—but I fancy he achieved the stroke under protest. The crowd sat through this perverted cricket of Collins with splendid patience, on the whole. There was, of course, much grumbling; but it had a friendly accent. One man in the 'popular' seats even stubbornly defended the Australian captain. "'E's a kerryin' 'is side on 'is shoulders,' said this charitable man. And the more Collins pushed and poked, the more did this vessel of English broad-mindedness seem to find solace in his formula. "'E's a kerryin' 'is side on 'is shoulders.' One of his companions—rather a scoffer, I thought—asked him, 'Wot abaht Macartney—if 'e ken pl'y the gime why kaint Collins?' "'E's a kerryin' 'is side on 'is shoulders,' reiterated Tolerance; 'Wot's more, 'e's the Capting. 'E's the Capting 'e is, and 'e's kerrying' 'is side on 'is shoulders.' Here was appreciation for you of the cares and responsibilities of office. Where else on this earth will you discover the humour, the ample fellowship, that reside in a cricket crowd on a sunny English day?

THIRD TEST MATCH AT LEEDS

AT the moment of writing, the Selection Committee have not invited more than fourteen of our cricketers to be on the spot at Leeds this morning (anybody might think it was going to be a Rugby football match). The chosen men are (I give this list marked 'E. and O.E.', as they say in the offices of Whitworth Street and Portland Street):—

A. W. Carr, A. P. F. Chapman, Hobbs, Sutcliffe, Tate, Hendren, Woolley, Kilner, Root, Strudwick, Larwood, Parker, Macaulay, and Geary.

I wish the Selection Committee would make up their mind once and for all, and pick what they consider to be the best available England XI—with a twelfth man—and then leave it alone and let it play itself into a TEAM, with every man in his place and each fully aware of the style and manner of all the other players. The Yorkshire XI owes much of its success to the fact that it is not chopped about and changed from game to game. Moreover, a cricketer will always show his best form if he knows he is not expected to struggle for his place match after match. An England XI ought not to be selected piecemeal from hour to hour, according to the latest piece of form shown in the latest county engagement. We expect a selection committee to name the England XI on the strength of intimate knowledge of the ability of a player as shown over a long period. Confidence is not inspired by 'last minute' invitations.

I doubt, also, the wisdom of allowing the wicket on the opening morning of a match to have influence on the composition of a side. After all, the weather on a Monday might well be vastly different from the weather on a Saturday morning—the intervention of a Sunday might easily soak or dry a wicket. An England XI ought to be equipped with batsmen and bowlers for all conceivable emergencies; it should, as I say, be carefully chosen and then its members should be given a reasonable chance of 'playing together' and arriving at some balance and cohesion. My own idea of an England side for Leeds is Hobbs, Sutcliffe, Hendren, Woolley, Carr, M. D. Lyon, Kilner, Rhodes, Tate, Macaulay, and Root. Collins's strongest flank is his batting; it is against this that we must take a vigorous offensive. Hobbs, Sutcliffe, Hendren, Woolley, Carr, and Lyon would, I fancy, build a safe foundation of runs from Australia's moderate bowling.

I imagine that nobody in cricket today is more astonished at the selection of Strudwick for Leeds than Strudwick himself. His form at Lord's was that of a wicketkeeper grown much too old for Test cricket. Lyon is a first-class batsman and a tolerably dependable stumper; the choice of a wicketkeeper with ability to bat would open a safe way for another bowler. And the wisdom of playing Rhodes at Leeds will not, I fancy, be argued amongst North-country cricketers. On all wickets he is a better left-handed bowler than Parker and a batsman not yet finished with by a long way.

There may be a softish turf for this match. In that event the Australians might easily give a shock to those cricketers here who imagine a wet wicket would favour England every time. At Lord's we had reason to doubt the quality of the Australian bowling on hard grounds; with venom in the pitch, Arthur Richardson and Macartney would make a really difficult attack. And Macartney and Bardsley might prove the best batsmen in the game against a turning ball.

On a perfect turf Australia's bowling ought not to give Hobbs and the rest too much trouble—though I somehow shiver a little at the name of Grimmett. He 'did it' once, he 'did it' twice, and he might do it again. Still, all things considered, England now have a rare chance of beating Australia. Such another opportunity may not come our way for years and years. Sooner or later, Australian cricket will discover bowlers of proper Test match quality. We are constantly boasting that Hobbs, Hendren, Woolley, and Sutcliffe are great batsmen; let them prove it once and for all at Leeds by thrashing the most moderate Australian attack of recent times. England must take the offensive in batsmanship and bowling alike—drawn matches will play into the Australians' hands. They hold the rubber, and they will be content to hold what they hold. Our batsmen, once they have removed the 'freshness' from the Australian bowling, must get runs speedily, so that our attack may find time in which to win the game. I trust our XI will not go into action with the notion of an 'inevitable draw' in mind. Such a notion would tend to breed dull, unimaginative cricket and have a deadening effect on the 'psychology' of our cricket. Test matches have been won by England within three days in this country many times in the past—against far better Australian XI's than this of today. What *has* happened can happen. Strategy and the will-to-conquer are likely to settle the issue which begins this morning at Leeds. It is true England has never yet won a Test match at Leeds, but this fact ought not to depress our men. There's a first time for everything in the cosmic process.

THIRD TEST 1926
1st Day, Headingley

AUSTRALIA
First Innings

W. Bardsley, c Sutcliffe, b Tate		0
W. M. Woodfull, not out		134
C. G. Macartney, c Hendren, b Macaulay		151
T. J. E. Andrews, lbw b Kilner		4
A. J. Richardson, not out		70
Extras (b 2, lb 2, nb 3)		7
Total (for 3)		366

J. M. Gregory, C. V. Grimmett, A. A. Mailey, W. A. Oldfield, J. Ryder, and J. M. Taylor to bat.

ENGLAND: A. W. Carr, A. P. F. Chapman, Hobbs, Woolley (F. E.), Sutcliffe, Tate, Hendren, Strudwick, Kilner, Macaulay, and Geary.

Fall of the wickets:
AUSTRALIA—First Innings

1	2	3
0	235	249

LEEDS, SATURDAY

Every cricketer in the land knows by now that on Saturday Leeds was a torment of argumentation. 'Why did Carr put Australia in?'

'If he thought the pitch was likely to get difficult, why did he leave out of his side Parker, the best slow left-hand spin bowler at his service?' These questions buzzed in the air of Headingley the afternoon long, but I can see now that they were only so many midges of controversy living their brief, fretful moments in the glorious sunshine of Macartney's batsmanship.

This Test match will be remembered for Macartney's innings long after we have ceased our multitudinous chatterings about the mistakes made by Carr and the Selection Committee. The very result of the game (whichever way the gods may turn round the adamantine spindle) will pass from memory sooner or later, but Macartney's cricket will leave its bright dye stamped there. The game, its chances and results, its ambitions and frustrations, with all our political talk 'about it and about'—all these things are by nature perishable, for they belong to the abstracts and brief chronicles of the time. Macartney's innings was a work of personal art and as much a revelation of man's power to create brave and lovely things as if it had been wrought substantially in poetry, prose, paint, or stone. It was cricket that lifted the match, big as it was, far above the narrow pressure of partisan interests; the crowd at Leeds, though aware that every run made by Macartney was a heavy hindrance to England's chances and, moreover, a sting into the heart of England's captain—nonetheless, every man and woman, boy and girl, amongst us sat willingly under the spell of delight cast by this little wizard of cricketers. And when he broke his spell by getting himself caught, we came out of our enchantment with sorrow enough; we had been seeing visions, dreaming dreams of the great days of cricket—the days when batsmanship like Macartney's was not a miracle of refreshment in a stony desert. Macartney on Saturday let us see again the game as it was played by 'Ranji', J. T. Tyldesley, Spooner, MacLaren, Victor Trumper, R. A. Duff, F. S. Jackson, Kenneth Hutchings—to mention but a few of the artist-batsmen of a single period.

Young sceptics are nowadays constantly crying out, 'O you croaking greybeards; you sentimentalize the past and see old-time mediocrity with eyes that tell beautiful romantic lies.' Well, Macartney at Leeds provided the evidence the 'greybeards' would have chosen in support of their familiar claim that post-war cricket is, compared with pre-war cricket, as sackcloth to silk, stale beer to new wine. If it is objected that Macartney, being a genius, must not be cited as a 'typical' batsman of a given epoch, the answer is that Macartney's school (and spirit) of cricket gave us its personal artists in the score, that even the average everyday batsman of that school (for example, Ernest Hayes) might well loom handsomely against the current background composed of dull standardized batsmen who hold to that negative 'safety-first' philosophy which belongs to the age we live in at the moment.

It was necessary to begin with this tribute, not only because the artist commanded our affection and gratitude, but because Macartney's innings came like the sign of a prophet showing cricket the way out of the wilderness. Let our batsmen throw away the common specifics of the moment—the 'two-eyed stance' quackery, and the rest; let them trust their love of cricket as a *game* to lead them to brave ways of their own of doing things with a bat delicious to the touch. Only a great passion for cricket could inspire Macartney to play as he does; the beauty he makes on a green field is his offering to the game which, because of its traditions of chivalry, has attracted and nurtured his own genius.

The day was dull, with often a threat of rain as well as of fitful sunshine in the sky of moving clouds. Friday's thunderstorm had left the turf heavy and lifeless. When Carr won the toss Bardsley must have suffered from one quick shiver of apprehension. 'Heaven help us!' his mind possibly whispered at lightning speed. 'We've got to bowl on a sodden earth—Gregory won't be able to stand up or get any pace out of it; and it'll be hopelessly dead for hours to come for Grimmett and Mailey—"googly" bowlers hate moist ground.' Precisely what Bardsley said to himself when Carr told him Australia was to bat—this we shall never know. I saw Bardsley smile after the captains had tossed in front of the pavilion. I wonder he did not throw a fit of convulsive laughter on the spot. Here was a humorous kettle of fish for an Australian cricket captain. These many months England had been moaning about her inability to beat Collins at the toss. By good luck England gets Collins out of the way and at last discovers a captain who is pretty good at spinning a coin. And then—ha! ha!—having won the toss, England puts Australia in, on a dead wicket, leaves Parker out of the XI, and goes into action with Tate and Geary, both of them bowlers who are at their best on a fast wicket—both of them, indeed, the very two bowlers who ought to have attacked for England on the hard Sydney wicket a year ago! My readers may recall that I then recommended Tate and Geary as bowlers for Australian wickets. O excellent though bitter irony that I should have lived to see them both in action in an England team at last—on a wet Leeds pitch.

Everybody, of course, was sorry for Carr on Saturday. No doubt he counted on Kilner and Macaulay and on the advent of sun. Still, the questions remain: If Parker is not worth a place in the England XI, with rain in the earth and some prospect of sunshine to come— then, in the name of commonsense, whenever will he be worth a place?

O Time! thou must untangle this, not I;
It is too hard a knot for me to untie!

Carr flung good fortune smack back in the face of the gods—and they scourged him for this courageous yet rash act of independence. Mark how they put him on the rack. First, his hopes were lifted on high. From the opening ball of the game Bardsley was out. Tate sent a quick-rising ball that swung away a little, yet kept danger-ously close to the off stump. Bardsley merely 'shaved' his stroke, and he fell to a splendid catch at first slip by Sutcliffe, who gripped the ball low to the earth with an action which was all curving young life and limb. The crowd roared out its satisfaction at England's quick taste of blood; the English fieldsmen gathered round the wicket in a confident circle and Carr lived through his moment of vision. Then the iron was plunged into him—none of us watchers at Leeds will ever know the half of the bitterness that came into Carr's expectant heart after that moment of short-lived ecstasy. Two minutes following the game's outset Macartney came to the wicket. Against the second and third balls of the same over of Tate's in which Bardsley had fallen, Macartney played defensive strokes, confidently but fruitlessly. The fourth ball Macartney cut for two, a stroke clean and aggressive. The fifth ball, which rose abruptly to the bat, Macartney flashed a swift catch to the left side of—Carr! England's captain flung all his being to the scudding hit—'Lord!' he surely said, 'Macartney now is mine and for next to nothing.' Carr got the ball in his hands—got his net over the butterfly Macartney. And he let it go. Down to the ground fell the spinning ball, and with it fell England's hopes in this match. Macartney gave us no other opportunity; at the end of his innings his one mistake was no more than brief breath blown on the polished magnificence of his cricket.

Suppose Australia had put England in on a pitch of a sort England is not used to. And suppose, in these circumstances, England had lost Sutcliffe for nothing and then had nearly lost the wicket of Hobbs. Would not the common shout of 'Safety first' have gone through England's ranks with a vengeance? It was 'safety first', for England at Lord's the other week when our total read '150 for 0'. Macartney did not draw into his shell after his escape from a difficult chance. He is a great cricketer, and as such understands well that challenge and risk are body and soul of the game. From the next six balls he received after his 'escape' Macartney hit seven runs, including a superb off-drive. Macartney attacked the English bowling the moment he went 'to the middle'; in quick time he knocked it away from its length, reduced it to the dogged but unavailing work of schoolboys, played it here, there, and everywhere to his heart's content—cut, drive, thrust, and glance, each stroke a different facet on a diamond of an innings. Woodfull kept company with Macartney. Macartney's bat rippled its music, Woodfull's bat pat-patted all the time—a sort of pom-pom-pom accompaniment in the bass to Macartney's sparkling valse-caprice. As I looked on these two superb but wholly different batsmen, I thought of Dr Johnson's description of Pitt and Walpole—Macartney was the meteor and Woodfull the fixed star.

Macartney raced to his first 50 in 48 minutes, out of a total for Australia of 64; he reached his century in 100 minutes out of a total of 131. Victor Trumper once got a Test-match century before lunch—at Manchester in 1902. It is only right and proper that Macartney should have been given the grace also to achieve this wonderful performance. For the same joyous yet dangerous spirit that moved the incomparable Victor also sets in motion the quick-silver cricket of Macartney, who indeed has inherited Trumper's own chivalrous blade—which he uses in his own way.

From 11.32 on Saturday until 2.50, the English attack was a vain thing. Macartney never seemed likely to get out—this despite the prodigious risks he was always taking—while Woodfull's innings might have been growing before us like a tree with roots deep in the ground. If, at long intervals we saw a ball beat the bat, we were astonished at the batsman's momentary negligence. After lunch Macartney was nearly bowled by Tate, and a run or two later he almost returned the ball to Geary. These slight mistakes only increased our admiration at the marvellous precision of Macartney's cricket on the whole; they were proof that, after all, it was mortal skill and not witchcraft that was doing it all. Macartney seemed to tire after he passed his 150; he suddenly sent a catch to mid-off, and the next minute he was walking back to the pavilion, and 35,000 people were standing on foot roaring him home. Macartney batted two hours and fifty minutes; in this time he and Woodfull made 235 for Australia's second wicket. Macartney hit 21 fours. His innings seemed to contain every known stroke in batsmanship—and several of his very own. He gave us the wristwork of Spooner, the quick feet of Trumper, the fierce physical energy of J. T. Tyldesley. He proved once again that length bowling is relative, not absolute—that quick feet and versatile stroke play will turn the best-pitched ball into sorry enough stuff. Even so accurate a bowler as Kilner was unable to drop a length for long to Macartney; one quick jump to the ball made a half-volley; one quick backward motion of the right foot made a long-hop. In all his just less than three hours of brilliance, Macartney did not let us see a half-dozen 'ragged' strokes. His timing was amazing; every hit seemed born at his wrists' ends, and each went over the field with the speed of thought from the bat's middle. And often it was an audacious cross-bat—yet one moving according to the strict laws of Macartney's art, which, though apparently lawless to the common eye, has, like the art of every individual genius ever born, its own strict rationalism—right for Macartney, wrong for anybody else.

Andrews failed, and at half-past three Australia were 249 for 3. Richardson and Woodfull here began another partnership—cautiously for a while, then hitting the bowling immediately it was 'down again' in technique and ardour. The partnership had made 117 when rain put a finish to a distressful day for England—at 5.25.

Woodfull remained undefeated; he has so far been at the wicket four hours and 50 minutes. He exploits a short lift-up of the bat for defence and watches the ball almost until it is on the blade. But he is quick to jump to the over-tossed length. Obviously he is blessed with the true Australian temperament for big cricket. His innings, of course, had to stand against Macartney's in our sight—and a Macartney innings makes everything on a cricket field seem like dust revealed by sunshine. Nonetheless, Woodfull's game was great for Australia; it began in a difficult way for any young man venturing on his second Test. It was excellent and significant to see so discreet a batsman as Woodfull run out of his ground to Kilner. Richardson drove powerfully; he is a natural hitter with no common powers of discretion. England's bowlers rarely had a dog's chance on a wicket which reduced spin and length to the same lifeless state. Even Parker would have been unable to turn the ball at any useful pace. Root might have risen superior to the easy turf by means of his swerve through the air. If you are on a wicket so dead that conventional spin and length are 'cancelled out' immediately the ball pitches, obviously you must try to get the batsman 'guessing' while the ball is in the air. I imagine Root does that—in form. The Australians have never yet mastered Root's swerve—Woodfull least of all. He was in a mazeful condition of mind against Root at Lord's. Tate was the best of Saturday's impotent bowlers. Macaulay had one excellent period—'round the wicket', after lunch. He turned the ball for a while, but ceased as soon as a dozen runs were hit from his off-break in an over. He quickly fell back unimaginatively on fastish short stuff—'safety first' again. Geary, considering that the slow ground was all against his style, bowled as well as he himself could have expected. Yet somebody in charge of the England XI apparently imagined Saturday's pitch was likely to suit Geary. Who ever was it? Carr fielded magnificently and the others only tolerable—though Strudwick was better than at Lord's. He had rather less to do!

During the week-end attempts have been made to argue that the turf really was difficult, and that our bowlers failed to take advantage of it. The answer to this is that hardly a ball 'popped' all day, and that only once was a batsman to be seen prodding the ground with his bat. Moreover, Kilner bowled very frequently over the wicket. Still, for Australia to have scored 366 for three on a turf of a kind wet enough to be quite strange to them—here is a caustic enough commentary on the arts of some of our recognized Test match bowlers; moreover, here is proof of Australian adaptability.

THIRD TEST 1926
2nd Day, Headingley

AUSTRALIA
First Innings

W. Bardsley, c Sutcliffe, b Tate	0
W. M. Woodfull, b Tate	141
C. G. Macartney, c Hendren, b Macaulay	151
T. J. E. Andrews, lbw b Kilner	4
J. M. Taylor, c Strudwick, b Geary	4
A. J. Richardson, run out	100
J. M. Gregory, c Geary, b Kilner	26
J. S. Ryder, b Tate	42
W. A. Oldfield, lbw b Tate	14
C. V. Grimmett, c Sutcliffe, b Geary	1
A. A. Mailey, not out	1
Extras (b 2, lb 4, nb 4)	10
Total	494

ENGLAND
First Innings

Hobbs, c Andrews, b Mailey	49
Sutcliffe, c and b Grimmett	26
Woolley, run out	25
Hendren, c Andrews, b Mailey	0
A. W. Carr, lbw b Macartney	13
A. P. F. Chapman, b Macartney	15
Kilner, c Ryder, b Grimmett	38
Tate, st Oldfield, b Grimmett	5
Geary, not out	6
Macaulay, not out	18
Extras (b 4, lb 4)	8
Total (for 8)	203

BOWLING ANALYSIS
AUSTRALIA—First Innings

	O.	M.	R.	W.		O.	M.	R.	W.
Tate	51	13	99	4	Geary	41	5	130	2
Macaulay	32	8	123	1	Woolley	4	0	26	0
Kilner	37	6	106	2					

Macaulay bowled four no-balls

Fall of the wickets:
AUSTRALIA—First Innings

4	5	6	7	8	9	10
378	385	423	452	483	492	494

ENGLAND—First Innings

1	2	3	4	5	6	7	8
59	104	108	110	131	140	175	182

LEEDS, MONDAY

Our batsmen today have been violently shaken out of the pleasant opinion of themselves which was bred by England's vast score at Lord's a few days ago. My readers perhaps will remember that I did not join whole-heartedly in the announcement made after the second Test to the effect that English batsmanship had revealed at Lord's its old masterfulness. I could not help feeling that the heavy runs scored then were made from an Australian attack which was much too bad to be true—much too bad to happen again in a hurry. I have, throughout the season, harboured a furtive dread of Mailey and Grimmett, because I have been compelled by what I have seen day by day on our cricket fields to believe that English batsmen on the whole are rather unacquainted with the technique needed in a prosperous innings against slow spin bowling.

This afternoon the Australian attack was given leave by Hobbs and Sutcliffe to throw out its chest confidently. The first-wicket stand of Hobbs and Sutcliffe struck the wrong note; it did not blow any challenge at all to Australia. Both batsmen seemed to play for a draw from the first over sent down to them; while they batted England's ship seemed to drift without a directing sail. Lassitude and aimlessness were in this cricket; the batsmen even at times walked instead of ran across the pitch. Instead of playing a game normal to a sunny day on a not yet uneasy turf Hobbs and Sutcliffe gave us the batting of sheer negation. Hobbs was masterful enough, but his strokes were short of their customary strength; he was obviously holding his proper powers in reserve—for some misguided reason. And, of course, we can scarcely expect Sutcliffe to move fast whenever our greatest batsman sets discretion's own pace. Hobbs this afternoon was at the wicket one hour and fifty minutes for 49.

The Australian bowlers must have been mightily glad to see Hobbs in this accommodating condition of mind. They jumped quickly at the opportunity given them to pitch a good length. In the end it was the old, old story—bowlers are fed by flattery and grow very valiant men on it. The English innings would have fared better (it could scarcely have fared worse) if Hobbs had acted, as Macartney acted on Saturday, according to that hearty old axiom known to W. G. Grace—'Get at the bowler before he gets at you.'

The Australian innings, which came in like a lion, went out sheepishly enough this morning. On a wicket much faster than Saturday's Tate bowled in his best vein, and Geary pitched that just too short a length which moderate batsmen are unable to score from, but which a Macartney will cut fiercely by strong and late wrist action. And, truth to say, this Australian side has so far shown itself both at Leeds and Lord's to be definitely a moderate rather than a distinguished lot of batsmen—excepting, of course, Macartney and Bardsley. Woodfull, a difficult cricketer to bowl out, is a utilitarian: the score board will tell all about his cricket that really matters. This obstinate young man's circumspect old bat was beaten by Tate after a quarter of an hour's action in the forenoon's hot, dank air. After Woodfull's passing the field looked empty of a familiar landmark: an immemorial tree had been torn up by the roots. The Woodfull–Richardson stand for Australia's fourth wicket lasted one hour and three-quarters, and was worth 129. Woodfull's innings traversed an unheavenly length of some five hours—he gave us much clever labour, but in the end he spread about us all a sense of more or less noble ennui—to pervert the phrase of Mme. de Staël.

Richardson went to his century slowly and tentatively. All of his Saturday's violence was gone; the giant had lost his eye now, his stout cudgel had become a supporting staff. Richardson dawdled for 35 minutes while he moved his score from 89 to 100—this impalpable motion at a time when it ought to have been Australia's policy to get runs or get out and so let her bowlers attempt a bid for victory. This morning Australia's total stood at the fourth hundred just in front of twelve o'clock: another forty minutes ran out in the game's brief sand-glass before the total got to 450. In two hours and a half this morning Australia made only 128 for the loss of seven wickets.

Gregory was the one batsman who came to the wicket with the light of challenge and enterprise in his eye. He beat his bat in the air, was missed by Sutcliffe at first slip from Tate with his score five, some of his drives flashed through the slips humorously, and altogether he wakened up the match. Richardson's century came to him after three hours of rough-hewn cricket. He has the strokes which nature gives to a man—the drive, the pull, and, as they say in the North country, the clout. He commands few of those strokes which are the mark of strict culture: his play is almost wholly lacking the wrist action which to a batsman is as touch to the pianist. It was Richardson's want of a late wrist or short-armed stroke which made it hard for him to get runs quickly today against Geary and Tate, both of whom pitched, as I have suggested, too short for the full-blooded body drive. Ryder also is mainly a body and long-arm hitter—here, possibly, is a technical reason for much of Australia's slow progress before lunch—the batsmen possibly could not, rather than would not, force the pace. Macaulay made an end of Richardson in high Yorkshire fashion. The batsman hit a ball back to Macaulay, who was bowling, and he ventured out of his crease looking for runs. Macaulay hurled the ball down the pitch and shattered the stumps, while Richardson was still away from his ground. Here was Yorkshire smartness for you! How the crowd roared its gleeful recognition of a worthy trick of the clan! Emmott Robinson could not have done it all with a more passionate alacrity. But this was Macaulay's one moment of distinction in Australia's seven hours' traffic of the crease. His bowling was without sting or resource; his length was wild, not to say dishevelled. I have never yet seen Macaulay bowl well outside of the Yorkshire eleven. He is a spare part when away from the assembled machinery of Yorkshire county.

Tate was England's one bowler. Our attack seemed poverty-stricken for want of spin and flight variation: our cricket is paying today for the fashionable preoccupation with the easily-acquired dodge of swerving a new ball, and before the afternoon burned out its scorching warmth we were to learn from these Australians that the ancient arts of spin are still the best of all the bowler's possessions.

At a quarter past two Hobbs and Sutcliffe went into the middle, and the multitude cheered them all the way. England's innings began in a dead calm: the cricket of both batsmen was quiet. Grimmett bowled at the outset with Gregory, who again had his run of thunder, but no lightning ball to follow after. Gregory's teeth have gone, let the old lion roar as he may. Grimmett exploits leg spinners with a low action—he bowls rather with the aspect of some middle-aged gentleman on the sands at holiday time. But he controls spin and flight skilfully. Today his pitch sometimes dropped just a little too short for danger. Hobbs and Sutcliffe both were at liberty to play back with ample scope for a watchful stroke. Slow bowlers are deadly only when they are sucking their victims forward; luring them, not forcing them, to destruction. Hobbs and Sutcliffe batted like cricketers satisfied already that the game was a draw for certain. There was no speculation in the batsmen's eyes, no hurry in the feet of either. Runs it appeared did not matter—the Australians were given leave to do all the attacking. In the whole of Australia's innings we saw little or no deliberate use of the pads as a line of defence; this afternoon, though, our batsmen were not infrequently driven to this last resort of the perplexed cricketer. Hobbs and Sutcliffe scored 59 for England's first wicket in eighty minutes; as I say, the match seemed becalmed. But we all lived for a while as though housed at ease on a hillside of volcanic land. Out of a peaceful day came the first throbbings under our comfortable foundation —Sutcliffe sent Grimmett a lady's catch, and at a quarter past four

207

Hobbs lost his wicket; he tried to get a single for his 50 from a ball whizzing with spin, and put up another catch of mild and gentle mien. This English disaster happened in Mailey's first over; he did not bowl till 104—had he done so, England's position now might well be worse even than it is. His attack had more than Grimmett's break; also he exploited the googly, and seemingly Grimmett did not. And Mailey's flight hung the ball in the air like the very fruit of temptation. At 108 Woolley ran himself out; he played a stroke a few yards away to leg, and after a fatal second's hesitation risked a dash down the pitch for a second run even as Woodfull got his grip well on the ball. With no run added, Hendren was caught by Andrews from a hard drive to silly mid-off. (Yes, the Australian field contained a silly mid-off, and, moreover, it also frequently contained a silly mid-on as well.)

Consternation moved visibly in the crowd, making its outraged noises. We had all been flung back again into the pit of incompetence dug by English batsmen five years ago. We had looked again on feeble tight-footed batsmen, but this time it was slow bowling and not fast bowling which was making for our cricketers' ineptitude. The agony went on after tea—we were afflicted still further by the sight of English batsmen of renown put to humiliation by slow bowling on a wicket which was firm enough to take finger spin. And, as I have already written, the Australian attack possessed exactly the sort of spin welcomed by the occasion. On Saturday's dead turf Mailey and Grimmett would have been harmless; their spin would have perished the moment it fell in the spongy earth. Chapman was bowled by Macartney at 131—a lovely ball that pitched on the off stump and hit the leg stump; Carr was lbw at 140—he has suffered his whips and scorpions in this distressful game. England today was saved from shame by Roy Kilner's gallant play, an innings carved by a bat finely tempered. Kilner attacked the slow bowling—not for him the timid foot. In one over off Mailey he hit four smashing boundaries from four consecutive balls; it was a brave innings, with a brilliance that shone well in our darkness. Lost causes are won in Kilner's cavalier spirit. He used his feet quickly both in jumping to the well-flighted length and in getting back on his wicket to crack the short length past cover. He played death-or-glory cricket for an hour, and his ever-thumping bat let loose the Yorkshire roar from a crowd that had sat sick at heart for all too long.

The long day's end saw England in a position of jeopardy. Tomorrow our batsmen will need to attack straight away on resolute feet before Australia's slow bowling can bite the earth with its spin.

At Sydney a year or two ago the lesson was taught to English cricketers that the slow finger-spin bowler thrives on the cricketer who will not venture to move his right foot from his crease and will not trust to his eye and a bold fling of a bat. Now at Leeds this lesson has been taught yet again. The other day I chanced the prophecy that we should hardly ever again see Australia's attack as impotent as it was on the perfect wicket of Lord's a week or two ago. It will be possible for Mailey, Grimmett, and Macartney to spin the ball to the finish of this game—Hobbs must be Hobbs tomorrow, and, what is perhaps as important, Woolley must be Woolley. Mailey and Grimmett both abhor the left-handed batsman.

THIRD TEST 1926
3rd Day, Headingley

AUSTRALIA
First Innings

W. Bardsley, c Sutcliffe, b Tate	0
W. M. Woodfull, b Tate	141
C. G. Macartney, c Hendren, b Macaulay	151
T. J. E. Andrews, lbw b Kilner	4
J. M. Taylor, c Strudwick, b Geary	4
A. J. Richardson, run out	100
J. M. Gregory, c Geary, b Kilner	26
J. S. Ryder, b Tate	42
W. A. Oldfield, lbw b Tate	14
C. V. Grimmett, c Sutcliffe, b Geary	1
A. A. Mailey, not out	1
Extras (b 2, lb 4, nb 4)	10
Total	494

ENGLAND
First Innings

Hobbs, c Andrews, b Mailey	49
Sutcliffe, c and b Grimmett	26
Woolley, run out	25
Hendren, c Andrews, b Mailey	0
A. W. Carr, lbw b Macartney	13
A. P. F. Chapman, b Macartney	15
Kilner, c Ryder, b Grimmett	38
Tate, st Oldfield, b Grimmett	5
Geary, not out	35
Macaulay, c and b Grimmett	76
Strudwick, c Gregory, b Grimmett	1
Extras (b 4, lb 6, nb 1)	11
Total	294

ENGLAND

Second Innings

Hobbs, b Grimmett	88
Sutcliffe, b Richardson	94
Woolley, c Macartney, b Grimmett	20
Hendren, not out	4
Chapman, not out	42
Extras (b 5, lb 1)	6
	—
Total (for 3)	254

BOWLING ANALYSIS

AUSTRALIA—First Innings

	O.	M.	R.	W.		O.	M.	R.	W.
Tate	51	13	99	4	Geary	41	5	130	2
Macaulay	32	8	123	1	Woolley	4	0	26	0
Kilner	37	6	106	2					

Macaulay bowled four no-balls.

ENGLAND—First Innings

	O.	M.	R.	W.		O.	M.	R.	W.
Gregory	17	5	37	0	Richardson	20	5	44	0
Macartney	31	13	51	2	Mailey	21	4	63	2
Grimmett	39	11	88	5					

Macartney bowled one no-ball.

ENGLAND—Second Innings

	O.	M.	R.	W.		O.	M.	R.	W.
Gregory	6	2	12	0	Mailey	18	2	80	0
Grimmett	29	10	59	2	Ryder	9	2	26	0
Macartney	4	1	13	0	Andrews	4	0	36	0
Richardson	16	7	22	1					

Fall of the wickets:

AUSTRALIA—First Innings

4	5	6	7	8	9	10
378	385	423	452	485	492	494

ENGLAND—First Innings

1	2	3	4	5	6	7	8	9	10
59	104	108	110	131	140	175	182	290	294

ENGLAND—Second Innings

1	2	3
156	208	210

210

This morning, in a furnace of sunshine, Macaulay, of Yorkshire (where Hirst, Rhodes, and Emmott Robinson were born), showed us that the spirit of man may move the mountain. For England was now facing a big hill: 142 were needed to save the follow-on, with only Geary, Macaulay, and Strudwick left to get them. A mountainous score indeed, but Macaulay seemingly did not let its bulk trouble him. Boswell once pointed out to Dr Johnson a towering hill in Scotland and boasted of its height. 'No, sir,' said Johnson, 'it is no more than a considerable protuberance.' Macaulay's spirit looked at Australia's high total, and spoke likewise—a mere protuberance which good Yorkshire brawn and grit might climb over any day.

From the first over of the morning, bowled by Gregory's excellent ghost, Macaulay clenched his teeth, crouched down on his bat, and got himself into a posture confidently assumed to be one of very warlike offence. Straightway he began to smite boundaries, and straightway the crowd sent up its roar to the sky. And immediately the Australian attack had to put on its thinking cap. Gregory went out of action at an almost indecent speed: Grimmett bowled instead of Macartney, and then Mailey bowled at Grimmett's end while Grimmett changed over to the opposite wicket. Silly mid-off removed himself to a less conversational part of the field: And all the time Macaulay's bat cracked its antagonistic noise—such a noise was never heard at Leeds yesterday while Hobbs and Sutcliffe were in the middle.

Geary, too, displayed temper—the stern temper of defiance. His bat was straight; his strokes decisive and stylish. Better cricket than this has never been seen at the end of an English innings since Albert Relf and Rhodes were our last two men of the order of going in. Both Macaulay and Geary played out on quick, resolute feet to Grimmett's well flighted length; both hurled a heavy bat at the first hint of a loose ball. If Macaulay and Geary had each spent an hour after breakfast digesting my remarks in my message of yesterday they could scarcely have exploited tactics more calculated to confirm my views that the Australian slow spin bowlers can be safely attacked, granted a batsman who trusts to a free forward method and to the proper cricketer's heart.

Neither Macaulay nor Geary ever looked likely to lose his wicket; as they let us see the easiest cricket imaginable against Australia's attack, I was compelled to ask myself whether after all, Monday's paltry play by England's approved and advertised masters had not been just a wild, horrid mid-summer's dream. 'Perhaps the bowling is not so good as it was yesterday.' I said, and to make certain on this point I went out of the press-box—a place of Ethiopic scorchings—and watched the play from near the sight-screen almost behind Grimmett's arm. And there I saw that the Australians were bowling almost as on Monday afternoon, excepting a suggestion now amongst Grimmett, Mailey, and the rest that they were getting rather hot and bothered. The ancient story, as I wrote yesterday: strong-hearted batting makes bowlers unhopeful and unsteady.

In an hour Macaulay and Geary scored 60 runs; Macaulay's share of these was 41. Bardsley plainly did not relish the turn of the game: exasperating it must have been to him to see all Australia's good work of Monday undone at this important hour by two cricketers fresh from England's notorious hutch. Bardsley frequently consulted his men: brain-waves passed visibly over the field. Once Macaulay drove a full toss from Mailey to the long-on boundary: Mailey then moved a man rather square to the on side and bowled a higher and faster ball, designed to send a catch if Macaulay again attempted a long-on drive. But Macaulay showed horse sense—he waited for Mailey's full toss, got behind it, and clouted it gigantically round to the leg side. Every run made hereabout was wildly cheered. But though the runs counted for much, the time stolen from Australia by this gallant rally of England bowlers counted for more. The moral value of Macaulay's and Geary's play was immense: they were letting Hobbs and the other notables witness from the pavilion's shade that Australia's slow break bowling could comfortably be driven hard.

If Geary and Macaulay had got out quickly this morning, England's second innings would have started with our batsmen still in the uncertain mood provoked in their breasts by our collapse yesterday. Geary and Macaulay freed English cricket yet again from the inferiority complex. And the point I would wish to stress is that this very necessary liberation was achieved not by haphazard and lucky slogging but by real cricket—but it was cricket nourished on the old-time faith in the forward hitting game which mingles offence and defence in proportion. No good ball found Macaulay or Geary wanting in a sound method; and not a single loose ball, as far as I was able to observe, found either man wanting in quick vigorous strokes.

This ninth-wicket stand was, of course, a triumph of the temper and spirit. Nobody would argue that Macaulay and Geary are better batsmen in the technical sense than Hobbs and Sutcliffe: they conquered where the greater craftsmen had failed because naked competence plus good cheer will always travel farther and faster in this world than high skill that wears the burdensome armour of circumspection.

When his score was 73 Macaulay gave a chance at the wicket, and Oldfield, the best wicketkeeper in cricket at the present time, somehow missed it. The ball bounced from Macaulay's hand to Oldfield's momentarily insecure grasp and passed thence to Gregory, who could not hold an easy catch because the stumper hindered his sight. Macaulay then left the field to get his bruise nursed. He was out of the sunny field some minutes. When he got back to the wicket he was promptly caught from the worst ball Grimmett bowled all morning—a long-hop, which Macaulay mistimed.

Perhaps his brief absence from the light of a gleaming day interfered with his eyes' accuracy; had he remained in action perhaps he would now be the maker of a Test match century. Geary would never have got out; his innings was a perfect example of the uses of the honourable old straight bat moved with the left shoulder well forward. The Macaulay–Geary partnership scored 108 runs in 115 minutes; this was the duration of Macaulay's innings, in which he hit ten boundaries.

Grimmett was Australia's best bowler by far today; he turned the ball from leg with remarkable accuracy considering he puts a great strain on wrists and fingers alike. I noticed, too, that from time to time he sent down a slight in-swinger—a spin swerve and not, like the seam swerve, dependent on the quickly perishable new ball. Australia fielded keenly; it was palpable that the lot of them went into action this morning very much on toes and ready to taste the blood of an Englishman.

The heat smote the earth magnificently as Hobbs and Sutcliffe opened England's second innings—200 to the bad, with four and a half hours remaining for a decision. I can make these batsmen no handsomer compliment than to say that they put an end to our anxiety in an hour of thoroughly assured play. No risks were chanced, and this time none were called for by the hour or the occasion. But the batting was not sapless, as it was yesterday; every stroke made cricket's confident music—the clean cracking of a willow blade. In the torrid heat Australia's attack grew weary; this humid warmth of ours is less healthful than the dry air of an Australian summer. Today's torrents of sunshine have fallen on us all and rendered us a company of moist unpleasant bodies.

Hobbs was at liberty to go his new ways of serenity. He may not be a great match-winning batsman any longer, but he is certainly the most majestic of match-savers. As the game passed gradually into stalemate and our competitive interests waxed and waned, we were able to enjoy Hobbs for the sheer art of his batsmanship. He is beyond criticism as a craftsman: it is apparently impossible for him to blunder into an undignified piece of work. When he loses his wicket it is because he has chosen for a given ball the wrong good hit out of his long range of immaculate strokes—not because he has actually bungled in touch and technique. Again one felt in his cricket a sense of a master arrived at the artist's mellow end: he does not strive now to astonish us: he seems even unaware that we are watching him at all as he spreads about the field the cricket of ripe fulfilment. If his sun is setting it is going down beautifully: perhaps we are unreasonable to expect Hobbs to turn easily to the ardent ambitious East nowadays; he is for the West and its peaceful departing fires.

This afternoon Hobbs exceeded the highest individual aggregate of runs ever made in Test cricket: he batted two hours and a half for 88, his share of another Hobbs–Sutcliffe stand against Australia, worth this time 156. In the day's intense light and heat we saw Hobbs and Sutcliffe as though they and we had been lifted by Mr Wells's time machine back to Australian cricket fields of a year or two ago. This partnership, indeed, might well be described as Hobbs and Sutcliffe discerned under the conditions of eternity: the Australians, at any rate, might well have looked at the long stand in this way.

Sutcliffe missed his century by six runs after an innings of three hours and twenty minutes' length: he was always easeful and charming to the eye. After Hobbs got out the match dwindled from sheer weariness of Australian limb: thus Test match number three has also finished in unsatisfactory indecision.

Perhaps Leeds would have told another tale had England batted first on Saturday's lifeless pitch. The wicket was faster on Monday and today—I should have liked to see Tate bowling on it. He got much venom out of yesterday morning's firmer ground. Australia lacks a consistent match-winning bowler, as indeed England does whenever Tate falls below true form. But Grimmett has not been mastered yet; on a worn dry wicket he would cause trouble. But, as I say, nowadays wickets do not wear. The ground arrangements at Headingley were admirable.

ERNEST TYLDESLEY AND THE TEST

ERNEST TYLDESLEY, the best English batsman at the moment both as stylist and scorer, has been chosen as reserve for the Test match on Saturday at Old Trafford—a ground which, being Tyldesley's own, is not likely to trouble his method of batsmanship half so much as, conceivably, it might trouble the methods of a Southern cricketer. I imagine it would be difficult for the Selection Committee to justify this choice of Tyldesley as a 'reserve'. For if Tyldesley is not good enough to play for England as a batsman he is certainly not good enough to play as twelfth man. The Selection Committee possibly have left Tyldesley out of the XI proper because he is rather slow in the outfield. But who in his senses ever selected a slowish runner for twelfth man? Twelfth man of a Test match side ought always to be a brilliant all-round fieldsman—for reasons too obvious to be set down here. The Selection Committee cannot have it both ways; Tyldesley's batting plus his reliability as a catch obviously make him an England cricketer today; Tyldesley minus his batting—that is, as twelfth man—ought not to be called on at all by an England XI. One suspects the Selection Committee, trying to be nice, imagine that they might gladden the hearts of Lancashire cricketers by paying Tyldesley what is really a rather barren honour.

But let us consider for a while this defect in Tyldesley's fielding—a defect which presumably, despite all of his sequential centuries lately, has kept him out of the England XI. Nobody could ever charge Tyldesley with bad fielding in any place close to the wicket; he is a very accurate judge of a ball's flight, a safe man at a catch. It is only his want of speed that prevents him from being a fine outfield. Well, then, is it impossible to find in the English field a position near the wicket for Ernest Tyldesley? And if it comes to that— to use Mr George Robey's term of threatening accent—is Tyldesley a slower runner than Chapman? On the form shown at Leeds I would confidently expect (as the technical language has it) Ernest Tyldesley to give weight to Chapman in any hundred yards sprint and run him a hard race. Is Chapman preferred to Tyldesley because he is, at his best, a match-winning batsman? Does the Selection Committee understand that in his form at the moment Ernest Tyldesley is not only a great offensive batsman but in the right circumstances also a thoroughly sound defensive batsman? In a word, Tyldesley commands more than Chapman's range of offensive hits and, moreover, he commands, what Chapman lacks, a wide range of *experienced* defensive strokes.

Chapman, of course, is a left-handed batsman, and for that reason has an advantage over a right hander against the 'googly' bowler. Nobody would be sorrier that the writer to see Chapman dropped from the England team; he owns the proper spirit; cricket for him is a game well worth the winning. But we ought to select the best XI it is possible to get together, and plainly Tyldesley at the present time is an England batsman. Chapman seems the only cricketer in the lot chosen so far for Old Trafford who could stand down for Tyldesley. There is, of course, Hendren. This batsman again disappointed us at Leeds in a moment of crisis; nonetheless, he must remain in the team if only for his superb fielding 'in the deep'. Carr, though, will be sensible if he sees that Hendren *does* field on the busiest part of the boundary at Old Trafford; at Leeds, when he was not near the wicket, Hendren was in the least important section of the outfield. Chapman fielded on the more important boundary, and if Hendren had been there Australia would have scored considerably fewer runs.

Ernest Tyldesley's experiences in Test matches against Australia make for significant reflection. He played at Nottingham in 1921 and made 0 and 7, getting bowled in his second innings by a ball from Gregory that first of all hit him on the head and half-killed him. At Manchester the same year Tyldesley scored 78 not out— the most dazzling innings played by any English batsman against Australia since the war. Hendren in 25 opportunities for England has only three gone beyond 78.

Tyldesley afterwards made 39 in the Oval match, the last of the Armstrong games. Thus for England against Australia Tyldesley has this small but not unbeautiful record: 0, 7, 78 (not out), 39. Moreover, Tyldesley was the only batsman of Tennyson's South African side (1924–5) to score 1,000 runs, which he did at an average of over 50. Perhaps Tyldesley in part is responsible for the opinion held amongst many Southern cricketers to the effect that he is a 'doubtful beginner'. Even those of us of the North who admire Tyldesley's batsmanship and know well enough its worth when it is at its best—even we have frequently shaken heads over the strange moods of self-doubt which from time to time have come upon Tyldesley and stolen all his mastery away. But also we know how magnificently potential Tyldesley's batsmanship is at its truest— capable either of saving or winning a game against time and far better bowling than that of the present Australians. I appeal to the

Selection Committee on behalf of Ernest Tyldesley—and not because of any silly reasons of 'local' patriotism. I, like every other English cricketer, wish to see our best side take the field on Saturday. The Selection Committee are, of course, keener than anybody else to choose the 'best XI'. It is nonsense to suppose that Mr Warner and his colleagues ever consciously allow 'Southern bias' to influence their judgment. Possibly, however, none of the selectors have carefully watched Tyldesley's cricket, day in and day out, these last few seasons. I, who have so watched it, am confident that, at the moment, Tyldesley is an England batsman. When Tyldesley is good he is very, very good: when he is bad he is no better a batsman than Hendren is when out of form.

FIRST IN CRICKET QUEUE

SOUTHPORT BOY TAKES HIS STAND AT 8.20

THE first in the Test match queue outside Old Trafford cricket ground was a 14-year-old Southport boy who took up his place at 8.20 last night. He was a very smart well-dressed youth who had come by an excursion train. A lad like that ought to be given a specially struck medal with effigies of Hobbs on the obverse side and Ernest Tyldesley on the reverse. The gathering queue of which he was the head must have felt something like that, for when an observer with a streak of the Good Samaritan in him decided that it was not a good thing for even so keen an enthusiast to brave the night air and took him home to supper and bed, the queue unanimously voted him right of first place on his return next day—at 5 a.m.!

That, of course, was at the half-crown entrance in Warwick Road where, by midnight, about 60 enthusiasts were sheltering under the lee of the high wall from whatever wind that moved. The pavilion entrance higher up was solitary at midnight except for a policeman and an official, who congratulated the arriving pressmen on being the first at the gate!

After the boy at the half-crown entrance came a man from Hulme, a rather bad second, at 9.5, and then the queue began to assemble steadily from all parts, of which Birmingham seemed the most distant. There were others from Southport, Leigh, Oldham, and, of course, Wigan was also represented. There was a preponderance of clogs, which had trodden the high roads of Lancashire to be in at the best places when the first over is bowled. One could see them as one walked down in the dim light sticking off from the wall under which their owners sat in shadow—the great substantial clogs of hardy, enthusiastic men.

A proportion belonged to miners on strike. 'They don't care if they are out two years if they see this Test,' said one, who spoke, perhaps, without authority. Others did the thing in better style. A party of half a dozen from Leigh rolled up in a taxi after midnight. Everyone seemed to have brought his supper and breakfast, though coffee-stalls were making a comfortable picture on the waste ground a little distance away. One gathered that prices at the stalls were hardly considered 'cricket', but that by the way.

The early birds were a good-natured flock, though there was a steady muttering of resort to direct action if 'Ernie' Tyldesley should fail to find an eleventh-hour place in the team. Before midnight, by the way, the team had been selected again and again, and Tyldesley reappeared in it with the clockwork regularity of an ascending Aunt Sally. Not a Selection Committee of English internationals could have kept him down. 'If Tyldesley doesn't play today—!'

The all-night vigil did not command complete respect. There were those who came and looked at it and said what they had to say. One man, with a warm bed to go to, tucked up his opinion of the mental make-up of the vigilants in a phrase better left unwritten. He added a hint of possible rain, in which one almost detected a hope of it. But the queue did not mind. They had come to see cricket.

Another word about the coffee-stalls. Preparation was made thereat for the provision of breakfasts—no mean ham sandwich affair, but the true Englishman's breakfast, a rasher and eggs! Really, Test match cricket evolves enterprise. Of course, the coffee-stalls were a long way off, and one wondered whether waiters would serve down the queue in the grey dawn on trays. But the good nature of the crowd had obviated the need of that. There was a mutual understanding that places would be kept for early morning fast breakers—even those who did not include Tyldesley in their 'selection'—if there were any.

ENGLAND'S CHANCE IN THE
FOURTH TEST

The fourth Test match begins at Old Trafford today. The teams will be selected from:

England

A. W. Carr (Notts), A. P. F. Chapman (Kent), G. T. S. Stevens (Middlesex), Hobbs (Surrey), Strudwick (Surrey), Woolley (Kent), Hendren (Middlesex), Sutcliffe (Yorkshire), Kilner (Yorkshire), Tate (Sussex), Root (Worcestershire), Parker (Gloucester), Reserve: Ernest Tyldesley (Lancs.).

Australia

W. Bardsley (New South Wales), C. G. Macartney (New South Wales), T. J. F. Andrews (New South Wales), J. L. Ellis (Victoria), S. C. Everett (New South Wales), J. M. Gregory (New South Wales), C. V. Grimmett (South Australia), A. A. Mailey (New South Wales), W. A. Oldfield (New South Wales), W. H. Ponsford (Victoria), A. J. Richardson (South Australia), J. Ryder (Victoria), J. M. Taylor (New South Wales), W. M. Woodfull (Victoria).

Umpires: Young and Chidgey.

EVERY passing moment brings its helpful news about today's match. Old Trafford's groundsman let us know days ago that the wicket would be easy this morning; we have been told, too, that the weather is likely to be fair, with bright intervals, some rain, a little cloud, occasional sunshine, but no fog. Also the assuring tidings have reached us that the Australian cricketers arrived safely in Manchester yesterday morning and promptly went to bed. Let us trust that early this morning we shall learn that our own batsmen ate a hearty breakfast and walked unsupported to the wicket.

Despite all the current talk about the 'inevitable draw', I believe England could win this game at Old Trafford on *any* wicket if our men would visualize victory from the outset and play all the time to one thought, and one thought only—'England can win, and will win'. In the Test at Leeds, some of us were frequently compelled to think that our XI was not utterly possessed by the will-to-conquer; some of our players had the aspect of so many Micawbers waiting for something to turn up. It may be that the hour's chatter to the effect that on an easy wicket a modern Test match is doomed to stalemate—it may be that herein are powers of suggestion which will create the wrong atmosphere for a game, and tend to make the cricketers unconsciously let themselves drift rather aimlessly. Test matches have, in the past, been won within three days of the English summer, they will be won again in the same time, and without the help of an extra stump and a three-cornered ball.

The present Australian XI is not exactly the strongest in bowling of all that has come to this country in recent years. The batting is good, but not marvellously good. Bardsley and Macartney are the enemy's only two great batsmen. The opportunity is surely excellent for English cricketers, if only they would think that way, and go into action ready to take the risks that ought always to be taken by the stronger XI in its own country. If we cannot beat the Australians of this year, with the aid of Hobbs, it is difficult to believe we shall beat them in Australia in 1928–9, without Hobbs. The batsman worthy to wear Hobbs's mantle is not likely to be discovered in a hurry. Meanwhile, Australia will get to work and make improvement on her bowling weaknesses of the moment.

The collapse of England's batting at Leeds the other Monday afternoon was disconcerting; nonetheless, the problem facing our batsmen today should be easier than the problem facing our bowlers. In other words, the task of getting quick runs against Mailey, Grimmett, and the rest ought to prove simpler than the task of bowling out twice within three days Macartney, Bardsley, Woodfull, and the other Australian batsmen. The English runs, therefore, must be made at a speed calculated to leave our bowlers with ample time in which to perform their tougher job. Nobody wishes for vain glorious and indiscreet cricket in an England innings; one asks for no more than this determination in every batsman that gets set to force the action immediately he begins to 'see the ball'. We do not expect to see an English batsman make his runs at a slower speed the longer he stays 'in the middle'.

The Australians batting is the team's most considerable flank. It is for England, therefore, to go into the game with her bowling her most important arm. I trust the English attack will not be weakened because of some negative policy of playing for vast and safe runs at Old Trafford in the hope that the 'timeless' Oval match will bring us victory at last. The Australians may easily prove a better XI in a Test played to a finish than in one played to a three-day time-limit.

Besides, every game ought, in the best interests of cricket, to be fought on its merits. And each side ought to play all the time for a win, and not be afraid of taking the offensive—for fear of defeat! Old Trafford is famous for one or two thrilling and decisive Test matches; whoever 'gets his blow in fust' might turn out easy winners of this latest tussle.

We need to bear in mind that so far the Australians have had shocking luck this season. Gregory out of form; Ponsford, Hendry, and Collins ill; Mailey not yet able to get a length in Test matches; Taylor, the greatest batsman in Australia, clean out of luck's way— here's a sequence of misfortunes that might well have destroyed the confidence of a stronger side than Collins's. The tide may turn for Australia any day; then we should be free to repent at leisure for not having jumped, regardless of consequences, to a golden chance of beating Australia—and that without a bad pitch to help us, or another stump to bowl at, or another day for the job.

FOURTH TEST
1st Day, Old Trafford
AUSTRALIA
First Innings

W. M. Woodfull, not out	5
W. Bardsley, not out	0
Extras (lb 1)	1
Total (for no wicket)	6

C. G. Macartney, T. J. E. Andrews, A. J. Richardson, J. M. Gregory, J. Ryder, W. A. Oldfield, C. V. Grimmett, A. A. Mailey, and W. H. Ponsford to bat.

ENGLAND.—A. W. Carr, G. T. S. Stevens, Hobbs, Strudwick, Woolley (F. E.), Hendren, Sutcliffe, Kilner (R.), Tate, Root, and Tyldesley (E.).

MANCHESTER, SATURDAY

In three successive Test matches at Old Trafford now, the first day's play has been ruined by rain. Heavy showers prevented cricket on Saturday until twenty minutes to three; then, following the bowling of ten balls, rain washed out the afternoon—which was, of course, all very sorrowful. It is not true, however, to write, as a London newspaper has written, that the rain 'descended on Saturday as only Manchester rain can'. Here is the voice of exaggeration; I once saw wetter rain at Stoke Poges.

Australia won the toss—and did not omit to bat. In the England XI Ernest Tyldesley takes the place won for him by his form lately. Parker again was left out of the side; the Selection Committee possibly are waiting yet for the heat wave and hard grounds which a slow left-arm spin bowler loves so dearly. If Parker is not to be trusted in the green leaf what use will he be in the dry?

The first of Saturday's ten balls was bowled by Tate to Woodfull. It was a beauty— a fast, swinging-away ball that pitched on the middle and leg stumps and flashed over towards the off, keeping so dangerously close to the wicket that Woodfull simply had to make a stroke of some sort. His bat stabbed at the ball—the sheerest reflex action. Between first and second slip went the stroke, 'through' Sutcliffe and Hendren. Neither fieldsman attempted a catch—yet Carr's attempt to catch Macartney at Leeds was from a slip stroke, only a little slower, only a little more 'unexpected' than this eyeless, speculative hit of Woodfull's at Tate's master-ball. The fourth ball Tate bowled was to Bardsley; it swung into his wicket, beat his bat— but Bardsley had his two protecting pads there.

Root's first attack upon Woodfull let us see that the man is something of a tactician. He set his usual leg trap—then bowled a fastish but quite straight offside ball, to which Woodfull played 'inside', at a swerve not there; it missed the off stump easily. After Woodfull had got a leg-bye, the deluge happened. The cricketers fled the field at eight minutes to three; an hour afterwards Old Trafford's flag was pulled down and hidden from sight.

A crowd of some 20,000 went away with a noble fortitude; the bulk had waited patiently from early morning and suffered many a drenching downpour. But there was no bad temper; such a crowd as this could not be found in any un-English land. It could, of course, be argued that any sort of submission to miseries (and at a price) such as the miseries of Old Trafford on Saturday, is proof positive that we are a foolish as well as a philosophical people. We allow ourselves to be 'taken in' by our enthusiasms, it might be said. Well, as Mr Chesterton has written, to be taken in everywhere is to see the inside of everything. It is the hospitality of circumstances. Even Saturday's rain did not really put out the ardent fires burning for cricket in the hearts of nearly everybody present; I doubt whether many of all these men, women, boys, and girls went home really sorry they had 'ever come'. Better a moist, unpleasant Test than not to be there at all!

Old Trafford's admirable arrangements for the day contained one flaw. Some of the press seats were exposed to the wet. In fine weather these seats would have been enviable. Old Trafford always goes to its cricket confident of fine weather—that is why the enclosure is one of the least 'covered' in the country. But it is to be hoped that today all the press seats will be protected from rain; writing about a Test match is a difficult job in the happiest circumstances.

I see that already the suggestion has gone forward that this game now stands doomed to indecisiveness, even should the remaining two days keep fine. Why should it be! Cricket matches have been known to come to an end within two days. The Australians defeated England at Nottingham in two days during 1921. I trust none of the English cricketers will take the field today (if they take it at all) thinking the game is no longer worth some effort calculated to get it finished—and won. A lot can happen in two days on a wet cricket field, granted players who will go all out to take circumstances by the scruff of the neck and bend them the way of ambitious purpose. No game of cricket ever was, or ever will be, until the last ball has been bowled, 'a certain draw'.

FOURTH TEST 1926
2nd Day, Old Trafford
AUSTRALIA
First Innings

W. Bardsley, c Tyldesley (E.), b Stevens	15
W. M. Woodfull, c Hendren, b Root	117
C. G. Macartney, b Root	109
T. J. E. Andrews, c sub, b Stevens	8
W. H. Ponsford, c & b Kilner	23
A. J. Richardson, c Woolley, b Stevens	0
J. Ryder, c Strudwick, b Root	3
J. M. Gregory, c Kilner, b Root	34
W. A. Oldfield, not out	2
C. V. Grimmett, not out	4
Extras (b2, lb 1, w 1, nb 3)	7
Total (for 8 wkts)	322

A. A. Mailey to bat.

ENGLAND.—A. W. Carr, G. T. S. Stevens, Hobbs, Strudwick, Woolley (F. E.), Hendren, Sutcliffe, Kilner (R.), Tate, Root, and Tyldesley (E.).

Fall of the wickets:

AUSTRALIA (first innings):

1	2	3	4	5	6	7	8
29	221	252	256	257	266	300	317

MANCHESTER, MONDAY

Over the weekend Carr caught tonsilitis, and yesterday he was unable to play. Out of this disaster came an important happening.

223

We have lived to see a professional cricketer lead into the field an English cricket team. Here is a landmark in the social history of our country. O, beware of a precedent!—as the frank Junius wrote; one precedent creates another. They soon accumulate and become law. Hobbs looked the part to the life; as we watched him wave his men here and there over the field we might have said in the accent of Falstaff's hostess. 'He doth it all as like any of these gentlemen players as ever I see.'

The day's cricket was not exciting. A diligent scrutiny of the score-sheet will tell of all that occurred of importance. I would need summon all the muses to make this account go forth in noble numbers. The wicket was dead and easy nearly all day. In the morning it was lifeless as it was on a certain day twenty-four years ago when Victor Trumper and R. A. Duff scored 173 for Australia before lunch. The Australians yesterday did not seem inclined to chance a bid for victory on the strength of the possibility of a bowler's turf later in the game. Instead they apparently contented themselves with practice for the match at the Oval, where we shall probably get cricket *sub specie aeternitatis*.

No doubt the attack of Root did much to place the Australian batsmanship in chains; all day long he dropped a fair-length ball well outside the leg wicket, and, of course, he exploited his familiar ring of supplicatory fieldsmen. It could be argued, of course, that Root's method of bowling is 'hardly cricket', since it does not face the challenge of the full range of a batsman's strokes. But the logic has yet to be worked out that can demonstrate wherein Root's leg theory is less 'cricket' than, say, Attewell's 'off theory'. Root did his work well yesterday; over after over he sent down with the accuracy of good clockwork. Not imaginative bowling maybe; nonetheless, it helped to keep Macartney quiet; we must be thankful for small mercies nowadays.

Root's ceaseless maiden overs were loudly cheered by Old Trafford's vast crowd; he was a most willing horse, and I liked his aspect of solid, pertinacious English flesh. Yet I have seen Root a better bowler than this. At Birmingham in June he so pitched his inswinger that the Australians had no choice but to play the ball; he then swerved late from well outside the off side of the wicket on to the leg stump. Yesterday Root did not always give his attack the authentic swerve; often enough he merely directed a straightish ball diagonally, and it finished well away to the leg side. In his first 35 overs there were 22 'maidens'; during one period he bowled ten maidens out of a dozen overs.

224

The fact of Root and Woodfull in opposition—nay, that is a strong word and might well suggest the liveliness of positive antagonism; let us say conjunction—Root and Woodfull in conjunction did not make for spectacular cricket. Woodfull is a batsman with the admirable gifts of patience and watchfulness; but he is not, at his freest, a batsman of many strokes. Against Root the customary immobility of him was, so to speak, put into tight bonds and manacles. For four hours he was in our view, and though I never forgot the cleverness of his cricket, in the end I found myself wishing for mandragora that I might sleep out this great gap of time.

Woodfull's cricket reminds me of those little effigies of W. G. Grace which are enclosed in penny-in-the-slot machines which stand on the piers at Blackpool—we squander our money and try to get the ball past a bat which is lifted only a few inches high by a batsman not a little stiff in the joints. Woodfull will be in his element at the Oval shortly, and then I hope to be the first of his critics to praise his batsmanship. For we must always praise the right thing in the right place.

Woodfull and Bardsley made 29 for Australia's first wicket in 50 minutes; then Bardsley pulled a short ball from Stevens round to square-leg, where Ernest Tyldesley accomplished a brilliant catch. England's bowlers had to wait some three hours for a further advance; Macartney and the good tree Woodfull built a second-wicket partnership as valuable almost as the one they built at Leeds; it was worth 192, and Macartney's portion was 109. Macartney now has scored three consecutive Test match hundreds and Woodfull two.

This time we saw Macartney in academic mood—for him. He gave us many a beautiful stroke, but usually they were made from doubtful balls. At Leeds Macartney cut and drove good and bad bowling alike; yesterday it was within the power of human arts to pitch a good length to Macartney. Root, as I have hinted, clipped his wings a little; he was rarely in difficulties with Root, true, but he could not—or I would rather say did not—score freely from him. Macartney was some 100 minutes moving from 50 to his century; as I saw his bat held there fruitlessly while Root's 'maidens' passed by, I thought that this Macartney was Phoebus Apollo turned fasting friar.

Possibly the occasion did not challenge Macartney's antagonism; all day the match meandered towards indecisiveness. The technique of this glorious batsman was as wonderful to watch as ever; the man's energy was somewhat in abeyance. It was like watching a

Macartney in slow motion (again let me say slow for him—quick enough for the average batsman). And this suspended animation of his art gave us an opportunity of looking into its works, so to speak. We could see his feet moving into position—the right foot going back on the wicket for his great forearm shot to the on side, the left foot going to the line of the off-side ball which invited his sweet cover drive. Because the customary brilliance of Macartney did not blind our eyes now, we were able to watch how 'he does it all'. And it is all done with that indescribable simplicity of genius.

Macartney, when he was 64, made an unsafe stroke through the slips from a ball of Root's; a run afterwards Tate gave him a difficult problem to counter; and with his score 71 he was unmistakably beaten by one of Tate's best late swingers. All in all, though, Macartney seemed to toy with the English attack, I could not believe he was being compelled out of his customary aggression. His bat, so it appeared, now and again made deliberate play with the onrush of England's bowlers—it was like the picador's weapon used with sardonic delicacy. Macartney hit ten boundaries—one of them, a late on-drive from Tate, gave to his cricket his own un-mistakable signature. He threw his innings away as though tired of it.

At tca Australia's score was 252 for 3; Woodfull got caught in the Root leg trap just before the interval. When the game went on, Andrews drove a ball to long-on, and Chapman (fielding as substi-tute for Carr), running a distance, let us behold a lovely catch gripped at arm's length. It was one of those 'school' catches we read about, done by our hero, with only four to get and the last man in—pretty, pretty, as they used to cry out at Hambledon. With only one more run to Australia, Richardson was caught by Woolley in the slips; he did not seem to know that he had undone himself; he stood there, all innocence, till the law, which is the umpire, gently broke the news to him. Two more wickets fell to our bowlers before the afternoon's end; all things considered England came through a heavy day well enough—on paper.

But the bowling was obviously weak; it lacked contrast and strategy. Kilner did not spin the ball till the closing hour. Stevens spun it all day, but at a variable length. Tate toiled manfully on the sort of turf he thoroughly detests. He had bad luck, for frequently he broke through a batsman's defence. I wish, though, that he would not strike attitudes expressive of despair, chagrin, astonishment, and frustration each time he sees a ball miss the bat; he will do damage to his nervous system if he allows every moment to become a crisis. Better far Root's stolid indifference to all the alarums and excursions of battle—besides, it is not good tactics for a bowler to give a batsman a sign which might put him on his guard next ball.

The English fielding was good in the lump; the one or two 'chances' which were missed were of the sort which are easier to catch from the pavilion seats than in the field. Strudwick, obviously, has 'begun again', and is now about to settle down into mellow, unending youth. Once he chased a ball to leg, and the sight of him in hot pursuit reminded me of those distant days when he was one of the quickest outfields (with pads on, too!) in England. England's lack was a good-length finger-spin bowler—especially after the tea interval. And with no oblique reference to that latter remark, let it be said that Parker twice served drinks on the field with much charm of manner.

The play was watched by a crowd 34,000 strong, and the mass of it made a grand and thoroughly English sight. Old Trafford handled the day's multitudinous traffic excellently. If a special mention is given here of the good work done by Mr Agar it is not because others did not deserve praise as heartily, but because, after all, the most important job was to keep us all well nourished by good food. Australian batsmen piling up runs (and Woodfull in particular) is not the sort of spectacle to witness on an empty stomach.

ANOTHER TEST MATCH FIZZLES OUT

FOURTH TEST 1926
3rd Day, Old Trafford

AUSTRALIA
First Innings

W. Bardsley, c Tyldesley (E.), b Stevens	15
W. M. Woodfull, c Hendren, b Root	117
C. G. Macartney, b Root	109
T. J. E. Andrews, c sub, b Stevens	8
W. H. Ponsford, c & b Kilner	23
A. J. Richardson, c Woolley, b Stevens	0
J. Ryder, c Strudwick, b Root	3
J. M. Gregory, c Kilner, b Root	34
W. A. Oldfield, not out	12
C. V. Grimmett, c Stevens, b Tate	6
A. A. Mailey, b Tate	1
Extras (b 2, 1b 1, w 1, nb 3)	7
Total	335

ENGLAND

First Innings

Hobbs, c Ryder, b Grimmett	74
Sutcliffe, c Oldfield, b Mailey	20
Tyldesley (E.), c Oldfield, b Macartney	81
Woolley, c Ryder, b Mailey	58
Hendren, not out	32
G. T. Stevens, c Bardsley, b Mailey	24
Kilner, not out	9
Extras (b 4, lb 3)	7
	—
Total (for 5 wickets)	305

BOWLING ANALYSIS

AUSTRALIA—First Innings

	O.	M.	R.	W.		O.	M.	R.	W.
Tate	36·2	7	88	2	Stevens	32	3	86	3
Root	52	27	84	4	Woolley	2	0	19	0
Kilner	28	12	51	1					

Tate bowled a wide, Stevens 2 no-balls, and Woolley 1 no ball.

ENGLAND—First Innings

	O.	M.	R.	W.		O.	M.	R.	W.
Gregory	11	4	17	0	Richardson	17	3	43	0
Grimmett	38	9	85	1	Macartney	8	5	7	1
Mailey	27	4	87	3	Andrews	9	5	13	0
Ryder	15	3	46	0					

Fall of the wickets:

AUSTRALIA (first innings):

1	2	3	4	5	6	7	8	9	10
29	221	252	256	257	266	300	317	329	335

ENGLAND (first innings):

1	2	3	4	5
58	135	225	243	272

MANCHESTER, TUESDAY

Yesterday's play at Old Trafford was stale and sometimes sheer weariness to eyes and flesh alike. Australia set a bad example by going on with an innings which an imaginative captain might have closed on Monday evening. There was, of course, little or no chance of the Australians getting England out twice in a day; nonetheless a 'declaration' by Bardsley straightaway would have been the gesture of true sport.

England's innings began at twenty minutes to twelve. Less responsible circumstances could not easily come to cricketers than these in which Hobbs and Sutcliffe now found themselves—an easy wicket and no serious threat of trouble for England or a finish at all. (If it be argued there really was the danger that Australia would bowl us out twice in six hours, granted a quick overthrowing of Hobbs and Sutcliffe, and if it be also argued that therefore Hobbs and Sutcliffe had every reason to move warily, as though defeat actually were staring them in the face, I can only reply that if we really do go into Test matches possessed by these omnipresent apprehensions, then we ought not to play Australia at all at a hazardous game like cricket, but, instead, challenge her to croquet or tiddleywinks.) With England's score beyond 220 for five, Hendren pushed and poked an hour for 12. 'He ought not to be in the match at the Oval,' said an exasperated onlooker: but I say 'Yes; he ought —he ought to be *sentenced* to play in it; he deserves no happier fate.'

England missed a glorious opportunity of getting some practice at free hitting against Australia yesterday; she had a chance, too, of proving that the Australian bowlers do not still hold a 'moral supremacy'. The chances went begging. Hobbs batted two hours and forty minutes for 74; Sutcliffe an hour and a quarter for 20. At one period even Woolley so far forgot himself as to dawdle three-quarters of an hour for nine. Ernest Tyldesley, though playing for his place in the eleven and palpably anxious not to disappoint a crowd that expected him, as a matter of course, to score another century—he was the first English batsman of the day to wake the game up and send it moving along brightly. It was, surely, his cracking bat (following a dubious opening period) that stirred Woolley from his astonishing immobility.

Hobbs and Sutcliffe made 58 for England's first wicket in an hour and a quarter—which is their best Australian speed, guaranteed to keep going from noon till evening in any six-day Test match. In seventy-five minutes Sutcliffe did not accomplish one scoring stroke in front of the wicket worth more than a single. Hobbs was very solemn; he might have been holding all the English cricket that ever was on his shoulders. Yet the hour was actually so care-free that no English cricketer (save those new to the eleven) was under any obligation at all—excepting an obligation to entertain the crowd. Hobbs went gravely from 31 to 38 in half an hour; it was all very amusing, if only we could have looked at it with fresh eyes.

The closing hours of a cricket match, one side just having finished its innings, the other side just beginning their first, the wicket easy and a decision well outside the range of probability—and here was Hobbs getting himself down on his bat in much austerity of manner, pushing the ball away with the aspect of stern duty and conscience, patting the turf suspiciously, and now and again mopping a moist brow. Humour is born whenever a man takes himself seriously for no cause.

Ernest Tyldesley's innings did not begin at all certain of touch. He reached out tentatively at the slow spin bowling. But after lunch he played the game we expect to see from a Test match cricketer— that is to say, he held good balls in respect and exploited a wide range of strokes to balls of doubtful quality. His cricket put into the crowd animation at last; moreover, it seemed to put animation into Hobbs and, as I have hinted, also into Woolley. When Tyldesley came to the wicket Hobbs had been batting 85 minutes, and his score was 37. And though Tyldesley had to play himself in, with all our expectations in front of him like a visible, forbidding presence, he nonetheless made 39 to Hobbs's 37 in his partnership for the second wicket. Tyldesley batted altogether two hours and a half; he looked to give a stiff chance to Andrews at 'silly' mid-off; but the stroke was good enough. He drove Richardson straight and hard— the same Richardson that stopped the Hobbs–Sutcliffe ride to victory at Lord's. I thought Tyldesley might have got more runs had he driven the slow bowling after jumping into position for a swinging stroke; usually he merely 'pushed' the ball, from a point of vantage excellent for the drastic hit. His leg strokes were charming— no other cricketer makes this stroke with Tyldesley's mingled crispness and leisureliness. He got himself out, on the threshold of his first century against Australia, by indiscreetly attempting a cut from the wrong ball. None of us would have grumbled, at this stage of the game, to see him playing for a hundred according to the year's fashion amongst our Test match batsmen. His downfall broke the hearts of innumerable small boys, one of whom vented his disappointment by calling Oldfield horrible names for not dropping the catch.

Woolley's innings—once it really became Woolley's—was silver and gold of batsmanship. His bat made easy curves—indolent, one might have sworn; and the ball was running over the grass as fast as the eye could follow! Woolley must stay in the XI if only to give to an English innings sweetness and light.

Stevens, during a dashing little innings of ten minutes' duration, hit 24 runs; he has spirit. Even his variable bowling does at least try and 'get something done'; he is not content to keep runs down.

Grimmett bowled for long spells with an accuracy astonishing in a cricketer who spins from leg with immense finger and wrist action. But yesterday's turf was not fast enough for him. Mailey also bowled well at times; his curving flight is always pretty to see. The rest of Australia's attack was definitely commonplace, though Gregory bowled faster and better than so far I had seen him bowl this year. On a worn pitch he might have been very awkward. At the afternoon's blessed end Andrews might have been observed tossing up ambitious slows—without a man in the 'deep'. Moreover, he might have been observed bowling five maidens out of nine overs. Thus did two days of preparation for the Oval game come to an exhausted finish; poor Test match cricketers.

> They need their pious exercises less
> Than schooling in the Pleasures.

FIFTH TEST 1926
1st Day, the Oval

ENGLAND

Hobbs, b Mailey	37
Sutcliffe, b Mailey	76
Woolley, b Mailey	18
Hendren, b Gregory	8
A. P. F. Chapman, st Oldfield, b Mailey	49
G. T. S. Stevens, c Andrews, b Mailey	17
Rhodes, c Oldfield, b Mailey	28
Geary, run out	9
Tate, b Grimmett	23
Larwood, c Andrews, b Grimmett	0
Strudwick, not out	4
Extras (b 6, lb 5)	11
Total	280

AUSTRALIA

W. M. Woodfull, not out	22
W. Bardsley, c Strudwick, b Larwood	2
C. G. Macartney, b Stevens	25
W. H. Ponsford, run out	2
T. J. E. Andrews, b Larwood	3
H. L. Collins, not out	1
Extras (b 1, lb 4)	5
Total (for 4 wkts)	60

J. M. Gregory, C. V. Grimmett, A. A. Mailey, W. A. Oldfield, and A. J. Richardson to bat.

231

England—1st Innings bowling analysis

	O.	M.	R.	W.		O.	M.	R.	W.
Gregory	15	4	31	1	Macartney	8	3	16	0
Grimmett	33	12	74	2	Richardson	7	2	10	0
Mailey	33·5	3	138	6					

Fall of the wickets:

ENGLAND—1st innings

1	2	3	4	5	6	7	8	9	10
53	91	108	189	213	214	231	266	266	280

AUSTRALIA—1st innings

1	2	3	4
9	44	51	59

LONDON, SATURDAY

The Test match at the Oval today confounded all our expectations, for the wheel of the game went round and round dizzily
turned by the ironic gods. With all eternity to play in, the cricketers
took time not only by the forelock but by the scruff of the neck, and
already the game has arrived at the situation most of us imagined it
would reach after several days of lean, canny activity. In a word,
today's cricket has knocked us into the middle of next week.
Fourteen wickets and 340 runs within the brief space of six hours—
were these the very cricketers that launched a thousand yawns at
Lord's and Manchester?

The play had refreshing variety; from hour to hour the battle's
tide changed. Though the wicket seemed good enough for countless
runs, the batsmen no longer were masters of a dull, mechanical
competence; they were hedged round by error always. This was
Test cricket blown here and there on fortune's winds, the dead calm
of stalemate had passed. Mischievous imps of luck were in the air,
humorously fooling the players, who, in the accent of Horace, like
tops with leathern thongs were scourged about. The world's two
greatest batsmen, Hobbs and Macartney, had their wickets knocked
aslant by two of the world's worst balls. Hobbs was bowled by a
full-toss. Macartney by a rank long-hop. On any ordinary day in a
score of summers. Hobbs and Macartney would each hit to the
boundary the kind of ball which was their undoing today. Had
Hobbs not suddenly been surprised out of inhuman technical
mastery into a mood of human and whimsical fallibility, then he
would have not been overthrown by a wretched ball but would have
made a hundred, and, with Sutcliffe in his usual form, the match
would have gone along the customary Test match course, and at this

232

moment our pens would be eloquent about the need for reform in cricket—four stumps, four days, and the rest of it.

The day at the Oval was a victory for cricket's (and man's) incalculable spirit. Perhaps the players were affected by the momentous occasion, perhaps the absence of all need to 'remember the clock' caused some of our batsmen to try to play every ball strictly on its merits. Whatever the reason, the match, so far, has let us see few instances where a bad ball has been suspiciously stonewalled. The English innings, especially after lunch, was fast and furious. I shall see it in my mind's eye for days to come as a giddy mix-up of thumping boundaries, fallen wickets, batsmen now impudent and vain, and batsmen now comically crestfallen.

When the game began in the quiet of an autumnal morning it was thrilling to know there was bound to be a significant end sooner or later to all the tense action. 'One side or the other,' we told ourselves, 'will die the death. There can be no escape now for England or Australia. Every ball bowled in this match will be a nail in somebody's coffin, and which side will provide the body!' The fates got to work on the loom of destiny as Hobbs took his guard against Gregory. Every man's slightest action was going to count for something in this engagement. This Test match, which some of us had said would drag through weary pointless days, was marked by the hand of inevitable destiny from the very outset. For a while we lived in the old ease as Hobbs and Sutcliffe went along the old confident track. Hobbs was at his best, the master in all his ripe dignity. He played the second ball of the match to leg for two from Gregory as though he were making his 152nd run; then he drove Grimmett through the covers with an ease and loveliness of cool, leaning movement that had the effect on the senses of old sculpture. In half an hour the Australian attack looked to be in a pretty helpless way. Sutcliffe, true, was beaten periodically; true somehow he hardly appeared likely to get out. Sutcliffe was calm, but his steady coolness of manner contradicted the occasional fluctuations in his method. Gregory heaved his way to the wicket, mounting up to his high leap like a man facing a heavy wind. His pace was faster than it had been before in this season's Tests, but it was not the authentic thunder and lightning of him. In forty minutes his energy dwindled, and then Grimmett and Mailey bowled slow spinning stuff.

The English total topped 50 in under the hour, and we started to tell one another our familiar stale wheezes about the extreme unlikelihood of there being any play on Christmas Day. Then came the first ironic interference from the outside, the first sting from the arrows of the sardonic-deities. Mailey sent Hobbs a slow, high ball on the leg stump, and the master's bat swept right across and over it. The ball pitched at the wicket's base and had just time to turn a little from leg to off before upsetting the stumps' straight tidiness. We all of us caught breath incredulously; Hobbs stood there for a second a stupefied man. The Australians plainly could not at once believe their delighted eyes. Hobbs recovered himself, laughed at Mailey, and walked back to the pavilion. Possibly the pavilion's black background had spoiled his sight of the ball, which was own brother to the full-toss with which Mailey bowled Hobbs after he and Sutcliffe had scored 283 at Melbourne a year or two ago. It is as certain as anything can well be certain at cricket that Hobbs was going to make a hundred on Saturday. He has never played finer cricket in this year's Tests. So complete was his control over the bowling that we might say, paradoxically, that only a bad ball could have got him out; his skill was much too good for a good ball.

Australia's tail stood erect with confidence after Hobbs left. Woolley never settled down, and at 91 Mailey bowled him—whether with a 'googly' or not I could not say, because I was not placed behind the bowler's arm. But it is not of much importance what the ball 'did' after pitching; Woolley was beaten by flight, a beautiful 'dip' at the last second upset his calculations. Hendren made a few pleasant strokes, but his demeanour was in strong contrast to Sutcliffe's unruffled poise. Hendren ran his every run like a cricketer terribly eager to give a good account of himself—and confidence is never anxious. Just on lunch Collins asked Gregory to bowl again—especially, as I thought, for Hendren's wicket. And not for the first time in the history of Test matches Hendren fell to Gregory just at a time that we wanted him to do well. Hendren snicked on to his stumps a low ball slightly outside the wicket but not at all far away. Hendren's stroke was not high-class—I thought it looked suspiciously like a reflex action by a batsman not yet at ease in a difficult atmosphere. England 108 for 3 and Sutcliffe 40 not out brought us to lunch.

In bright sunlight the game went on, and Chapman gave us a chivalrous innings. Captaincy did not visibly sit on his young shoulders. He might have been playing against the Devon Dumplings down in his own leafy county. He jumped out to the slow bowlers, and time after time hit hard on the half-volley. Yet he mingled discretion with his rosily flushed antagonism. At one period he scored at least nine consecutive singles. I give this fact to show that Chapman did not merely 'slog' heartily; he respected the good length like a proper batsman, but how he did open out his young shoulders to the over-tossed length and how he did lie back on his back foot to short stuff and crack it hard behind point with his strong young arms! His first boundary was a violent, even passionate hook from Gregory, and the ball was not too short at that. In one over from Macartney he thumped two leg boundaries of the old vintage, both from the ball that goes with the left-hander's arm. Many of his slice-cuts through the slips were swift as light. Sutcliffe and Chapman pulled England's game round. At half-past three our score was 180 for three wickets. Chapman now went once too often to Mailey's well, and, trying a mighty drive, was circumvented by a lower flight than he had anticipated, and was stumped. Chapman and Sutcliffe made 81 for the fourth wicket in 80 minutes. And here was an end to Collins's apprehensions—for a while. The last six wickets fell for 91. The fun of this stampede will be understood when I say that these 91 runs were hit (that is the word) in an hour, and with the circumspect Rhodes at one end of the crease most of the time. It was all like a Saturday afternoon game down in the Cotswolds. Stevens clouted two fours and then a six, and next ball gently pushed a slower-paced and lower-flighted length into Andrews's hands at 'silly' mid-off. Rhodes came in next, cheered all the way by a crowd that possibly saw the man's years and greatness hanging about him, cloud on cloud. It was a moving sight to find Rhodes here at the Oval again in a Test match—at this very Oval where, years and years ago, he won a victory for England, last man in with Hirst, while the crowd sat still and hoped against hope. Chapman was two years old, a bonny baby no doubt, when this happened—in 1902.

Rhodes nearly got caught before he had scored, for he hit against Mailey's leg-spin and popped up the ball over Collins's head at forward leg. After that he played well, but perhaps he ran Geary out, though Geary started his run badly. Tate's innings was a Sussex breeze—two fours and a six from Mailey, the latter an outlandish pull into the crowd from a ball almost outside the off stump! This was the broad smile of cricket, and I loved Tate for letting us see it. After all, rusticity was cricket's own nurse. The boisterous gale blown by Tate obviously got into the head of Rhodes, for Rhodes was once or twice to be seen making the authentic cut. Even Strudwick thought the occasion appropriate for the hitting of a boundary, which he did rather after the style of J. T. Tyldesley.

I have been at some pains to describe in detail the way England batted after Chapman got out. Perhaps the higher criticism was shocked by it all. Fours or wickets! In the last seven overs of England's harlequinade there were one six, four fours, two threes, four twos, five singles, two maidens, and three wickets. Nice carryings-on for a Test match without a time-limit! After lunch only Rhodes and Sutcliffe played virtuous Test cricket. Of the others there was scarcely one batsman that got out from a Christian stroke. Sutcliffe's innings lasted three hours and thirty-five minutes —a worthy stand, despite a few moments of hair's-breadth escape. Sutcliffe lost his wicket unhappily. He was hit in the face from a ball which glanced there from his bat, and the next ball, a leg-break by Mailey, bowled him—a clear case of cause and effect.

Mailey got his wickets craftily. His length was that of temptation itself; yet in three-day Test cricket Mailey's blandishments have usually been sternly resisted by our batsmen. The Australians' fielding was good, and Oldfield excellent in his own dapper way.

At five o'clock the Australian innings was begun on a wicket even better, because faster, than it had been for England. The 'rubber' dangled in front of the Australian's eyes now. And straightaway the pot got a-boiling. With nine runs scored, Bardsley flicked his bat speculatively at a fast swinging-away ball from Larwood, and Strudwick made a catch. Twenty-five minutes were spent making those nine runs from a battleaxe attack. Macartney, in next, batted as only he can bat for 25 minutes. A glance to leg from Larwood was the stroke of Puck turned cricketer. A drive through the covers from Stevens saw all the impudence of Macartney suddenly transformed into dignity. The next ball asked to be hit out of the field—a long-hop unashamed! Macartney missed it with his bat's middle and merely glanced it into his stumps. It may turn out that this delightfully mortal mistake of Macartney will cost Australia the rubber. Macartney was the second blood to England's bowlers at 44. Seven runs afterwards a quick return from short-leg by Larwood in combination with clever work by Strudwick ran Ponsford out. And at 59 Andrews was most comprehensively bowled by a breakback of quite blinding pace from Larwood. The ball crashed through Andrews's defence as though his bat were made of straw; it shot his off stump yards through the air. A rare sight in these days—the spinning wicket and the thunderstruck batsman. I have seldom seen a cricketer more thoroughly bowled than Andrews in this match. I wonder what he would have had to say if a deputation had waited on him on Saturday evening and asked for his views about the need in Test cricket for four stumps or four days? 'Let us move cautiously', he might well have said, like Lord Hawke, 'let nothing rash be done.'

Collins stayed in with the good oak-tree Woodfull to the close. The first hour's cricket on Monday might settle the match.

England attacked admirably. Tate was a model of steadiness, and Larwood's fast bowling was easily the best I have seen this year. The fielding on the whole had a reliable aspect, but Rhodes at deep third-man did not make a quite decent spectacle. The crowd's size was below expectations—as, indeed, was the day's play. On Monday morning probably all London will turn up. Test cricket was alive and kicking on Saturday, but Woodfull and Collins will no doubt do their best on behalf of propriety. It will not be for want of endeavour if both do not teach us this morning that a Test match must behave itself, and not outrage time and space and the eternal verities.

FIFTH TEST 1926
2nd Day, the Oval
ENGLAND

First Innings		Second Innings	
Hobbs, b Mailey	37	Hobbs, not out	28
Sutcliffe, b Mailey	76	Sutcliffe, not out	20
Woolley, b Mailey	18	Extras (lb 1)	1
Hendren, b Gregory	8		—
A. P. F. Chapman, st Oldfield, b Mailey	49	Total (for no wicket)	49
G. I. S. Stevens, c Andrews, b Mailey	17		
Rhodes, c Oldfield, b Mailey	28		
Geary, run out	9		
Tate, b Grimmett	23		
Larwood, c Andrews, b Grimmett	0		
Strudwick, not out	4		
Extras (b 6, lb 5)	11		
Total	280		

AUSTRALIA

W. M. Woodfull, b Rhodes	35
W. Bardsley, c Strudwick, b Larwood	2
C. G. Macartney, b Stevens	25
W. H. Ponsford, run out	2
T. J. E. Andrews, b Larwood	3
H. L. Collins, c Stevens, b Larwood	61
A. J. Richardson, c Geary, b Rhodes	16
J. M. Gregory, c Stevens, b Tate	73
W. A. Oldfield, not out	33
C. V. Grimmett, b Tate	35
A. A. Mailey, c Strudwick, b Tate	0
Extras (b 5, lb 12)	17
Total	302

ENGLAND—1st innings bowling analysis

	O.	M.	R.	W.		O.	M.	R.	W.
Gregory	15	4	31	1	Macartney	6	3	16	0
Grimmett	33	12	74	2	Richardson	7	2	10	0
Mailey	33·5	3	138	6					

AUSTRALIA—1st innings bowling analysis.

	O.	M.	R.	W.		O.	M.	R.	W.
Tate	37·1	17	40	3	Stevens	29	3	85	1
Larwood	34	11	82	3	Rhodes	25	15	35	2
Geary	27	8	43	0					

Fall of the wickets:

ENGLAND—1st innings

1	2	3	4	5	6	7	8	9	10
53	91	108	189	213	214	231	266	266	280

AUSTRALIA—1st innings

1	2	3	4	5	6	7	8	9	10
9	44	51	59	90	122	229	231	298	302

LONDON, MONDAY

The Oval was nearly full this morning when the game between England and Australia was continued in a quietness most grim considering the thousands of passionate English folk present packed rank on rank—the crowd of them looking from the distance like a clipped high hedge planted round the field. Woodfull and Collins bent on their bats warily, and, as the cricketers moved here and there over the field between overs, neither Collins nor Woodfull spoke or smiled. Tate and Larwood attacked at the outset, and Collins forced three balls to the on side each for two—all within a few minutes. He himself was the first to make a protest against this indecent exhibition of impatience in a timeless Test match and with Australia rammed hard in a troublesome corner. The cricket of Collins seemed to contract, to draw suspiciously within itself as it went on. Woodfull's stonewalling was as frank and open as the day compared with that of Collins. Woodfull is indeed an authentic batsman whose style grows on you the more you see of it. He is like tomatoes and Marcel Proust, an acquired taste. You need to watch Woodfull's feet rather than his bat to enjoy his cricket. His bat is heavy and cramped, his footwork a delight in its neatness and versatility. A kinema film of Woodfull's feet during any long innings would give you to believe that you were watching a great and beautiful batsman. His light movements up and down the crease

238

are prompted by an eye that sees a ball quickly in its flight: it is a pity the message flashed from his mind to his feet does not touch his arms on its way and tell them to move freely too. Yet there must be wrist-work in his strokes, else how could he place the ball accurately, and how could he force the good length forward by means of the late stroke of a bat lifted back hardly knee-high?

Collins and Woodfull threatened to root themselves to the Oval's more or less green earth (there is no cricket field in the south as green as Old Trafford), and Chapman therefore called upon Rhodes to bowl. I cannot think that Woodfull would have fallen to the temptation of Rhodes's bowling; he was out through another interference from the mischievous imps that worked merry sport with high skill's intentions on Saturday. Woodfull cut a ball from Rhodes hard into his stumps after the morning had spent forty-five minutes, and brought to Australia another 30 runs. Woodfull was as steadfast of bat when he played on as Collins; he got himself out, and was the only man in the field capable of that performance. He walked back to the pavilion wearing as tragic a look on his face as I have ever seen a cricketer goaded into. He realized, no doubt, that Collins was ready to stay there for hours, and that by losing his wicket he had given England a tight grip on the match. Woodfull batted, in all, two hours and ten minutes. He was rarely, if ever, in difficulty.

Chapman changed his attack hopefully; there was speculation's light in his eye. After Rhodes had bowled three overs for three maidens and a wicket, Tate went on at Rhodes's end—no doubt with instructions to get Richardson caught at or near the stumps before the spectacled batsman had got his 'eye in' thoroughly. But Rhodes came back shortly afterwards and Tate rested again. Rhodes set a tight off-side field for Richardson's drive; he bowled with a 'silly' mid-off, a cover point, an extra-cover, a mid-off, and a deep long off. And in his own sweet way of rhythmical simplicity he 'tossed them up'—bowled to his field as he has been bowling man and boy nigh on thirty years. Richardson could not resist the challenge; time after time he jumped out to get Rhodes on the half-volley, but never once could he break through to the boundary. And the old Yorkshireman fiddled away on Richardson's patience and at last he ensnared him. I wonder that Collins did not ask Richardson not to be such an innocent. From the ring even we could see the poor man snatching after Rhodes's bait and going to certain destruction. At the old melodramas the audiences used to shout to the hero, 'Don't touch it, mister!' when Claude was about to drink the poisoner's draught. I am astonished that no Australian in today's crowd was as helpful in advice as this to Richardson. Richardson was almost caught and bowled by Rhodes. Then a brilliant catch by Geary at mid-off settled his innings. The ball was hit hard, and Rhodes almost hindered Geary by trying to hold the flying ball himself, presumably according to good Yorkshire doctrine of self-help. Richardson, metaphorically speaking, kicked himself out of our sight. The stand by Collins and Richardson for the sixth wicket added 32 in just under the hour.

One or two statistics will give an eloquent account of the stern, unlovely antagonism of the morning. Tate's first 21 overs contained 13 maidens and cost him 12 runs only for no wicket. The first boundary, from the bat, happened after 65 minutes' play. Rhodes wheeled up his first ten overs for three runs and two wickets. In 80 minutes Australia scored 49, including 25 singles. Collins at one period batted a quarter of an hour without scoring, then made a single, and then rested again for another 25 minutes. Certain curiously minded folk in the crowd made ironic noises as Collins hit an occasional single of exceptional discretion. Collins, of course, was playing a great game for Australia, hanging on to the wicket as much by tenacity of mind and will as by his technical ability—which would not withstand a Sydney Barnes for long, because he is not very quick at getting across the wicket and over the line of the 'going away' ball. Tate was unable to exploit his own version of the 'Barnes ball' today. Tate, indeed, has lost much of his pace from the turf, and seems ready to develop into one of those uninteresting bowlers who keep the runs down.

To hark back to a beginning of the morning for a while, I thought Stevens might have caught Collins when only eight at short leg. Collins failed to get on top of a fast ball from Larwood that jumped a little. The stroke would have been an excellent short-armed defensive hook from an 'in-swinger' had the ball kept at the height expected by Collins. As it was he lifted it, though without power, and Stevens made his ground much too late. A quick wicket might have moved Larwood to a ride of comprehensive destruction.

It was, of course, out of all reason to hope for an Australian innings which lacked at least one long stand. I thought it would come when Mailey joined Collins, but I was forgetful of Gregory's renowned love of a crisis. He came to the wicket at a quarter to one, a tawny giant carrying his bat like a vindictive club. He started to hit straightaway, sometimes flinging his blade at the pitch of the ball with all the reach of its long handle and his own long arms. For the first time in the morning the bat was heard cracking noisily. Rhodes packed his field to the on side for Gregory, who is a left-hander, and attacked the leg and middle stump. Only two men were in Rhodes's off-side field for Gregory, yet the old soldier so far forgot himself once as to pitch well outside Gregory's off stump. Result—a powerful boundary. That was bad bowling, as Tom Emmett would certainly have told Rhodes. And Emmott Robinson would have said stronger than that. Gregory gave a terrific return chance to Larwood just before lunch; afterwards he boomed to his 50 in 75 minutes, out of 71 runs made in that time.

As the wheel of the match once more turned in Australia's favour, Collins let us understand what a superb opportunist he is, for he, too, began to look for the hittable ball. Runs were wanted now by Australia; stonewalling was no longer a virtue in itself. Collins achieved his first boundary after his innings had lasted three hours; then he drove Larwood straight for another four—both strokes those of a fine cricketer. The 200 gave Larwood and Tate a new ball, and Larwood recaptured his pace and 'devil' of Saturday evening. Thrice Gregory flashed almost like a blind man at Larwood's lightning, and sent the ball red-hot through the consternated slips, each stroke one of those lucky ones which make the crowd buzz the round 'O's' of alarm and disappointment. Gregory's death-or-glory innings finished at 229. He hit too soon at a ball from Tate which was slower than usual.

Gregory and Collins held Australia's seventh wicket for one hour and three-quarters and added 107 precious runs. Only another two runs were got before Collins was caught by Stevens in the slips from the persevering but unlucky Larwood. Collins had given us an unforgettable essay in vigilant obstinacy. His bat had a hundred eyes. It was not a charming innings by any means, either to watch or to bowl against. There was something furtive about it. It was, as I have suggested already, cricket that turned within itself. This innings had sensitive feelers which were always withdrawn at the first hint of danger. It persisted for three hours and three-quarters, and it was Australia's long backbone. Yet, when the little captain left the wicket with as scant a show of emotion as he had let us see all day, England stood a rare chance of winning on the first innings, for eight wickets were down for 231. Grimmett and Oldfield told us the old, old story, though—Australians fight to the last, and English bowling nowadays is without the shattering power that routs the less than high-class batsman. Australia's ninth wicket was not taken till 298. Triumphant cries of 'Coo-ee' went across the Oval as Grimmett carried his side's score beyond England's. Larwood bowled fiercely to the end, with no smile at all, from the gods. The English slips would perhaps have served him had George Gunn been amongst them. Oldfield batted like a 'No. 1' batsman. Grimmett, though, goes to the wicket in his proper place—for an Australian innings. The Australian batting today had a superb, even self-scourging, temper. Every man set his teeth—not a man amongst them did not square himself defiantly to the English attack.

England's best bowler by far was Larwood. His length seemed short at times, but there was edge to his work, and no Australian batsman could for a moment cease his look-out for a fiery break-back. Tate's analysis flatters his skill, though not his endeavour. Geary lacked resource—like most of the seam bowlers of our time. Stevens is not a Test match bowler, and Rhodes's good work was the reward of his long experience in an artful school. What a commentary, though, on English cricket that we have to turn to him yet for left-handed bowling in a Test match. The English fielding had plenty of individual excellence, but the men did not move in the field with a team's cohesion; too many of them had to work in different positions throughout the day. The returns to the stumper were often inaccurate, and during the Oldfield–Grimmett stand I got a sense that we were falling a little out of humour. The Australian innings waxed and waned through six and a half hours.

England had an hour's batting at the day's fall. As Hobbs went to the wicket, perhaps to begin his last innings for England, the glorious sun turned the Oval into a noble place for the master's farewell. Autumn light shone in the great cricketer's autumn. . . . Even a game can be visited by the vague sadness which sweetens the end of splendid things. The Oval is not usually beautiful, but in the evening's slanting sun the field was like a gracious home in which Hobbs was saying goodbye to the England eleven, side-by-side with Sutcliffe, his young armour-bearer—comrades through many an historic day. But not yet has his bat sheathed itself from the Australian enemy. There is work for him still to do, a fight for him still to win. Let us wish with all our hearts that the end will be his crown, and that Rhodes, who was his Sutcliffe years ago, will just once again join with him in a stand leading England to victory as it happened to these two cricketers many many times in the old years.

FIFTH TEST 1926

3rd Day, the Oval

ENGLAND

First Innings

Hobbs, b Mailey	37
Sutcliffe, b Mailey	76
Woolley, b Mailey	18
Hendren, b Gregory	8
A. P. F. Chapman, st Oldfield, b Mailey	49
G. T. S. Stevens, c Andrews, b Mailey	17
Rhodes, c Oldfield, b Mailey	28
Geary, run out	9
Tate, b Grimmett	23
Larwood, c Andrews, b Grimmett	0
Strudwick, not out	4
Extras (b 6, lb 5)	11
	—
Total	280

AUSTRALIA

First Innings

W. M. Woodfull, b Rhodes	35
W. Bardsley, c Strudwick, b Larwood	2
C. G. Macartney, b Stevens	25
W. H. Ponsford, run out	2
T. J. E. Andrews, b Larwood	3
H. L. Collins, c Stevens, b Larwood	61
A. J. Richardson, c Geary, b Rhodes	16
J. M. Gregory, c Stevens, b Tate	73
W. A. Oldfield, not out	33
C. V. Grimmett, b Tate	35
A. A. Mailey, c Strudwick, b Tate	0
Extras (b 5, lb 12)	17
	—
Total	302

Second Innings

Hobbs, b Gregory	100
Sutcliffe, b Mailey	161
Woolley, lbw b Richardson	27
Hendren, b Grimmett	15
A. P. F. Chapman, b Richardson	19
G. T. S. Stevens, c Mailey, b Grimmett	22
Rhodes, not out	0
Extras (b 15, lb 16)	31
	—
Total (for 6 wkts)	375

ENGLAND–1st innings bowling analysis

	O.	M.	R.	W.
Gregory	15	4	31	1
Grimmett	33	12	74	2
Mailey	33.5	3	138	6
Macartney	6	3	16	0
Richardson	7	2	10	0

AUSTRALIA–1st innings bowling analysis

	O.	M.	R.	W.
Tate	37.1	17	40	3
Larwood	34	11	82	3
Geary	27	8	43	0
Stevens	29	3	85	1
Rhodes	25	15	35	2

Fall of the wickets:

ENGLAND—1st innings

1	2	3	4	5	6	7	8	9	10
53	91	108	189	213	214	231	266	266	280

Fall of the wickets:

AUSTRALIA—1st innings

1	2	3	4	5	6	7	8	9	10
9	44	51	59	90	122	229	231	298	302

ENGLAND—Second Innings

1	2	3	4	5	6
172	220	277	316	373	375

LONDON, TUESDAY

At half-past two this afternoon, in the summer sunshine, there was a scene at the Oval which none of us will forget who were privileged to be present. Hobbs played a ball gently to the off side, and, scampering down the wicket like a happy boy, he made a century—his eleventh, and perhaps his last, for England against Australia. The great crowd roared out affectionate applause; Collins gave Hobbs a shake of the hand; somebody deep in the encircling multitude called for three cheers, and we sent them in our thousands to Hobbs over his own Oval field. And Hobbs waved his cap at us and then put it on the back of his head—the old beloved attitude.

This century was a masterpiece through and through. Today's part of it had to be played on a wicket which, for an hour before lunch, was uncommonly difficult for these days. Yet Hobbs's batsmanship had scarcely a flaw till he made his hundred. It possessed all the attributes which we associate with the classic style —cool precision of craftsmanship and serenity of mind and manner. Every stroke of Hobbs was eloquent of the man's long experience; it was an innings touched with the bloom of age. And coming as it did in a dangerous situation for England, it stood there like a strong ancient rock of refuge.

The Australians missed a rare chance between a quarter to one and lunch. The pitch then was unmistakably sensitive to spin after the night's storm. Richardson caused the ball to break back sharply. But he did not give his attack a wise direction; he exploited a 'leg trap' field, and more often than not pitched a rather short length on, and sometimes even outside, the leg stump. Surely with the turf definitely unpleasant he ought to have bowled his off break on the off wicket, making it come back to the batsman's leg wicket— within the danger zone.

The direction of Richardson's bowling kept the runs down no doubt, but it could not have been dangerously pitched, since not

once but frequently Hobbs and Sutcliffe were able to counter the
break by pads alone. It seemed, too, that Richardson's length was so
short that the batsmen were free to wait and follow his break round
and play it safely to the earth well in front of the waiting fieldsmen.
And perhaps this much-too-short length of Richardson's (for the
state of the wicket) was a defect which he found himself forced into
by the absence from his field of a deepish long-on. He bowled without a man behind him, hence, probably enough, his apparent un-
willingness to trust to the well-flighted off-spinner which experience
has taught many of us to regard as the most dangerous right-handed
ball for a bowler's pitch.

Richardson sent down maiden over after maiden over; it was
accurate work of its kind. But Australia ought to have upset English
wickets on the mischievous turf. Collins's great lack, of course, was
good left-handed spin. From time to time Macartney and Richardson made a ball spin and 'pop' nastily—certain proof here of how
deadly a Trumble or a Saunders would have been on the wicket.

Collins's mortification at the sight of the scoreboard hereabout—
120 for 0—can easily be imagined; this score would have been hard
enough for him to stomach on the immaculate grounds of Sydney or
Melbourne. There was another thought, too, that must have
tormented him; if only Hobbs or Sutcliffe could somehow get overthrown while the wicket was at its nastiest—which was round about
12.30—Richardson would have a chance of attacking Woolley, the
left-hander. Every cricketer knows how difficult it is for left-
handed batsmen to play right-handed off-spinners on a sensitive
pitch. And if Woolley had failed again—as he eventually did when
England's score was 220 for one—would not Australia have jumped
at the opportunity to thrust themselves still further on the nerves of
Hendren in a moment of incipient crisis?

Hobbs and Sutcliffe saved England this morning; a mistake by
either of them, and Australia could hardly have captured less than
four wickets before lunch. The stand by Hobbs and Sutcliffe must
be counted the finest of all their many accomplishments for England.
They had now to build for us a sure foundation on a more or less
bowler's wicket. And had they not reason enough to believe, from
past experience, that the others were scarcely to be trusted—even on
a batsman's happy hunting field!

It was a joy to watch the way Hobbs adapted his methods to the
turf as it changed from docility in the early morning to its later
viciousness. While the ball was coming through with tolerable
simplicity Hobbs took possession of every run that his resourceful

bat could find. A sweeping leg-hit from Grimmett in the third over of the day filled us with a thrilling sense of beautiful circling energy. His use of the 'dead bat' to Richardson's spin was sheer science wearing the flush of art. His bat, though almost motionless in these defensive strokes, had the poise of dignity, and his strategy was just as praiseworthy as his art. His moves to get to the end to which Richardson attacked were clever and unfailing. For though Richardson's tactics may not always have been judicious, he was at any rate Australia's best bowler in the trying last hour before lunch.

England's finest pair of opening batsmen of all time were unbeaten at the interval, when the score stood proudly at 161 for none —an incredible performance on the pitch and the reward of merit indeed. This superb work was not done without much dropping of anxious sweat. The Australians, knowing well that every run against them was now hit with a bat that sounded doom in their ears, fought bitterly ball by ball.

Many times did Hobb's face seem drawn with care. In the day's first half-hour only 16 runs were made, and not one of these by Sutcliffe, who batted for forty minutes before he advanced his Monday evening's score. Between 12.30 and one o'clock the English total was lifted by grim labour from 125 to 142. Richardson bowled six consecutive maidens. In the first hour of the morning 138 balls were bowled, and from them only 23 scoring strokes were to be seen, 18 by Hobbs and 5 by Sutcliffe.

In 150 minutes Sutcliffe made 33, but his obstinacy was not bleak, like that of Collins yesterday. He wore his rue with a difference. Sutcliffe, when he is compelled to stonewall, is the prettiest stonewaller conceivable. As we saw his bat go gently to the ball with its graceful leaning movement, and then as we looked on the strong bat of Hobbs—a rod of authority—we saw the pleasantest picture in the world of the master and the apprentice (and it might be said here that after Hobbs got out the apprentice himself immediately assumed the aspect of the master—in comparison with Hendren and Woolley).

Gregory bowled following the interval, and Hobbs arrived at his century. Then a break back just removed his off bail. Hobbs got his runs out of 169 in three hours and three-quarters—an innings which, if it has been the end of his Test match career, has brought him to an end that crowns all. In this summer's great games Hobbs and Sutcliffe have never once proved unequal to the occasion's challenge. Here is the glorious sequence of their stands at the outset of England's innings:—

At Nottingham, 32 (unfinished).
At Lord's, 182.
At Leeds, 59 and 156.
At Manchester, 58.
At the Oval, 172.

These performances, coming after the men's greatness in Australia, must leave us silent with admiration and gratitude. Shall we ever look upon the like of Hobbs and Sutcliffe again? It is the fashion to decry cricketers of today and to venerate those of yesterday. But our children of tomorrow will envy those of us who tell them that we once upon a time saw Hobbs and Sutcliffe, and we shall make epics for our sons to the memory of two superb cricketers who never failed us, no matter how dark the hour.

When Woolley and Hendren disappointed once more we were able to appreciate to the full the value of the Hobbs–Sutcliffe partnership. Hendren was obviously all at sea with the slow spin bowling; he lunged out at it speculatively. He seemed deplorably to lack the confidence which sets the batsman's feet moving in and out of his wicket. While Hendren was batting the Australian attack looked as difficult as it looked easy to Sutcliffe, who went his ways delightfully cool and sure of himself. After lunch his many lovely strokes to the off side flashed before our eyes; once again he threw his staff of responsibility away and gave us the free-running batsmanship of youth. His cover drive is as winsome as anything in cricket today. And that fierce hook of his—which Old Trafford and Macdonald know so well—shot its lightning over the field once at least this afternoon from a fast-rising ball, chin high, hurled by the desperate Gregory.

Woolley made a few of his own charming strokes, but he fell—as I was certain he would—to Richardson.

At tea England were 296 for three, Sutcliffe not out 125. His century came to him after five hours and ten minutes' diligent craftsmanship, and I imagine the bulk of his runs were the consequence of his delicate push stroke. His cricket was, in its boyish straightforwardness, all of a piece with the picture given us by Sutcliffe of the cricketer at the blossoming time of life. As the sun shone on his black hair and brown face and soft creamy flannels, I somehow had the notion that his innings was a reflection of himself seen in cricket's bright looking-glass. His assurance was endless, even when he made mistakes and was nearly caught at short leg in Richardson's leg-trap at 38, again when he almost snicked a ball into his wicket from Grimmett at 47 he did not lose a jot of his

247

composure. He has the priceless gift of the Test match temperament; obviously he revels in the big engagement. He reached his 150 out of 356 in six hours and 50 minutes.

Chapman was not fruitful this time—which was a pity, for now the Australian attack was weary, easy game for a vigorous bat. Sutcliffe could not reasonably be expected to do the big hitting; the wonder is that he could find—almost till the close of play— the energy wherewith to stand erect at the wicket. A splendid day's work by England or, rather, by Hobbs and Sutcliffe. The score is now a hill from which we can just see the Land of Promise that we have all been looking for in the wilderness for these many years.

The Australian bowling, as I have written, was short of the kind of spin the pitch demanded. It was never a sticky wicket of the old breed, perhaps—not even in the hour before lunch. But it was always possible to turn the ball. Mailey and Grimmett both prefer a fast ground; Macartney is so much deprived of his old spin that today he attacked from over the wicket. The Australian fielding was keen to the end; when it did waver it was simply because all flesh is grass.

Sutcliffe was bowled in the day's last over. As he saw his stumps shattered he smote the earth with his bat's end in disgust. Youth's appetite for glory is excellent and without end. This innings by Sutcliffe will become legendary as the years go by; it was a triumph of skill and of the rarer qualities of patience and self-reliance.

FIFTH TEST 1926
4th Day, the Oval

ENGLAND		AUSTRALIA	
First Innings		Second Innings	
Hobbs, b Mailey	37	W. M. Woodfull, b Rhodes	35
Sutcliffe, b Mailey	76	W. Bardsley, c Strudwick,	
Woolley, b Mailey	18	b Larwood	2
Hendren, b Gregory	8	C. G. Macartney, b Stevens	25
A. P. F Chapman, st Oldfield,		W. H. Ponsford, run out	2
b Mailey	49	T. J. E. Andrews, b Larwood	3
G. T. S. Stevens, c Andrews,		H. L. Collins, c Stevens,	
b Mailey	17	b Larwood	61
Rhodes, c Oldfield, b Mailey	28	A. J. Richardson, c Geary,	
Geary, run out	9	b Rhodes	16
Tate, b Grimmett	23	J. M. Gregory, c Stevens, b Tate	73
Larwood, c Andrews, b Grimmett	0	W. A. Oldfield, not out	33
Strudwick, not out	4	C. V. Grimmett, b Tate	35
Extras (b 6, lb 5)	11	A. A. Mailey, c Strudwick, b Tate	0
	—	Extras (b 5, lb 12)	17
Total	280		—
		Total	302

Second Innings		Second Innings	
Hobbs, b Gregory	100	W. H. Ponsford, c Larwood,	
Sutcliffe, b Mailey	161	b Rhodes	12
Woolley, lbw b Richardson	27	W. M. Woodfull, c Geary,	
Hendren, c Oldfield, b Grimmett	15	b Larwood	0
A. P. F. Chapman, b Richardson	19	C. G. Macartney, c Geary,	
G. T. S. Stevens, c Mailey,		b Larwood	16
b Grimmett	22	W. Bardsley, c Woolley, b Rhodes	21
Rhodes, lbw b Grimmett	14	H. L. Collins, c Woolley, b Rhodes	4
Geary, c Oldfield, b Gregory	1	T. J. E. Andrews, c Tate,	
Tate, not out	33	b Larwood	15
Larwood, b Mailey	5	J. M. Gregory, c Sutcliffe, b Tate	9
Strudwick, c Andrews, b Mailey	2	A. J. Richardson, b Rhodes	4
Extras (b 19, lb 18)	37	W. A. Oldfield, b Stevens	23
	—	A . A. Mailey, b Geary	6
Total	436	C.V. Grimmett, not out	8
		Extras (lb)	7
			—
		Total	125

ENGLAND–1st innings bowling analysis

	O.	M.	R.	W.
Gregory	15	4	31	1
Grimmett	33	12	74	2
Mailey	33·5	3	138	6
Macartney	6	3	16	0
Richardson	7	2	10	0

AUSTRALIA–1st innings bowling analysis

	O.	M.	R.	W.
Tate	37·1	17	40	3
Larwood	34	11	82	3
Geary	27	8	43	0
Stevens	29	3	85	1
Rhodes	25	15	35	2

ENGLAND–2nd innings bowling analysis

	O.	M.	R.	W.
Gregory	18	1	58	2
Grimmett	55	17	108	3
Mailey	42·5	6	128	3
Macartney	26	16	24	0
Richardson	41	21	81	2

AUSTRALIA–2nd innings bowling analysis

	O.	M.	R.	W.
Larwood	14	3	34	3
Tate	9	4	12	1
Rhodes	20	9	44	4
Geary	6·3	2	15	1
Stevens	3	1	13	1

Fall of the wickets:

ENGLAND–1st innings

1	2	3	4	5	6	7	8	9	10
53	91	108	189	213	214	231	266	266	280

AUSTRALIA–1st innings

1	2	3	4	5	6	7	8	9	10
9	44	51	59	90	122	229	231	298	302

ENGLAND–2nd innings

1	2	3	4	5	6	7	8	9	10
172	220	277	316	373	375	382	425	430	436

AUSTRALIA–2nd innings

1	2	3	4	5	6	7	8	9	10
1	31	31	35	63	83	83	87	114	125

VICTORY AT LAST

[Amid remarkable scenes of excitement and enthusiasm England yesterday defeated Australia in the Test match at the Oval by 289 runs and thus won the 'Ashes' for the first time since 1912. Australia had to score 415 to win—a total never yet obtained in the fourth innings of a Test match,—and was dismissed for 125, her lowest aggregate since the Oval test in 1912. Chief bowling honours fell to Rhodes and Larwood, the veteran and "baby" of the team.]

THE OVAL, WEDNESDAY

The old writers used to call on the Muses for guidance whenever they had a difficult work on hand. If the Muse of History will deign to recognize the uses of the humble cricket reporter, I petition her now to give me aid. Heaven knows it is wanted, for as I write against time, this vital Test match is raging away at the Oval; England is winning; every ball bowled is being hurled across the wicket with bitter English determination; while a crowd gets madder and madder. If one's eyes are taken away from the action for a second something is bound to happen and a roar of triumph or frustration will set one's heart thumping apprehensively, for fear of having missed a superb piece of cricket.

Under the nose of this press box men and women are sitting spellbound now flushed joyously, now silent in expectation. And we poor galley slaves must somehow get down on to paper our facts, our impressions. Never before have I known a field as tense as this. The air is throbbing as history is beaten out in the hot forge of the game.

Years and years have we been waiting for this hour of revenge, and after long eating of the bread of humiliation here come Victory with her wine at last. No wonder the packed multitude lifted up its voice this afternoon as one by one they watched the smashing of the shackles of Australia which have held English cricket these many summers.

When Macartney fell to a slip catch the clamour of the crowd was not merely jubilant; in it could be heard the note of savagery. 'Die and be damned,' said the Oval, and then magnanimously cheered every Australian counter stroke. The enemy were caught in a trap of their own making. The 'timeless' Test match was invented by them, not us. Here, as Corporal Nym would say, is where the humour of today's fight comes in.

The English innings closed at twenty-past three. Rain held back the morning's play till a quarter-past twelve, and again at twenty-past one heavy showers fell and prevented a resumption till a quarter-past three. Twenty minutes afterwards Australia's heavy task started. They required to make 415 for victory and the Ashes. The rain made fast bowling rise awkwardly, and also it helped the spin bowler. But the turf could hardly have been more difficult than it was yesterday between noon and lunch time. It was faster and a little rougher, and perhaps for that reason a good ball gained in deadliness.

Collins sent Ponsford in with Woodfull to open his innings—a doubtful move, I thought, though plainly made with the intention of sparing Bardsley from Larwood's first devastating energies. Woodfull and Ponsford were terribly in earnest. Australia were not going to be beaten, we thought, in a hurry. As Larwood ran to the wicket and opened England's fire the silence on the ground was painful. He galloped along the earth like a young horse. His right arm shot forth its violent speed.

Ponsford was nearly caught at slip straightaway; as the stroke went at blinding pace from his bat the crowd's heart jumped into its mouth, and a man somewhere said 'Oh my God.' He spoke for thousands. In Larwood's second over we had tasted blood. Woodfull flashed a speculative bat at the lightning ball and Geary accomplished a lovely catch. The good tree Woodfull was thus felled to earth at one blow. The roar of the crowd must have been heard half a mile away by women in Kennington making tea. Woodfull could safely have left alone the rising ball that got him out, and as he walked back to the pavilion his face was twitching with mortification.

Macartney came in next. At last we saw him the most solemn of men. Where were his quips now, his whims and oddities, that were wont to set Armstrong's table in a roar. He took his guard as cannily as any Makepeace. But once he got to work he was his own quicksilver self. His bat made brave play here and there. He drove Tate through the covers with a stroke that had the bloom of a peach. He hit Larwood fiercely to leg. The little man was ready to play a jewel of an innings to shine through the encircling gloom for Australia.

He hit, as I say, Larwood for four to leg. The next ball, like that which was Woodfull's undoing, rose high outside the off stump, but it was a little wider; Macartney tried to cut it in his own coxcomb fashion. He too sent a catch to Geary, who again had safe, capacious hands. Macartney took off his gloves as he walked away from the wicket, for the last time in a Test match. The sound made by his bat as it sent the catch to Geary might have been the noise of

251

Australia's cracking foundations, and with the old enemy's score still 31 Ponsford edged a beautiful spinning away ball to the slips, where Larwood tumbled forward, all eager, excited boyishness, and hugged his prize. Hats were thrown into the air from the black ranks of the crowd. Acclamation and lust for conquest and vengeance have never on any cricket field deafened ears as they were deafened now.

Collins was the living image of the will-to-survive when he reached the wicket. But even he could not hang on. Rhodes ensnared him in the slips at 35, and four wickets had toppled in the Australian camp at half-past four.

The match was won and lost at this very moment. Even the hardened old fighter Bardsley must have realized that it was only a matter of time now for England's victory. He played dourly, nonetheless, for eighty minutes. Then Rhodes tempted him to hit, and he skied a ball against the spin, high to Woolley moving from the slips behind the wicket to the leg side. But before he got out Bardsley and Andrews scored 28 for the fifth wicket, which was taken when Andrews let his bat fly at a by no means short-pitched ball from Larwood, only to see Tate hold a catch at forward leg from what might be called a good bad stroke. It was good because it was an authentic hit, and bad because no cricketer in a difficult period ought ever to 'let fly', as cricketers say, at a fast ball's pitch.

Bardsley was sixth out at 83; Gregory was a victim to recklessness at the same total; Richardson, with desperation making a sullen light behind his spectacles, drove a spiteful boundary to the on from Rhodes, who immediately afterwards bowled him with a ball that 'made pace' from the ground. Richardson's bat came down, too late, with a thud that might have been his heart making a beat of palpitation.

Let the rest of the Australian innings be silence. The ninth wicket was worth 27—forlorn play but plucky by Oldfield and Grimmett. Oldfield was not to be disturbed even by a dire period out of his customary air of cool cocksureness. At four minutes past six Mailey's leg stump was knocked flat to the earth, and at long last English cricket was free to throw out its chest.

The crowd ran over the Oval and massed itself in front of the pavilion and demanded a sight of its heroes. English and Australian cricketers alike were given a resonant 'All hail!' to the tune of the 'Bow Bells.' The happy thousands sang 'We want Herbert' (meaning Sutcliffe). 'We want Collins,' 'We want Chapman,' 'We want Jack Hobbs,' 'We want Rhodes.' Everybody stayed there for half an hour at least—men and women, boys and girls—all well aware that they were living through a moment which in the after years they will boast about to their children, telling them as they do so that giants walked the cricket fields in their days.

Frankly, the Australians batting was disappointing to those of us who, while we prayed for an English win, also wanted to see a stern fight. The Australian innings did not keep in tune with the titanic girth and temper of the match as it was played from Saturday till Tuesday.

No conceivable team could have scored 415 on this afternoon's wicket, but we have one or two county elevens that might have tackled the English bowling with a more consistent show of common sense than Australia did. Woodfull, Andrews, Macartney, Bardsley, Gregory, and Richardson may be said to have lost their wickets by indiscreet, impatient hits. The tactics of this 'suicide club' were astonishing in a team which has learned its Test cricket in a land where the clock is never an enemy. May it be whispered that Collins and his men have proved themselves today not entirely lacking in human hearts and human nerves. The batting appeared suspiciously like that of 'rattled' cricketers. Macartney burnt his own wings, and nobody will scold him for that; he has always been a lovely wayward butterfly. But why Woodfull should have flicked at the off-side ball, and why Bardsley, Andrews, and Gregory should have made the rash strokes they did make can surely be accounted for only on the assumption that they for the moment forgot the Australian habit of Fabian doggedness in the face of odds.

The English bowling, apart from Larwood's first few overs, was not exactly of the battering-ram order. Rhodes spun the ball in his old way of curving guile masked by simplicity. Nonetheless he invited the batsmen to be accessories after the act of their own destruction. Geary and Tate were everyday 'up and down' bowlers. I imagine that had Australia been beginning a match against this attack they would have got a good score. Once Woodfull and Macartney were out there seemed a readiness on the part of most of the others to make the worst of a bad job. The difficulties of the wicket and the bowling alike were exaggerated. Larwood, with careful nursing, might develop into the best fast bowler of recent years, though he is not tall enough ever to rank with the great fast bowlers of Test cricket.

The sight of Rhodes getting Australians confused into knots at his time of life was beautiful—and a little sardonic. He takes his farewell from Test matches, even as Hobbs does, with immense honour. Had he played in the earlier Tests, especially at Leeds, we might have recovered the 'Ashes' before today.

Australian critics maintain that their eleven of this tour is not truly representative of the best of their country's cricket at the moment. Be that as it may, it is certain that England has won the rubber with a side a little below the best available here. Woolley is no longer dependable, either as batsman, bowler, or fieldsman; Hendren never has been a Test match batsman; Stevens, Geary, and (on current form) Tate are not amongst our eleven cleverest cricketers. But for Hobbs and Sutcliffe the English second innings would have broken down in a moment of crisis—even as it broke down last evening against tired bowling on an improving turf.

The gods gave Australia a rare chance on the unpleasant wicket before lunch on Tuesday. They did not jump to it, and so the gods had no further use for the Australians. When the gods would destroy, the old saying has it, they first make mad. There were certainly some signs of blind folly in the Australians' batting this afternoon—and at the very stage where the situation called for the authentic shrewdness and patience of Australia.